NEW AFRICAN
LITERATURE AND THE ARTS
Volume 3

Edited by

Joseph Okpaku

THE THIRD PRESS
Joseph Okpaku Publishing Co., Inc.
444 Central Park West
New York, N. Y. 10025

NEW AFRICAN
LITERATURE AND THE ARTS

Volume 3

CONTENTS

CULTURE AND SOCIETY

Essays

THE GREAT BATTLE OF NEGRITUDE

LITERATURE

Essays and Criticisms

Poetry

FOLKLORE, MUSIC AND COMMUNICATIONS

*All these articles were delivered at the Festival in Algeria.

To
my wife, Sheila
and our precious little son, Joe-Joe

with love

Preface

Considering the reception of the first two volumes in this series, there is very little that needs to be said by way of a preface to volume three.

Since the publication of the first volume in 1970 much has been written on different aspects of African culture. Happily, a great deal of this has been by Africans themselves. The crucial importance of articulating African insights into African culture cannot be overemphasized. In fact, as the reader will find in this volume, the event of African scholars and critics finally coming to play the most dominant role in the discourse on African culture is doubly significant: first, in that it establishes, once and for all, the high quality of African scholarship and, second, it lays to rest all of the suggestion by some non-African Africanists that objectivity tends to suffer when Africans write about their own culture.

Never in the history of African scholarship has there been so much exciting, meaningful controversy as there has been in the last few years when one African opinion has been pitted against another in the search for truth and meaning. The essays in this collection, many of which were presented at the first Pan-African Culture Festival that was held in Algeria in 1969 (the Algerian Festival) under the auspices of the Organization of African Unity, are an impressive evidence of this lively and solid debate on Africa by some of the finest thinkers today.

This volume covers a very broad range, from culture and society to literature and criticism, negrutude, poetry, folklore, music and communications. It is our most successful attempt so far to put the discussion of all aspects of African culture within the same covers. The various aspects of the humanities are so interrelated that much is lost in separating them into restricted subdivisions. One, of course, cannot overlook the fact that narrowly-defined disciplines are much easier to handle, but the insight that may be lost in so doing far outweighs the obvious advantages of convenience. Fortunately, the essays in this volume have been so arranged as to make for very easy reading as one goes from one section to the other.

It is my belief that this volume, like the earlier two, has a lot to offer to the average general reader to whom it should make very interesting and informative reading. It also has a lot of solid material for the student or expert in the field. This dual quality is only a reflection of the nature of the *Journal of the New African Literature and the Arts,* from which the volumes in this series derive. The Journal, now in its seventh year, continues to be the focus of much serious and exciting literary and critical creativity and scholarship on the arts of Africa.

In thinking back to the early years of the Journal during my Stanford University days, I recall, with a certain nostalgia, the days of editing manuscripts in bed, sitting (some five or six of us) on the floor addressing envelopes to subscribers, and somehow never wondering where this was all going to lead. Now that the Journal is firmly entrenched within the framework of The Third Press (a curious case of the father becoming the ward, very much like Britain to America!) the intensity and enthusiasm with which we pursued the exploration of African culture remains undiminished. One, however, does miss the intimacy of literally putting everything together by hand.

Nevertheless, this is the inevitable consequence of the growth of any journal or review, and we certainly are most happy with what the Journal has come to mean to many students of African culture, and with the place it has come to occupy in the field of African humanities.

Finally, I have enjoyed putting this volume together,

especially now that The Third Press has taken over the publication of the series. I hope the reader enjoys the experience of sharing this volume with me.

Joseph Okpaku
May 1973

CULTURE
AND SOCIETY

THE ALGERIAN FESTIVAL:
Inaugural Address

By HOUARI BOUMEDIENNE

Algeria is happy to welcome the First Pan-African Cultural Festival on behalf of our entire continent. The importance of this event and the joy and enthusiasm which it has aroused and still is arousing, the diversity and the quality of the manifestations to which it will give rise, should not make us forget to what an extent this first Pan-African Cultural Festival is concerned, not only with our values and sensitivities, but also with our very existence as Africans and our common future.

This Festival, far from being an occasion for general festivities which might momentarily distract us from our daily tasks and problems, should rather be related to them and make a direct contribution to our vast effort of construction.

It constitutes an intrinsic part of the struggle we are all pursuing in Africa—whether that of development, of the struggle against racialism, or of national liberation.

Our continent, three-quarters of which is liberated, but which is fully master of its destiny, is undertaking the task, with this First Pan-African Cultural Festival, of holding the greatest artistic and literary reunion at a continental scale in history, commensurate with all facets of its expression. By the same token, it takes a further step forward in the continuing struggle against all forms of domination.

Colonialism is an evil which all of us have experienced

1

and over the most tangible and most insolent forms of which political domination we have triumphed.

But the mechanism is a complex one and cannot be solved by a simple operation. Colonialism, a well known political phenomenon, is both spiritually and essentially a total act.

If it is to continue to exert itself it must justify itself morally and intellectually and spread its hold to all spheres of human activity. In order to exist as such, it can supplement its material hegemony only by social and intellectual ascendance. Then, in its own eyes, it achieves a perfect synthesis and imagines that it can defy men and destroy their very existence.

Most fortunately, history is a long succession of the breakdowns of such attempts, but it was the sad destiny of our continent to experience this phenomenon of domination in its most varied and most criminal forms. It experienced the most total of colonizations and the most perverse of hegemonies. The aim was not merely to dominate and exploit the African but also to deny his very existence as a thinking individual, as a member of a community and as a creator of the most essential and natural human undertakings.

For the African, this past is not so very distant; he was refused the right to assume his national destiny, the right to a past, to a language, in other words, to a culture. Such a situation still persists in certain parts of the world. Colonialism is also the genocide of the spirit.

The tragedy of history in Africa is on the scale of Manichean drama, in which man inflicted upon himself the most terrible of tragedies: the destruction of his own image and his own reflection.

For it is quite certain that, by destroying men and their works of art with such rage and fury, the colonialists were hastening their own destruction. Our experience as resistance fighters saved not only our sons and our nations but also a certain notion of mankind and his capabilities. This is to our honour today, in spite of the price paid and yet to be paid. It is a conception to which we are irrevocably attached.

We succeeded in triumphing over the forces of oppression. That alone is a sufficient reason for us to give to African culture, and therefore to universal culture, the time, place and care we are now devoting to it. This is why we wanted this festival to be the meeting of hope and rebirth, as well as an enthusiastic and lucid undertaking to recover and assert our basic oneness.

We believed, we spontaneously felt that freedom was identified with patriotism and that the well-being and progress of our peoples have to be built around our specific personalities. We naturally admitted that freedom, nationhood, personality and finally, universal dimension, were but the product and origin of culture.

We quite naturally recognized the vast role of culture, long before the social sciences made it the pernicious instrument of domination or a materialistic form of entertainment, as the basic cement of all social groups: its prime means of inter-communication and understanding of the outside world, its reflexion and transcendancy, its soul and its essence, its expression and its ability to change.

This is not an assertion of circumstance, it is the long experienced realization of an indestructible human phenomenon. Culture in its widest and most complete sense is what enables men to order their lives. In our own case it is what enables us to resist the avalanches of history and to keep standing up, as a long past had taught us, in the way we were and are determined to live our lives.

The preservation of our culture saved us from the attempts to make us peoples without a soul and without a history. Our culture preserved us. It is quite obvious that from now on we want to use it as a means of progress and development, for culture, that permanent and everlasting creation, not only brings men together and defines personalities, but also stimulates progress. Culture is not an isolated phenomenon in men's lives. Its relation with them is the pre-requisite for its vivacity and its effulgence. It is, in fact, the abiding eternity of peoples.

It is the supression of an economy, a way of life, of social relations determined at a given time of men's life which give it a direction, a style, a sensitivity conforming to the conditions of life encountered and the social rules chosen.

The political, social and cultural life of men constitute an entity which cannot be cut off or mutilated without inflicting serious wounds which cannot be cured by mere verbal assertions or purely formal political changes.

This is why Africa pays so much attention and attaches much importance to the restoration of its cultural patrimony, the defense of its personality and the development of new branches of its culture.

After having been justified, accepted and codified, not only by the conquerors but also by the public opinion and the intellectuals of the western world, colonialism was obliged by our resistance and upheavals to withdraw and renounce its territorial ambitions, at least officially. We know that this first step of decolonisation concealed more insidious and more all-embracing hegemonies.

Discussions on the under-development of third world countries camouflages a change in the methods of exploitation.

The struggle in this field will be long and difficult. It will demand many sacrifices. This is another reason for our being here together today. Our under-development is not due to a lack of riches; on the contrary, it is due to an irrational and unplanned use of them. Our shortage of supervisory staffs and technicians, and our scientific backwardness are the many problems we must solve in order to assert ourselves in this century of progress.

This is the very heart of the matter which concerns us and the second stage we must complete in order to become completely free men. In this stage, cultural development must keep pace with the economic development.

Culture, which is the cement of our resistance, the source of our oneness, the reason for our right to a universal hearing, the basis of our personalities, and a weapon in our struggle for liberation is also for Africa one of the essential elements in its development and social progress.

This is why, after so many years devoted to recovering our national independence and strengthening our states, it was essential for us to tell the world that the damage caused to us was not completely repaired, that some people were about to give it a new form. In order to be ourselves, it is not enough to see our national flag before our houses. We must also find our bearings, we must preserve our personality, and freely assume our responsibilities. For we not only want to be ourselves but we also want to be in harmony with our time.

It would have been easy for certain people and convenient for others if we had not set out conditions for our political independence: we could have been satisfied with that and have borrowed language and art from those who had the good fortune to enjoy a harmonious internal development. We might have also been satisfied with a cultural past, a poor man's culture, and have given up all thought of true freedom and real independence.

In the name of man, his rights and acquisitions, we refuse to accept a false destiny, cultural under-development and the disguising of mind, heart and soul as we refused to accept both slavery and racialism.

A tribute to man, a respect for his noblest undertaking

must derive from an effort to be oneself, not an imitation man but a real man, a man as the product of historical, geographical and economic factors and issued from the block of his forefathers. In the very outset of our struggle we assigned to ourselves the well-defined task of rejecting falsehoods spread by colonialism and furnishing proofs of Africa's cultural past and present.

Our peoples, militants, intellectuals and artists spontaneously undertook these tasks of safeguarding and restoring our culture, often acting clandestinely, long before history gave them the right to do so, publicly and in concert.

Scientific studies were undertaken in all countries and little by little, African culture, its ancestral origins and its vitality, stood out against the colonial darkness.

The world discovered that despite the tragedies of slavery, exile, transportation or depersonalization, Africa succeeded in preserving its entity, its spirit, its sensitivity which have made her the home of the most beautiful arts, the most prosperous civilizations, the most vivid literature and the most rigorous scientific thought.

It behoves exegetists and scientists to make a deeper analysis of this common inspiration. At the present time we already know clearly that apart from similarities of form and thought, apart from our common background, "Africanity" also means a shared destiny, fraternity in the fight for freedom, and a common future which has to be grasped jointly if it is to be under our control.

African Unity, cultural "Africanity", are realities shaped by the events of history on a common soil and experienced by men bound to the same destiny.

"Africanity" has a double origin: our common cultural inheritance and our common destiny.

The First Pan-African Cultural Festival should not therefore be a merely temporary meeting-place for diverse idioms. It is, at one and the same time, a primary assertion of African unity; unity of thought, heart and soul, and of the recognition of the part this "Africanity" has played in the preservation of national identities and in the fight for freedom.

This Festival was a duty for us and a debt of gratitude owed to our fathers who preserved our personality. All our nations felt the necessity to commit themselves, immediately after independence, to these tasks of safe-guarding and restoring our cultural heritage.

The First Pan-African Cultural Festival must be seen as a united African tribute to its own cultural and artistic foundations, and to its characteristics of structure and expression.

In making this tribute, we would not want the Festival to be based on a fanatical, xenophobic or unfruitful ethnocentrism. We have suffered too much from this to allow it ourselves or wish it to occur.

Culture, art and science, however voiced, do not differ basically. They are but specific expressions of a common universality.

Long denied, long consigned to exotism, to folklore or condemned to partial death in museums, the "Africani-ty" which we are celebrating today on a continental scale needs to find a living expression in the modern world. The world confronting us and the future which we are responsible for creating are both entirely dominated by the problems of development, progress and scientific conquest.

Justifiably, we have included in the agenda for the Symposium which will take place as part of the First Pan-African Festival, topics which deal with the role of culture in the development of Africa. If we wish to defend our authenticity it is because it gives greater assurance for the future, for far from confining ourselves to the monotonous and unfruitful reiteration of the past we want and must make our cultures into an instrument for our final liberation and further development.

For us, culture is a beginning which involves the best works of man in the stimulating task of development and social progress. What meaning, what role and what function could we give to culture, to education and to our arts if not to give our liberated peoples a better life and to continue the fight for our brothers still under the yoke of colonialism and, in one way or another, to participate thus in the world-wide task of the rehabilitation of man by man?

If these last conquests of man can have an efficacy and a meaning other than practical, tactical or factual ones, it will henceforth be this: culture in general, and in particular our own, will no longer be the basis of injustice or domination, but rather the instrument of a greater understanding between human beings.

THE FIRST PAN-AFRICAN CULTURAL FESTIVAL confirms our determination to make an individual and original contribution of our thoughts and our art within a single continuity and the same dynamics of social revolution and progress.

Now that the Festival is beginning, I should like to join you in expressing the hope that this meeting will be the beginning of a new era for our culture and that our efforts will be crowned with success.

I should also like to take advantage of this opportunity to welcome you and to wish you a pleasant stay in our country and also to thank the guests who have come from other continents to encourage us in our tremendous undertaking.

CULTURE, HISTORY
AND IDEOLOGY

By MAMADI KEITA

For once, we have not been asked to try to elucidate
the diverse terminologies obscuring the concept of
culture.

The path of tribulations undergone by the concept of
culture is, today, long indeed! The opinions of "commit-
tees of intellectuals" cancel each other out in a sterile
dialectic; various "symposia" painfully bring to a close
their august sessions with an incomprehension bringing a
hollow humanism face to face with the fear of the historical truth, and the progressive determination of man up
against the greatest calamity known to history: imperialism. In countries where a capitalist regime isolates the
general populace from scientific and technical attain-
ments, the intellectual fights to retain his false "freedom" and questions himself in vain about the future of a
decadent economic and social structure. He is helpless.
He somehow constructs a cultural policy in an attempt to
strengthen a society whose upheavals are the undeniable
symptoms of degeneration, and instead of using the faded light of his poor autocratic reason to seek a new
cultural conscience, he sinks into scepticism or, rather,
into the terror of a future overshadowed by capitalism.

The trends have dominated the study of cultural problems in Africa. For a long time latter-day Anglo-Saxon
anthropology, concerned with justifying the reactionary

9

ideas of colonialism, cited Africa as the home of backward peoples who should be forced to accept colonialist humanitarian civilization!

History has shown that revolutionary maturity cannot be the object of an edict which imperialism would, in any case, never sign! The Anglo-Saxon school of thought allowed for a pseudo-realism worthy of Hume's successors—a pseudo-realism the reactionary ideological content of which was soon to be exposed. Vierkandt's disciples, such as the "culturalists" Grabner and Ankermann, and functionalists like Malinkowski, believed they had discovered the basis of our culture. This was a medley of empiricism whose hate of historical materialism gave rise to disjointed monographs in which the class war and the imperialist exploitation of our peoples were weakened to an anti-scientific cultural pluralism.

Archeologists' pickaxes had evidently not yet reached the African culture which lay too deeply buried under the irremovable heap of dirt, left behind by the colonialists, which our peoples have now succeeded in piercing. The anxiety to extricate an authenticity which is, for obvious reasons, indiscoverable, gave rise to a fairly accurate representation of prelogism of Levy-Bruhl, who was already blind! In any case, there is no difference of concept between the black man unaware of the logical categories of the classical world on the one hand, and the idea of the essentially sensitive black man as a sort of passive, wax creature, only fit to remain at a primary intuitive level in his perception of the outside world on the other.

Thus it is no accident that African states still have to dedicate a symposium to a topic such as that which unites us to-day: "African culture and its realities". We recall that twenty years ago many pages were devoted to another topic which at that time seemed provocative and that was "A black man is a human being". It has become today our historical duty to re-establish ourselves in a field such as culture because we are emerging from a long period of eclipse during which our intrinsic possession of the most elementary attributes of man, notably his creativity, was denied.

In accordance with a well-nurtured prejudice, we took no part in the general task of civilization. Africa is accused of being without history and without culture because it was necessary that this be so. Europeans slaughtered American Indians while at the same time admiring their temples and palaces. They admitted that they massacred the men to take over their land. By their conquests and domination they destroyed millennial civilizations in Asia, but they never denied the existence of these civilizations as such, and never contested the quality of their craftsmanship and their human attributes to the peoples of this continent.

Concerning Africa, Europe's first notion was not to exterminate the men with the sole idea of seizing their treasures, but to treat them as beasts to be sold into slavery and as they pleased, sold on the spot or exported to America, or even killed when their working capabilities and selling price was no longer assured an adequate profit.

To guarantee the success of such a venture a preliminary was necessary—that of easing one's conscience and re-assuring oneself by thinking that it was a question of dealing with beasts and not human beings. Hence the alleged barbarity of Africans and the denial of their culture and civilization gave birth to their estrangement from the human race.

But time did not stop, and the strength of progress continued to increase in the face of opposition and exploitation. More attention was paid to the legends, the epic poems and the tales passed by word of mouth from generation to generation of the Griots. Archaeology finally penetrated the various continents, thrusting deep into the depths of history and the soil so as to revive and bring to the surface the remains of intombed cultures.

In fact without archaeological research and the tales of the Griots, ordinary commonsense was adequate to realize the absurdity or rather the class-consciousness of those who managed to imagine a cultureless people.

What is Culture?

By culture, we understand all the material and non-material works of art and science, plus knowledge, manners, education, a mode of thought, behaviour and attitudes accumulated by the People both through and by virtue of its struggle for freedom from the hold and dominion of Nature, and also through and by virtue of its efforts to destroy the deviationist politics—social systems of domination and exploitation which appear as aberrant excrescences in Society through the productive process of its life.

Thus culture stands revealed as both an exclusive creation of the People and a source of creation, as an instrument of socio-economic liberation and as one of domination.

Culture implies our striving—it is our striving.

As has been observed by Comrade Ahmed Sekou Toure, Secretary-General of the Democratic Party of Guinea, culture—as both the expression and the result of the relationships between Man and Society, between Man and Society on the one hand and Nature on the other—is found among all peoples and is inherent in the very process of life. A culture is to be found wherever conscious life exists.

Culture is the sum total of the material and spiritual values created by humanity throughout its history. This creation is both continuous and necessary. It is the corollary, the yardstick and the result of man's action to adapt to his environment so that he can both survive and flourish. It is inspired by the instinct for survival at the first stage and by an awareness of the laws of existence at a higher stage. Therefore, it firstly obeys a simple biological law regulating the survival of the individual and the species before obeying a more complex psychological and socio-economic law. Now the instinct for self-preservation and the need for self-fulfilment are common to all societies and peoples. Every people must struggle to exist by creating the material means of its existence. The African peoples, like all peoples, have come along the long road of history through recurrent conflicts whose overall result has been increasing success. The creation of material values, the creation of spiritual values, the creation and development of this global culture progresses continuously in spite of momentary slowing-down, stagnation and setbacks. Material cultural production and spiritual cultural production are dialectically linked and exercise a reciprocal influence on each other. But the absolute priority must rest with material production, which itself participates directly in man's concrete action. For human history has more than once recorded a slackening of spiritual tension, a stagnation of intellectual and political life or even a total annihilation of all intellectual and political activity, but it has never recorded a long-term total interruption of the development of material civilisation. This evolution can, of course, slow down but it can never stop, as its stopping would signify the end of man's creative activity, the disappearance of his powers of adaptation and his extinction.

This action is a matter of vital necessity—a condition and a sign of life. Human action is the "prime mover", the source of all else. It aims at the satisfaction of needs, firstly vital, physical needs and then less immediate ones relating to the assertion and enrichment of the personality, and intellectual and moral needs. This action of both men and society is directed against the environment, against man himself and against nature. It is designed to meet the needs of all and this raises the problem of its efficiency and profitability. It calls for the existence of tactics, of a strategy, an intellectual effort to *attain* a certain degree of planning, both criticism and self-criticism in the light of the results and methodology bringing into play a whole series of intellectual operations. It is a culture, a material and spiritual acquisition, both the product and the price of action.

Creative action springing from a universal imperative and culture which is its reflection, subject and effect, both constitute universal realities. Wherever there is the necessity of creation, we find culture. As the expression of the relationships between Man and Society, between Man, Society and Nature, culture poses in the most pressing terms the problem of the dialectic of the general and the particular. Culture is an expression in particular, specific forms of a general problem—that of the relationships linking man to his environment.

But these relations in turn take on a specific character determined by geographical conditions, the level of development of productive forces and the nature of the means of production as determined by the historical and social context. The cultural level of a people (including the peoples of Africa), its means of conquering knowledge, its manner of explaining phenomena, will depend on the power that it has gained over natural forces, and the degree of objectivity and abstraction attained in the heat of action to gain mastery over ever more perfected techniques.

The specific, particular nature of a culture is a reality; one of the attributes of national reality in general and of class reality in particular. It expresses conditions of life shared in common, a similarity of attitudes and the reactions to natural and social phenomena.

But there is a general aspect even to this specific particularity, in that even if these attitudes and reactions are marked by the irrational at certain stages of historical development, even if they derive from simple emotion at certain points in the action or if they occur at the level of reflexes, they are fundamentally set in motion and guided by reason with a view to reaching well-defined objectives and finding solutions to well-defined problems. Specific particularity is not specific to African culture, but to every culture. This specificity is a general reality. But, apart from this general aspect of specificity, culture, by virtue of its content (the expression of man's eternal aspirations to happiness and to the final unfolding of his nature) with ever-increasing power over the environment, is in perpetual movement towards the universal. The speed at which culture tends towards the universal is the function of the dialectic of cultural forms and content at a given stage of history.

The universalisation of the content of culture in interpreting the aspirations of all peoples will go hand in hand with a greater perfection of its forms of expression, due to the general development of forms and the revolutionisation of industrial relations. African culture, like any culture, originated with the African himself and embodies his first preoccupations, his first struggles, his first successes and setbacks.

The course of history and the succession of its development have closely reflected the course of the development of productive forces, its initial simplicity, low intellectual level and slow rate of progression, all reflected the weakness of man's position and the precariousness of his existence. Then over the centuries and down through the ages, following the development of productive techniques, culture developed, became diversified, took on shades of meaning and incorporated science, technology, literature, music, dancing and sculpture. This whole evolution, this progressive qualification is subordinated to reason, to the law of gnoseology, to the transition from ignorance to an increasingly deeper and more exact degree of knowledge. Any anthology of African culture trying to situate it outside the realm of reason, of rational thought, of the law and of gnoseology tends to down-grade it and deviate it from its true end, which is to qualify mankind, and sacrifices it to the myth of singularity and specificity.

African culture neither has nor needs any foundation other than the concrete life of the African. With its roots deep in the innermost life of the people, it expresses the life, work, ideals and aspirations of the African people. It has contributed, along with other cultures, to the development of science and technology. Prior to the contact with other continents, Africa had begun to smelt metals and to forge tools and weapons. She had learned to weave fabrics. The notion of chemistry had developed through various recipes needed to make soap, indigo and ink, to tan hides, and so on.

But, to a far greater extent than science, which was handicapped by the persistence throughout the ages of a low level of technology, African art, African literature, African sculpture, music and dancing, already occupies, or will occupy, an important place in humanity's cultural heritage. The reality of African culture needs no further demonstration, but its infinite realities are still to be discovered, recorded and described.

But, in Africa as elsewhere, culture reacts upon those producing it (Man and Society) at the same time as it is produced and developed.

Culture is an accumulated experience which modifies man in a linear, progressive and quantitative manner but with additional qualitative phases of mutation.The result is a new man, a new society, more skilful and more apt, integrating to an ever-increasing extent the means and the end of action, and perfecting to an ever greater extent technology and means of action.

Experience, acquired by and for action, becomes an inexhaustible source of energy, both the instrument and the guide of present and future action. Culture appears then, at one and the same time, as a creation and a means of creation of man and society, as an expression of the dialectical relationships between the creator and his creation. It is clearly apparent in its real light, that of a factor determining and conditioning all else. The conquest of culture has obliged man to mobilise all his physical and intellectual resources. Once it was conquered, culture became a flame animating and intoxicating the conqueror, man. So it is scarcely an exaggeration to say man equals the culture that formed him and which inspires his behaviour and action.

The fact of a culture conditions both the existence of the people and its exercise of sovreignty and power. For us, to speak of culture is to fight, and although history has very edifying examples to offer such as these which dominate the formation of feudalism, we have chosen to carry the data of this combat forward into the present era.

Everyone knows what a foul use was made of it by the predatory powers, in the course of modern history, in their appropriation, among other things, of the African peoples.

After having laid their hands on the essential elements of the culture of their own people, the upper classes of the colonialist power used this weapon in their endeavour to dominate and exploit our continent.

It was first of all necessary to legitimise the various kinds of pillage and colonial domination in the eyes of established morality, and to this end the natural difference between our culture and that of the peoples of these powers was used to justify and accredit the ignominious assertion that we did not have any culture and that a culture should be bestowed and imposed upon us. Here started the crusade for humanization through the cultural-ization of the "marginal" peoples, of the peoples which have remained at the stage of "raw material-peoples", of peoples waiting to be manufactured in the Big Factory of civilized men. And presently, so as to ensure that coloni-zation was everlasting, the systematic drill of native workers was introduced; this contributed to the smooth functioning of the Big Factory.

The Corps of "colonial elites", "man of culture", natives of any level, of any experience and political hue, was created.

On the eve of the disintegration of the colonial empires, and opposed to this elite, an "intellectual elite", subjectively in opposition, came to the fore.

Of course this elite tried to make use of all available means. It had suffered from the racist blows that imperi-alism has dealt to Africa, but it had not understood that, although ideology and racist practices may be an effec-tive weapon when wielded by imperialism which is an active racism, a non-culture in history, racist ideology used by those who are in revolt cannot be but a double-edged weapon which, in the last resort, is profitable only to the imperialist enemy. Therefore, Holy Negritude, be it Arab-Berber or Ethiopian-Bantu, this negritude is ob-jectively an ideology auxiliary to the general imperialist ideology.

The Master transforms his slave into a Negro whom he defines as being without reason, sub-human and the em-bittered slave then protests: 'as you are Reason, I am Emotion and I take this upon myself'. This is how we loop the loops. The Master assumes his pre-eminence, and the Slave his servitude, but the latter claims his right to weep, a right which the Master grants him.

A reconciliation has come about and one understands easily why the imperialist propaganda system, which includes press, radio, and cinema, goes to such trouble to spread the comforting concept of negritude. Negritude is actually a good mystifying anaesthetic for Negroes who have been whipped too long and too severely to a point where they have lost all reason and become purely emotional.

As serious analysis shows that the colonial situation is by no means contested by this elite, and that objectively speaking, far from mobilizing and arming the subjugated peoples, it gives the colonizers an easy conscience by accrediting the existence of a certain liberty of thought and action within the colonial system. From this point of view, the intellectual elite while being subjectively in opposition, objectively completes the arsenal of colonial domination. While the latter appropriates popular culture for its own profit it deprives the colonized people of its best defensive and offensive weapons, an autonomously created culture nurtured by themselves.

The combination of two circumstances: a people deprived of its own culture on the one hand, and the tremendous development of science and technology (elements of culture) with the imperialist, on the other, made a certain kind of culture, at a time when the former colonies were attaining national independence, into a deadly weapon in the hands of the neo-colonialist.

It must be admitted that the frightened attitude of many African governments towards cynical imperialist arrogance, the helplessness of the peoples who were victims of neo-colonialist coup de'etats, were a result of the fact that these peoples had been deprived of their culture. The most powerful weapon for the rape and renewed subjugation of our peoples now available to imperialism and new-colonialism is a certain kind of culture.

The invincible weapon, defensive against imperialism and colonialism and offensive for the complete emancipation of our peoples, is culture which has once again become the creation of an entire society and the source of all progressive creation.

This analysis leads to the conclusion that culture, a superstructure born from an infrastructure, which it modifies and qualitatively transforms in its turn, is the reality of a class of ideological classes.

One should not mistake this expression for a form of neo-idealism: by ideological classes, we are referring to classes which are by no means born from a simple economic and social stratification; we are faced here with a fundamental choice between two possibilities which are mutually exclusive, namely:

1. The ideology of domination, and prostration under domination.
2. The ideology of struggle against any kind of domination and of the complete sovereignty of the people, power being exercised by and for the people.

(All the activities of the Guinean Democratic Party are based on this second ideology which is manifest in all the aspects of life without a single exception.)

Thus it is understood that culture is a field of action where man, society, nature, men and peoples confront one another. In this merciless combat, the reconnoitering and conquering of ground are essential for victory. The superiority of arms is a superiority of culture, at least in its material and technical aspects. And it is this superiority in the production of culture which enables a people to dominate other peoples and impose its spiritual culture upon them. Culture is a more effective weapon than guns for the purpose of domination. For it was scientific, technical and technological culture which produced the guns. The prerequisite for any domination, exploitation and oppression is the denial to the oppressed man or people of his (or their) human attributes and therefore, in the first instance, cultural activities.

Before conquering, dominating and subjugating a people, the ruler asserts the superiority of his culture and civilization and proclaims its civilizing mission to those he has declared arbitrarily and unilaterally to be barbarian, savage, uncultured, and without civilization. The rulers take it for granted that the understanding of nature with a view to exploiting it in order to promote technical advancement is their exclusive privilege, their property. But opinions more authoritative, and more justified than those of imperialism, colonialism and neo-colonialism, stated that nature was understandable to any individual and that man, provided he was aware of the historical significance of his existence, was capable of penetrating further every day into the secrets of nature, and increasing his power over it in order to increase his control of it.

What is important at a given historical moment in the process of the knowledge and control of natural forces is not so much the quality of knowledge and its conformity to the absolute truth as the way men and people are aware of their abilities and possibilities of understanding, and of their unfailing will to progress. In this process, the characteristic factor is an attitude, a turn of mind leading to self-reliance and confidence in the people. Acquired knowledge and the degree of truth which characterizes it, belong to a quantitative factor linked with facilities used in research, experiment and application. This is an historical stage in development which each people will achieve more or less quickly according to its means, the prerequisite being once again the belief that what is unknown can be known. No people is more gifted, more intelligent than others, but there are differences in historical contexts. Imperialists and exploiters blinded the will to exploit are incapable of understanding these primary truths. Their culture is made up of guns, whips, hard labour and training which deny, humiliate and depersonalize those under the colonial yoke.

Nowadays efforts are still being made, and the objective law of relationships between things goes on working. Problems of economic and cultural development of our peoples are watched, analysed and criticized by Imperialism—that commanding and universal exploiter. And each time it proves to be otherwise, age-old, false notions are, without hesitation, revived.

Here we have a speculator, who may be honest and who proposes once again a new reactionary Valerianism "entering backward into history" because one cannot accept capitalist civilization and open new prospects for the future of oppressed people.

Or a research worker with a philosophy doomed to failure, alive to a questionable universalism, but rather losing the pitiable traces of a frigid idealism which proposes the pattern of an Africa of invertebrates and pithecautropes exploitable at will for ever.

Or an idealistic archaeologist who, in the absence of a scientific ideology proposes dodges in which spiritualism is sufficiently anaesthetic to befool masses and throw them in a state of coma to the rapacity of imperialism.

For the Bourgeoisie and its colonialist allies, the masses must be kept in ignorance, for ignorant individuals can distort culture if attained. Peasants and workers are incapable of preserving cultural values, let alone creating new ones. This has been proved to be absurd in those countries where socialism is being introduced. Revolution is the only way to ensure that science and culture will thrive and not decline.

Culture, through Art, Literature and Techniques, is the

image of men's activity. Thus, hunt dances imitate the movement and pace of the game hunted. The stylized choreography of the African savannah hunter imitating the lion or the elephant, even so far as to include its appearance, is aesthetically poor only in the minds of the exploiters who hate all that is connected with the people. War is a hunt where man is the game, and culture is an imitation of war episodes. The dances of the Sofas of Samori or the "tudos" of the Damel Tagne lat Dior, the Boko (challenge dances) of a N'Beur-Kat (Senagalese wrestler) like the famous wrestler Modum Khule (who actually existed) are real masterpieces, especially when accompanied by songs and gestures of attack like those of the phalanges mentioned by Stanley. Culture is the image, the record of experience and the techniques of production.

Sayings, proverbs, tales and folk songs express the wish for a bountiful production and the experience of mastery over nature; hence the coexistence of the naive materialism of peasant cultures with the idealism, arising from ignorance.

Authors as perspicacious as Frazer, in their rejection of historical materialism, were not able to account scientifically for magic. The experience of the fight against nature enables man to acquire knowledge. But given his limited means and sometimes even the implacable hostility of physical chemical determinism, the major secrets of nature are all the more difficult to penetrate in that their world is unknown. Magic then becomes a conjuration, and rites reproduce gestures acquired from experience, which are regarded as valuable if occult creatures are favourable. Hence the necessity to limit damages, natural disasters, and kill beasts which, for example, destroy the crops.

Should development stop at that stage, it would lead to ignorance. Imperialism soon found out that its power lay in this. It had to transform us into scared, helpless beings facing natural and historical necessities. Kept in such an ignorant state, oppressed peoples are a prey to prejudice and terror before invisible powers which are all the more alienating in that they are closely linked with their culture. Misery and physical decline are given an explanation except when this latter unveils the monstruous responsibilities of the imperialist exploiters.

Culture is the synthesis of people's activities. To fight against diseases and hunger, to control nature and to widen the scope of knowledge are the tasks of the whole of mankind. Scientific and technical culture is the highest manifestation of collective creativeness. It has led to the eradication of several natural scourges.

From the historical point of view, no culture can be free of a class content. Unless it is a camouflage for some stupidity of the ideologists of exploiting regimes, every culture follows a well-defined political line. African feudalism, for example, did not experience private land control; but it was the case in Europe, where the lords came to consider themselves as the owners of the land they were entrusted with simply defending against possible invaders! That is the origin of the collective nature of peasant dances where the gestures cover the whole range of free agricultural activity.

Culture, like all social phenomena, is characterized by class struggle. Cultural power, the container and contents of economic and political power, is thus a powerful oppressive weapon in the hands of the exploiters. Culture for the people has rightly been considered as the bete noire of the ideologists of capitalism.

It is logical for capitalistic exploitation to deny workers access to the culture they have created. Thus, sociologists and reactionary historians, with a view to justifying such a monopolization and to praising it, put forward the theory of the development of culture by an elite. The idea is that mankind is indebted to a handful of such genial individuals as Darwin, Einstein, Shakespeare, and Beethoven, for its achievements in art, literature, science, and technology. Of course, tribute should be paid to these men. But if it is true that their active existence is a proof that culture is created by an elite, how can one explain that individuals endowed with equal genius did not exist in the days of the leakey man or Sinanthropus?

Science has never been a one-man concern. It is usually said that, in the past, a scholar went to work by himself. In fact, a scientist can make discoveries or inventions and enrich the heritage of mankind only in a favourable social and cultural context. Nowadays, the method of scientific research has changed. The scientist forms part of a team. The "demonstration" of this method has not yet led to the realization that collective work is a necessity because of the complexity of the problems, and the scope, of modern science. Not only that, team work is necessary also because capitalism aims at monopolizing and exploiting brigades of brains. But as far as we are concerned, we are fully aware that this method, of which capitalism considers only the effects, is the very basis of scientific inventiveness. Besides, scientific workers are the perpetuators of the efforts of past generations.

It is here that comrade Ahmed Sekou Toure and the poet Victor Hugo are in agreement.

The former wrote: " . . . one discovery may fundamentally or partially question a scientific principle previously considered sacrosanct and which had therefore prevailed till then . . . , undoubtedly it is the law of continuous advance which prevails".

The latter wrote: "Science is continuous scratching with fruitful results; science is a ladder . . .".

The foundations of culture have been created and the conditions for its progress are created by the working masses which are the makers of history.

Literature and art have thrived for a long time in the form of folklore: epic poems, legends, tales, proverbs, songs served as a basis for writers. Painters and artists drew inspiration from the applied arts created by the people; popular art is an inexhaustible treasury of patterns and methods, a source of exaltation for writers and artists. It generates and feeds the national form of the art and literature of every country; science stems from the people's genius.

Consequently, culture is not the privilege of the haves. By depriving the masses of the benefits of science and culture, and keeping them in ignorance, the exploiters found a justification for their class supremacy. But intelligence and talent are not the privileges of a class; the force of the spirit, will and talent of thousands of workers is reflected in all cultural creations.

Culture, a weapon of domination, will be that of liberation. In this instance, one must fight on ground of the enemy's choosing but one where the issue of the fight will be governed by an adequate weapon: popular culture. As Comrade Sekou Toure pointed out: "The Imperialists use cultural, scientific, technical, economic, literary and moral values in order to justify and perpetuate their regime of exploitation and oppression. The oppressed peoples also use cultural values, but of a nature contrary to the former, in order to fight more successfully against imperialism and in order to free themselves from the colonial regime".

Resistance, and then, the offensive, will be organized, first of all, in the cultural field. Colonized man must first recollect himself, establish a critical balance of the results of the influences to which he was subjected by the invader, which are reflected in his behaviour and ways of thinking, his conception of the world and society and his way of assessing the values created by his own people.

In the first place, he must undertake to re-conquer his own personality by denying the cultural values which have depersonalized him, by de-colonizing his own mind, his customs, and his attitudes, by dismantling the philosophical systems justifying dominations, particularly Levy-Bruhl's notorious myth of primitive and prelogic mind as opposed to the intellectual and moral superiority complex of the colonizer; the colonized man must free himself from his inferiority complexes and embody Man in what he represents of absolute values, aspirations to the Universal. Actually, this first stage of liberation, of struggle for the liquidation of the various complexes of the colonized man is not to be dissociated from the following stage—that of the reconquest of lost values, of possessions denied and lost, attributes of a sensible man who thinks and acts in a dignified way and is aware of his potentialities. Nature abhors a vacuum, even on the cultural level. One cannot extirpate from the mind of colonized man the culture which has been imposed upon him and which has poisoned him except by offering him a substitute culture, namely his own culture, which implies an action to restore to life, and popularize that culture. However this action is possible only in the large framework of the struggle for national liberation and social promotion. Culture cannot flower properly without putting an end to the causes which had been stifling it; but conversely, the cult of cultural authenticity, the struggle for the reconquest of this authenticity by activating the awareness of, and mobilizing, popular masses, activates the process of political and social liberation as well as forges the nation through the creation of a melting pot in which the simple citizen is formed without any consideration of tribe or race.

This free man within a free people who has rediscovered his physical and mental balance can thenceforward assume the entire responsibility for his own destiny. He can and must widen boundlessly the bases of his cultural heritage, diversify them, and direct them in order to clarify any action likely to be undertaken with a view to improving the conditions of existence and prosperity. The imperialists have dominated and oppressed peoples, thanks to a technical superiority they had previously acquired. The peoples in turn, animated by the conviction that the faculty of research, discovery and invention is the thing most fairly shared among men, will throw themselves into the battle for knowledge of the sciences and technology. Scientific culture, the ideal means of domination and production of goods, is a factor for progress in the creation of culture, material and spiritual.

Yes, culture is an instrument of freedom, an anti-imperialist, anti-colonialist, anti-neo-colonialist weapon, a means of dominating nature. Always providing it is a progressive, revolutionary culture created and consumed by the people on the basis of popularization. Only such a culture frees man of himself, of his egoistical tendency, of the vanity and pride and the fear which inhibits him—only such a culture frees and promotes a people by reconciling it with its authentic nature and opening to it the way to the future and the universal.

Today national liberation and the edification of socialism are scheduled in the programme of revolutionary Africa. All kinds of imperialists, colonialists, neo-colonialists, armies of ideological puppets, traders of peoples have taken fright when found with the determination of our masses, vilify socialism and present it as an ideology of terror; the only reason for such a display of anti-revolutionary forces is our determination to free Africa from the lust of imperialism, our determination to build an Africa having nothing to do with the exploitation of man by man.

However, we would be supporting a determinism similar to a wait-and-see policy and to fatalism, if we limited our victory to the eradication of imperialism and its self-destruction. For a while such a system bears within itself the germs of its own destruction. History teaches us that the duration of the regimes of exploitation of man by man depends on the intensity of intervention and the cultural level of the oppressed peoples. It is therefore important to create revolutionary conditions in order to enable citizens to give the best of themselves. Culture, being a synthesis of people's activities, is a power whose democratic mastery provides the masses with unexpected capacities of ideological and material creation and improvement.

"It was through cultural power", as our comrade Ahmed Sekou Toure said, "that the master managed to justify and maintain his political power and economic domination over the slave. . . . It is through usurpation of cultural power (in the form of science, technology, methodology, art and a certain conception of the world) that neo-colonialist imperialism is still controlling many governments and exploiting the peoples it is supposed to help".

The other aspect of the elite's monopoly is that it cripples culture; capitalism which is only concerned with the creation of a wealthy upper class, cannot stimulate culture. There is neither a unilateral economic determinism, nor idealism to assert that the weakness or the death of several civilizations is due not to irascibility or a so-called original moral insufficiency of man, but to the fact that culture was the monopoly of a small minority; the scientific and technical power of this minority was the perfect expression of the frailty of such economic and cultural systems. Only a creative people can make culture advance, provided that the social system enables the democratic assimilation of the techniques and that the enrichment of a universal cultural patrimony becomes the peoples' monopoly. Democratization of science and culture is thus the fertilization of progressive civilizations.

Only the Revolutionary Movement can restore to culture its humanistic essence.

Culture is then understood in its two basic aspects: one, as a domination of physico-chemical determinism for progressive purposes, and two, as a revolutionary orientation of society.

The Cultural Revolution implies the total emancipation of the people; consequently the Cultural Revolution is the radicalized revolution.

One cannot talk of revolutionary socialization of the means of production when the people, who are the rightful owners, are uneducated. The revolutionization of culture presupposes two basic aspects: firstly, that culture is available to the masses, and secondly, that by widening the intellectual qualification, revolution creates new conditions for the fecundation of culture and science. Once the people are aware of what they create, and know they are responsible for the improvement of social relationship, they are ideologically capable of undertaking the construction of a society free of the exploitation of man by man.

Revolution democratizes culture to its very core, making it serve all of society and not just the elite. The democratization of culture enables many people to reveal their talents in all fields of scientific and artistic endeavour, and it creates the conditions that enable these talents to flourish.

Artistic creation cannot remain outside the struggle because each writer, each artist, whether he likes it or not, expresses the interests of his class in his work. The socialist revolution throws off the monetary yoke from culture and permits the creation of works for the vast popular masses and not just for the personal tastes of a handful of stupid gluttons.

The cultural and technical aspects of a society are a part of the whole of the revolutionary cause. Lenin wrote that they are "a little review and a little screw" in the general mechanism of the Revolution. Revolutionary culture is a powerful fighting weapon and a material force for the people. It constitutes an indispensable part of the battle-front of total Revolution. Science and culture fit perfectly into the general mechanism of the struggle as weapons of unity and education for the destruction of the enemy.

"An army without a culture is an ignorant army and an ignorant army can never defeat its enemy", wrote a contemporary philosopher. Africa must join the Cultural Revolution. But what are the principal tasks of the Cultural Revolution? Cultural Revolution does not mean the denial of all culture of the past; rather, it is the continuation of everything that was beautiful because it is authentic. Therefore, the following points must be mentioned:

> One must choose permanent and sound values from the cultural heritage and reject outmoded mores, bad traditions, superstitions, alientating and inhibiting attitudes such as Negritude and everything that is useless and reactionary.
> One must transform culture from being the privilege of an elite into a culture that belongs to the people.
> One must elevate the cultural and scientific level of the working class to ensure the continued progress of the production forces.
> One must re-educate the older intellectuals who can still be salvaged, because once man has freed himself from the narrowness of the petit bourgeois, he can always be perfected.

One must create a new type of intellectuals.

And finally, one must commit the whole people, irrevocably, to the edification of socialism.

The revolution restores to the people what they created during the secular class struggle——the scientific and technological acquisitions achieved with their labour——and defines constantly the means of fighting against imperialism, colonialism and neo-colonialism.

Given adequate material and dimensions, our people can become invincible, raise higher the flag of freedom and play in better conditions their historical role of permanently eradicating imperialism.

Here, presented as briefly as possible, is an African sample of Cultural Revolution.

VALUE SYSTEMS AND CONFLICT IN CONTEMPORARY AFRICAN CULTURE

By SETH CUDJOE

Ordinary African citizens need an enlightened and integrated authority of the kind that will give them a sense of identity with their own cultures and their continent of Africa. In spite of their animation and outwardly relaxed manner, an underlying feeling of frustration and stagnation afflicts many African nations, and the reason is simply this, that a people who have successfully rid themselves of foreign rule, need deeply satisfying spiritual and social ideals, to galvanise them into re-building their societies according to their own cherished image.

Men cannot function creatively when the image in which they see themselves is blurred, tarnished, and distorted by the confused values of culture conflict; when, by robbing them of the greater part of their adaptive and inventive powers, that conflict makes it a terrible hazard for them to begin re-shaping their societies.

In our contemporary society, the conflict is between traditional oral culture and Western visual culture; between what may be designated as a man-centered, personal, kinship or communal culture, on the one hand, and a machine-centered, impersonal, functional, or individualistic culture, on the other. The one society is based on versatility, the other, on specialisation.

Versatility implies a man's ability to acquire and exercise several skills in his quest for a many-sided adaptation of himself to his society. In a strictly functional society, on the other hand, a man may, generally speaking, acquire one skill only, be it that of road sweeper or shop assistant; farmer or factory worker; physician or lawyer; magician or preacher; engineer or artist. In contrast to the versatile worker, the specialist may, in fact, cease to earn a living where his one and only skill becomes a glut in the labour market.

The conflict of African oral culture with Western visual culture, seems the more vicious where the authority system characteristic of both cultures, clash with one another. This is not so only because oral culture contains authority systems whose religious and social sanctions differ from those of visual culture, but also because the concepts which bind the authority systems of each culture together differ from one another.

The concept of family in oral culture, for example, and its extended meaning in terms of chiefship, ancestors, deities, and the Supreme God, imply human relationships with spiritual worlds which are textually different from those of Christian visual culture. They imply also a concept of human destiny which, unlike the postponed heaven and hell of Christian visual culture, postulates natural and supernatural reward or punishment in this life, for the good or evil which men do.

No one who understands traditional authority systems can fail to see, in their inter-relatedness with one another, the important ferment and directive they are for the personal and social development of the individual. Each one of us, without exception, needs an intelligent and imaginative authority system to guide him develop those inner controls which enable a man to distinguish between self-esteem and mere conceit, between gold and glitter.

It is these inner controls which underlie the mastery of the modes in which a man exerts, asserts, and expresses himself within his social and natural environments. A breakdown of the external authority systems of a given culture, or of their inter-relations with one another, therefore, must result in the grievous interruption of those major environmental influences, which men need for their own development and contribution to society.

The authority systems that govern the development of the individual as a social being, belong largely to the intangible elements of culture. Without the comprehensive intangible value systems of culture, men could neither organise or maintain society, nor acquire the habit of social living. Moreover, man needs the intangibles of his own culture not only to stimulate him into constantly reshaping the physical or tangible frame-work of his society, but also into creating the new value systems which his changing view of the world demands of him.

Religion

It is right that the authority of the Chief should occupy first place in all considerations of traditional authority systems, since it was the Chief, in fact, who integrated the total life of the village over which he ruled into one large family.

The problems with which the Chief had to cope in his village in situations of culture conflict, therefore, must have led to much heart searching. For that conflict, which was not always self-evident as such, went a long way in subtly undermining both the Chief's authority and the mental health of his people.

These untoward influences become undeniable once religion is recognised as the pivot around which traditional African life and the rule of the Chief, revolved. For to reject African religions in the total way Western Christianity did, was tantamount to condemnation of a good deal of the cultures which derived from them.

It is proof, of course, of their unwavering conviction that those to whom the Light had been revealed, should have risked their own lives in their determination to share it with others. Retrospectively, however, it has always remained doubtful whether light could really be shed on a people's life by first setting aside almost the entire value system of their culture.

Surely, African concepts of the Supreme God and His authority over human societies, their concepts of the spiritual world and the manner in which it inter-acts with the physical, and the extensive systems of fellowship which they have evolved for themselves out of these concepts, cannot be said to be entirely devoid of love and virtue.

How did it come about that Africans allowed themselves to be so demoralised by the adverse value judgments of a people who did not understand the ideological foundations of their society? How did Africans expect to become truly Christian by such painful imitation of the theology, liturgy, arts, and behaviour patterns which Christians of an alien culture had created in their own image to the glory of God? Has the African Christian no free will or devotional imagination to call his very own?

The days of spiritual vassalage are over, and those of a true world spiritual comradeship, long overdue. Africa has her own resources of spiritual power, and it is high time her peoples created a new religious life, Christian or non-Christian, that is consonant with their own cultural roots. Without it, they could not hope to attain the same kind of spiritual stature, which inspired holy men from other lands to bring Christianity and Islam to this great continent of Africa.

I do not believe for one moment that the white man's way of looking at the life of Christ is the only valid one, nor do I believe that the social behaviour which he has created for himself from the teachings of Christ, are the only ones that deserve to be called Christian. The last word about Christ is not the sole preserve of white Christians. There is no racism implied here. If the first Christian missionaries had been Nubians, we would, under similar circumstances, have challenged their claim to be the only persons capable of truly interpreting the life of Christ.

It would be a miracle if African Christian churches which are strictly Western in style and context, ever succeeded in producing the dynamic and creative African Christian mind, which we need to transform our society, and truly win it for Christ. African church leaders have always, on the whole, been far too subservient to Western Christian thinking and feeling to develop the regenerative outlook which the different social and cultural environment of Africa demands.

Family

The family is the first authority through which man begins to learn to chart his way across the tangible and intangible value systems of his society, and he begins to do so long before he has developed a critical evaluation of his own family and of society in general.

Quite clearly, therefore, it is the family which lays down the first foundations of a man's development as a social and creative being. That being so, we must ascribe, at least, part of our present lack of a true resurgent spirit, to the disintegrative processes which have eaten deep into our extended kinship system.

The development of roads and communications and the migrations which these bring about, are partly responsible for the present fragmentation of the extended kinship system, and the consequent dislocation of its corporate security. This is a natural sequence of events in the progress of human beings with which no one would wish to quarrel.

It is a different matter, however, where family disintegration at the village level is further hastened by African bureaucracies, which are obsessed with the centralisation of all political and economic power, without paying much heed to the need of villages for an ever active co-ordination of their social, economic, religious, and artistic life. That bureaucracy should thus attempt to destroy traditional genius for a co-ordinated social life, shows how little some African leaders today know about the fundamentals of human progress.

Marriage

An additional factor in family disintegration is the conflict which has arisen from the unhappy superimposition of Western monogamy on traditional African polygamy. The first serious problem of monogamy in a situation of this kind, is the stain of illegitimacy which it stamps on all children born extramaritally to men, whose current marital status legally restricts them to one woman only, irrespective of whether or not she is capable of bearing children.

The problem of illegitimacy was bound to be acute in a strictly polygamous society, where the application of inheritance laws alike to full and half brothers and sisters, rendered the concept of illegitimacy irrelevant. Polygamous marriage was institutionally stable not only because the violation of a woman almost always implied the man's desire to marry, but also because by its very nature, extended kinship offered a strong protection for both the unmarried and married woman against philanderers. The tendency on the part of some Christians to equate polygamy with a total lack of masculine respect for the female, therefore, needs to be challenged. It is

questionable, at any rate, whether Christians who en-
dorse the cruel ostracism which is meted out in Europe to
unmarried mothers and their innocent offspring, have the
moral right to condemn a marital system which rejects
the very idea of illegitimacy.

On the other hand, the moral backing which traditional
polygamy obtained from kinship solidarity, was bound to
diminish with the disintegration of the kinship system
itself. With the loss of the traditional social controls
which once regulated pre-marital and marital relationships, polygamy has degenerated into promiscuity of a
singularly irresponsible kind. Clearly the hypocrisy of
secretive extra-marital relations on which monogamy
survives precariously in Europe, cannot be maintained in
African societies, which, from the very beginning, have
never had any real quarrel with plural relationships.

Sex Equality

The present state of our society renders meaningless
the claim of women to equality with men, for where a
nation's family system has fallen into disrepair and free
love has become the order of the day, men and women
can only be equal in their share of blame for irregular
sexual behaviour.

Whether the system of marriage prevalent in a society
is monogamous or polygamous does not hang vitally on
the question of female equality or inferiority. There are
areas of biological endowment in which men may be said
to be superior to women; areas such as those that have to
do with muscular strength, aggression, and adventure. It
is these areas, irrespective of monogamy or polygamy
which originally determined the superior role of man as
the provider for, and protector of woman.

Any society, therefore, which supports this provider-
protector role of man, necessarily places woman under

male dominance to variable extents, within this area of their inter-relationship. It is clear also that polygamy could not have become a social institution merely because man believed woman to be inferior to himself in all fields of human endeavour.

The present freedom of African womanhood is not so much liberation as liberty, and the reason is simple. The fact that women are no longer denied access, at least in theory, to the vocations and professions, the skills and controls, and the sexual privileges which were once the preserves of men, does not mean that they can offer an immediate and large scale competition to men in fields that have been opened to them much longer than women.

At any rate, the question is not so much equality of persons of the same or opposite sex as equal opportunities. Besides, there are biologically determined powers and functions, which are the natural and specialised attributes of each sex, and which, much to our cost, have begun to lose their rightful emphasis before the present clamour for false equality. False, because, on the whole, middle class African women who fight for equality of the sexes, tend to identify themselves with the aims of similar organisations in the international sphere without first conducting research into the role attitudes prevalent amongst the ordinary women of their own countries.

It may be that polygamy of a new kind will emerge out of the sheer need to contain the present promiscuity, but whether or not we believe in an eventuality of this kind, the fact still remains that a re-constitution of our family system and a re-definition of male and female roles and relationships, are more than overdue. Without them, the present frustration and unrest of youth can never be resolved, and all attempts at discovering a meaningful continuity between home and school, will be of little avail.

Education

The problems of education in a society in which cultures conflict are, on the negative side, those of ideological and creative confusion, and, on the positive side, those of selecting from, and integrating two value systems, which differ from each other in their environmental dispositions and physical organisational techniques.

Ideological and creative confusion arise from the fact that the African child's first stages in formal education in many parts of the continent, bear little or no direct relevance to its everyday experience of the human and natural events, to which its home and environment constantly expose it. The knowledge it acquires at school, in other words, does little to widen its vision, understanding, and love of Africa.

So long as this state of affairs prevails, the child's mind must function within two different compartments of valuation, namely, the traditional African, and the British or French as the case may be. Since, however, ideas do not remain isolated from one another for long, situations are bound to arise, sooner or later, in which odd associations and bizarre combinations of the two cultures will influence the child's thought and behaviour.

Such erratic conditioning of the child at the very outset of its literary education, in concert with the obvious lack of continuity which exists today between home and school authority, must at some stage, become a barrier to the child's wholesome intellectual and emotional development.

Unless African culture and its institutions become part and parcel of formal school education, African children will never become fully aware or convinced of the genius of their own people; and the inferiority complex which the disproportionate emphasis of European achievement instils, will continue to play havoc with their confidence and originality. The solution, therefore, does not lie in increasing the child's competence in English, French, Spanish, or Portuguese at the expense of African culture, but rather in helping it to acquire both cultures by effective comparative teaching.

Formal education, then, must take over a good deal of the dying traditional system of education, some aspects of which H.S. Scott aptly describes in "Yearbook of Education", 1938. "Africans trained their children almost exclusively by teaching them concrete facts or showing them how to deal with particular real situations. No doubt, story and proverb summed up the wisdom of reflection and conveyed a general impression of customary views and moral values. Africans knew no nature study or husbandry as such, but they taught the names of particular trees as they were met, the uses of particular plants as required, the handling of a particular herd of cattle or goats which was part of the daily routine".

African education needs to be regulated by such adaptations of African and Western values as would fire the imagination of African peoples, and sustain them in their great task of reconstruction. It must compare and contrast the social aims and ideals of both cultures in order to discover bridges that will link them into new syntheses. There is need to evolve an educational system which is rooted in Africa, but whose trunk bears the careful graftings of universal experience.

The present inability to select values from two conflicting cultures in order to integrate them into meaningful syntheses, arises from the African's mistaken belief that he must tread faithfully in the paths of Western spiritual concepts in order that the font of his own inventive and creative genius may thereby be set free.

Yet, it is only when he has carried the spiritual and social adaptations which his own forebears had gradually accumulated through their intimate living with nature, into the technical controls of nature which science has made possible, that his own genius will burst forth and the great moment of commitment be born.

Delinquency

The increasing frustration, unrest and frank delinquency amongst African youth today, stem from socio-cultural causes which are similar to, but different in some ways from those that prevail elsewhere in the world. In Europe and America, the anxiety from which young people seek relief by defiance of or non-conformity with authority, arise from their inability to assimilate or make integrated meanings out of the vast and complex cultures of their own societies. Their search is for escape hatches from the emptiness of their dominantly acquisitive society, and the tyranny of persistent surrender to relentless technological change.

The problem of African youth is not that, like their American peers, they are over-fed, over-educated, over-mechanised, and hypersensitive to the pretensions of their country's egalitarian social ideology. On the contrary, the dissatisfactions of African youth stem from a keen awareness of their country's inferior state of material development, and from their bitter disappointment with the older generation's lack of creative spirit and social commitment.

Such disappointment is both understandable and inevitable, for rightly or wrongly, the young believe that the older generation could have mastered the problems of culture conflict long ago, and evolved a new social ideology to sustain them and harness their youthful energies fruitfully to transitional problems. Obviously, the frustration of African youth must be associated both with the older generation's neglect to support them with meaningful authority during their formative years, and with failure to give them the new value systems which they need, at the threshold of manhood, to help define their role in the reshaping of their country's destiny.

The major problems of maldevelopment upon which we have touched so far, call, firstly, for an exhaustive examination of the viability of all our social institutions, secondly, for a review of the social ideals which determine their practical functions, and thirdly, for an analysis of the inter-relation of functions which integrates all the institutions into a single multi-purpose social machine.

Needless to say that in all attempts at reconstituting our culture along these lines, the role of Chiefs as the pivots of co-ordinated village life, has to be restored and geared to modern local government and rural development.

THE BATTLE FOR CULTURAL FREEDOM

By BEN ENWONWU

The darkness hanging over us in this aftermath of our political independence is very frightening indeed for this reason, that it presents a baffling situation in which our very political independence is troubled very deeply. We are surprised by the truth of our innocence and our hospitality to others, our right to free cultural expression, our scholarship and authority to determine the course of our socio-economic and cultural life in an era of political freedom, our inalienable right to nurture the cultural child of our age—all these and more are still being disturbed. Thus we have reason to fear what appears to be the second scramble for Africa.

Furthermore, we are confronted with our own realisation that our faith alone, our goodness of heart, and our innocence, are not strong enough weapons with which to fight and to maintain our existence in our own land. Such natural qualities which we cherish continue to be over-ridden and their places overtaken by the strong forces of the scientific world—such a new world in which it appears sometimes that we are doomed to be ostracised except as slaves to its economic exploitation or even as political fugitives.

Our response to the O.A.U. call is therefore, to some of us if not most of us, *urgent,* and by the reason of this urgency, we pledge ourselves to the re-affirmation of our cultural imperatives which are basic biological imperatives: we are to re-affirm with adamant and resolute intentions our determination to real cultural freedom.

With such support of the O.A.U. and cultural unity, we can, with confidence, re-state our cultural position through our cultural identity with a united front. We will then proceed to our claim to due respect and full recognition, not only as of right but also in respect of our great contributions to world culture and contemporary world cultural values and civilisation.

The decades of the colonial past should no longer plague our minds. We have no need any longer to be reminded, nor to remind ourselves, of those decades. The advent of colonialism should be constructively placed in the annals of our history as museum pieces. Rather, we might be wise to remember and make use of those aspects of the colonial era that have contributed to our growth, including even the oppressive aspects which we can use to face the more aggravating oppressiveness of the subtle methods of neo-colonialism.

In unity we can even afford to establish greater friendly relations with the descendants of our colonial masters whose innocence of their fathers' deeds should be their own redemption. We need their co-operation in cultural as well as economic relations. We, as United, can then afford to forgive because we will be richer United.

Hence the subject of this Symposium should motivate our growing consciousness and awareness to the process of our cultural evolution.

So as to enable us to concentrate our efforts on the tasks of cultural unity of all African countries as well as with the cultures of all descendants of the African Continent in other parts of the world who share the same experiences of imperialist and racial oppression and the denial of freedom.

A wider context in which African Culture can play its

fullest role and function as a social as well as political organism may now be established by this Symposium. Such a wider context for a redefinition of African Culture applicable to the peculiarity of each African State, according to how each faces her new problems—both the internal problems of evolution and the complexity of additional problems of neo-colonial impacts.

Similarly, and in consonance with such a definition, it should include those cultural values of Africa that have survived and flowered, and which have enriched Western cultures. I speak of what I would like to call, for want of a better academic term, Afro-American Culture whose current speed of evolution must not escape our plan for strengthening African Culture.

All aspects of cultures with African origin have their genesis in Africa and their preserved genetic forces which have continued to serve the cultures of the West and the world have further provided the contemporary world with a meeting point and have, nearly as much as our political agitations and demonstrations for racial equality, defied Kipling's saying that East is East, and West is West, and never the twain shall meet. Here, there is a valid case for cultural identification which Afro-American Culture has a rightful claim to its African roots. Cultural identification must draw, both in inspiration and material forces from its past hence its identifiable current manifestations are of the essential character of its kind.

The subject of this Symposium is exciting because it appears to be premature by the method of its introduction. It is also contradictory by the order of this Symposium—but this contradiction in terms makes it a valid subject which provokes debate and if there were enough time, argument.

It is an exciting subject which should take place at this time of our coming together, and also here, in Algiers, where we are gathered so safely under the protective umbrella of a big African brother.

The role of culture in the struggle for liberation is even more poignant than the realities of African Culture, the latter which is so self-evident and which has again and again, and beyond all possible doubt, proved its mettle. African cultural heritage is the evidence of African history and civilization: our works of art—description, realism, abstractions, surrealism, symbolism, art, functional crafts. The ages of distinct artistic efflorescence are clearly evidenced by styles and qualities—our dances, our consciousness of the reality of African Culture.

But the former offers new views for the role of African Culture. It is here that African Culture must seek and find authority with which to free Africa from foreign domination as well as to aid the liberation movements in their struggle for African freedom.

It is here that the inadequacy of political independence of African countries can be seen. Until all Africa—and all peoples of African descent in their own places of abode, whether in Cuba, America, England, Africa—is free, she must continue to fight for freedom from oppression, exploitation and racism.

REVOLUTIONARY CHALLENGES
AND
CULTURAL PERSPECTIVES

By MAZISI KUNENE

On behalf of the fighting forces of South Africa, allow
me, to put on record our sincere and honest appreciation
to the people of Algeria. We of the African National
Congress regard this event as of deep significance in the
history of liberation in Africa. We hold that a Festival
such as this is only incidentally cultural but is, in
essence, a moment in the history of our liberation to
mould and recreate perspectives for the struggles ahead.

Much has been said in this Symposium about the
fundamental synthesis between the cultures, economics
and the political life of the people. This is contained in
the speech of the President and was also mentioned by
other participants. This integration of culture in life and
politics is a fact. As such one would have thought it
unnecessary to mention. It is as if one would say all the
participants here have hands which are an integral part of
their bodies. But this is precisely the point. Colonial
ideology has atrophied our cultural limbs and in their
place seeks to put artificial ones. This way it hopes to
separate the herd from the elite, the barbaric and illiterate
mass from the "elegant" Intellectuals. Yet the pre-
colonial history of Africa, whatever defects it had,
preached emphatically an integrated ideology of culture,
economics and politics. This is illustrated by a highly

49

socialised artistic and literary tradition. From this tradition springs the source and stimulus of our creativity. We are therefore, in launching our revolution, setting out to recover these values and to reshape them according to the needs of our current experience. This is not in order to intellectualise our achievements, but to reinforce ourselves for the struggle for liberation and reconstruction. It is therefore essential to understand all the dimensions of African culture, otherwise we shall remain a people uncertain and unable to make fundamental decisions relating to our future. It is part of this disease to indulge in ideologies which are essentially reactionary and prostrate before the colonial doctrines. In this context, therefore, I would like to make an attempt to define that dimension. In defining, I must warn those who consider technology as the only criterion for achievement. I would like to warn them because of the persuasiveness and the ruthlessness with which this argument is bandied about, so much so that some find difficulty in conceiving of an alternative system of values other than that defined by the monolithic civilization of technologists.

The evolution of the capitalist structure in Europe was accompanied by a specific system of values, those values were totally commercial. I use the word "commercial" in a broad sense to include the individualistic philosophies, bureaucratic organization and the commercialization of art and literature. Art and literature became, in this context, so commercial, so vulgarized, that today in Europe a large amount of works do not need to have any social meaning at all. All they need to have is a fashion and a commercial value. They are then held in exhibitions or reviewed to attract a caste which constitutes the potential buyers. This is a simplification since these attenuated souls still get some satisfaction, if only that of not being regarded as backward and uncultured. Going thus hand in hand with technological advancement is the barbarisation of a people who, as a result, have become servants to the very instruments they evolve to exploit the environment. This is no exaggeration either, since the all pervasive technological monster in Europe defines and determines the values and the life goals. The purpose of civilized life is in this context defined as comfort and individual comfort. We are all expected by this untamed technological monster to proclaim the great achievements of Man. And yet all these things are for sale and, in any case, we are too hungry to allow the expenditure of billions on a project of such distant interest. Is there no imbalance in all this? Should not a social ideology be launched within the instruments of our own revolution to regress this imbalance?

The President, in his opening speech, said:

"Our experience as resistance fighters saved not only our sons and our nations but also a certain notion of mankind and his capabilities. This is to our honour today, in spite of the price paid and yet to be paid, it is a conception to which we are irrevocably attached.

"We succeeded in triumphing over the forces of oppression. That alone is a sufficient reason for us to give to African culture, and therefore to universal culture, the time, place and care we are not devoting to it. This is why we wanted this festival to be the meeting of hope and rebirth, as well as an enthusiastic and lucid undertaking to recover and assert our basic oneness".

I believe very strongly that this is the challenge put to us today, and that the challenge devolves from our history and our revolutionary perspectives. It is for that reason that I see the need to define the dimension of our culture and civilization. For it is that culture that has emphasized the value of man, not as an individualized and egotistical animal, but as a social and socialized being. Throughout the literature of our continent, with that I mean the literature of traditional myths, legends and epics, an emphasis was made on the communal ideology. In vain will those schooled in the individualized conversational dramas look for such counterparts in Africa, because our dance is our drama, such drama as will allow participation of the community in one form or another. This form is not unique to Africa but is found in Asia and also the Americas among the American Indians. It is for that reason that our literature and our art abound in symbols, symbols which can be easily communicated to a participating audience, such symbols becoming a complex system of ideas and inuendos. I would like to give an example of this phenomenon of communal participation in relation to the epic. In many parts of Africa the heroic epic is one of the most important forms of literary expression. The reasons for this are not far to seek, since the hero in a communally inter-dependent society expresses, by his actions, the highest virtue—self-sacrifice on behalf of the community. I would like to give an example from South Africa, but I could, of course, have just as easily have quoted an heroic epic of Ezana, King of the Ethiopians who conquered Meroe in the 9th century A.D. But I choose this quotation as I can mostly recite it in its original. I would like you to note these particular variations of pitch which are constructed to produce a symphonic series.

UNodumehlezi Ka Menzi	Great echo son of Mengi
Uteku Lwabafazi bakwa Nomgabi	Of whom the woman of
Betekula behlezi Emlovini	Nomgabi prattled
Bethi u Shaka hayubusa	Saying Shaka will never rule
Kanti kunyakana	But alas Shaka was to rise and
Esezakunethezeka	overwhelm the world.

I would like to take this opportunity to destroy a myth or fallacy which has been perpetuated and is still being perpetuated by the imperialists. In order to divide Africa, which is obviously in their interest, they have propagated a myth based on racial division. Much attention has been paid to what is called Africa north of the Sahara and Africa south of the Sahara (one wonders what would happen if the Sahara became cultivable once again). This differentiation is true to the Fascist colonial mentality based on race, racism being an institution or a superstition arising out of a colonial situation. It is a dangerous superstition which has been used to define economic privilege and maintain exploitation. The division of Africa in these racial terms has a definite purpose, that of maintaining hegemony over a divided Africa. From time immemorial, Africa has evolved numerous cultural experiments which, in their different forms, do not mean opposition, let alone on racial grounds. They are variations which project different cultural realities, but firmly originate from an African genius. Our ancestors have criss-crossed the continent from north to south and from east to west, so that we have today cultural elements which originate in various parts of the continent. Indeed, records and reports of historical significance have been written by sojourners from various parts of the continent. It is clear, therefore, that our ancestors who traversed the length and breadth of Africa have laid foundations of dynamic and a varied culture, of which we are proud inheritors. This culture bears a stamp at once Arabic, Sudanic, Eastern, Western and Southern African. An even more astounding phenomenon is not the existence of differences but incidence of ideology, belief and culture expression that are similar. The women of Algeria were ululating a few days ago in the dramatic display of participation in a communal spectacle. The spectacle depicts the history and the triumphs of a people. The scene could have been in Ethiopia or South Africa. The very responsibility and obligations that our cultures confer on the members of society in this age group is a phenomenon which has a continental significance. On the other level, some people have wondered at the pyramids of Egypt and some have even called them sculptural works erected by an extinct people. But we are not baffled since it is customary in Africa to use stones as a symbol for community solidarity. It is common also to pile up mountains of stones by various generations to symbolise communal unity and continuity. The pyramids are obviously an elaboration of this idea by a more power-conscious organization.

In short, the very idea of African unity is not a myth nor a political expediency, but evolves from very deep and fundamental experiences of our ancestors. I regard myself, therefore, as an inheritor of a vast and varied culture which our ancestors built. I am called upon to reshape and reorganize this culture according to my current experiences. This cultural festival assumes significance in this context in that it unites and provides an opportunity to share in the variety of cultures on this continent. I do not think Africans are superior or different from other human beings, but I do recognize the particularity of their contribution in the universal context. It is for that reason that I see our fate as very closely tied up with other human beings in this planet. It is also for this reason that I consider our tasks in recreating these perspectives of our history as a profound challenge. We are part of revolutions taking place, not only in Africa, but in Asia, Latin America and Europe.

We are called upon to conceive of the dimensions of African culture in positive and creative terms. It is reactionary and immobilising for a formerly colonised people to continue trying out the styles of their colonial occupation. After all, colonial occupation of Africa is, in terms of our history, only a short interruption in the normal development of our country. It is therefore the acceptance of this reality and the destruction wrought by it on the mind without a perspective of history that the decay of initiative is brought about. I mean initiative for struggle and against the dogmas of colonial culture. It is, for instance, enraging to hear Africans indulging in the glorification of precision, which is all very well in dealing with materials, but becomes destructive ideology when glorified beyond its material value. Africa, in developing its culture, has discovered, for instance, that man does not live years defined by time units, but by historical perspectives and evaluations in terms of the philosophical past, the philosophical present and the future. Man's value and contribution become the criteria for defining his age. Time is divided into time cycles and not units. When I say that I shall meet so-and-so tomorrow morning, I do not mean 8 o'clock but in the morning cycle. In this way, I am freed from the neurosis of failure which is bound up with time units. We have produced a philosophy of timelessness which the Europe of instruments may do well to copy. I am by no means advocating precision or unscientific methods of work. All I am saying is that if we have to avoid becoming machine men, we must at the same time understand and realize alternative dimensions. A philosophical synthesis becomes therefore a necessary corollary to the industrial idea of precision. This way man can be defined in socialist terms beyond the value of the product. I was the absence of this balance which Marx, by his analysis of society, sought to redress. When we therefore talk of revolution in the political, cultural and economic spheres, we are advocating a system of values which recognizes man as the centre of things. In making a reference to these African concepts of time, I want us to examine critically some of the aspects which colonialism glorified and bequeathed to us, so that we can found an integrated system of values based on our own revolutionary dialectic.

I would like to end my contribution by stating emphatically that our revolution in South Africa is based on the recovery of our social values defined not in airy-fairy attempts, but in concrete political, economic and social attempts. In short, we are fighting for a socialist state and we are dedicated to this ideal and we shall not lay down our arms until these ideals have been achieved.

AFRICAN CULTURE AND NATIONAL LIBERATION

By ALEX LA GUMA

What we see on record here at the First Pan-African Festival is a vast manifestation of the spiritual and cultural achievements of the African continent. The Pan-African Cultural Festival gives the lie to the racist idea that Africa is a dark continent and that it has produced to enhance the treasures of culture which is the heritage of all mankind.

Now that the burdens of imperialism and colonialism have been eased from our shoulders in a great part of Africa, we are better able to venture across new frontiers of material welfare and cultural upliftment. We Africans are concerned with the development of this continent and with its future in relation to the rapid changes occurring in all aspects of African and world life. We look back at the past in order to uncover values, assess them from the point of view of modern times, and attempt to determine and understand their place and role in history and modern civilisation.

The great problem facing new Africa today is that of ensuring that more and more of her people benefit from the successes over the forces which are responsible for the slowing down of African progress; which withhold scientific and technological development; which frustrated the development of our culture.

The end of the colonial period in liberated Africa left

millions of illiterate people in its wake. We have to build a new life in our various independent states with the aid of those men and women who grew up under the colonial regimes. So our people are thirsting for knowledge because they need it in order to win. We know that knowledge is a weapon in the struggle for final emancipation, that many failures arise out of lack of education, and therefore it becomes a duty of the liberated countries to give everyone access to education. It takes knowledge to participate in the revolution with intelligence, purpose and success.

The main distinguishing feature of a true democratic cultural revolution is its mass, nation-wide character. The strength and vitality of the revolution is derived from the awakened creative energy of the masses and their aspiration for a new life, enlightenment and culture. Real progress cannot be decreed from above; living creative progress is the product of the masses themselves. We must raise the lowest sections of the population to the state of making history.

Revolution in the people's minds is one of the most profound and most important manifestations of the cultural revolution. At the same time the cultural revolution from which emerges a qualitatively new type of socially-based culture must be seen as an integral part of the social revolution, as a far-reaching upheaval in the spiritual life of society effected on the basis of radical political and economic transformations. With the political and economic changes which are taking place or are planned to take place in Africa, every individual must be given maximum opportunities to enjoy the benefits of past cultures and the opportunities directly to participate in creating new spiritual assets.

Under the colonial regimes and the rule of metropolitan capitalism the brain of man created to give some the benefits of technology and culture and to deprive others of the bare necessities of life, education and development. Now we ask that all the marvels of science and the gains of culture belong to the nation as a whole, in order to introduce an all-embracing and speedy elevation of the cultural level of the people, the cultivation of a new consciousness, morality and ethics.

While the material wealth and all the avenues of science and technology are not accessible to the people, cultural development will be impeded. Today we know that man has walked on the moon. But in spite of this wonderful demonstration of mankind's prowess over nature, what does it matter to the people of Southern Africa if man can walk upright on the moon but cannot walk upright in his own country? What does it matter that science has given rise to space exploration but in South Africa 52 out of every 100 African children die of malnutrition before the age of 5 years? What does it matter if we can plot the course to a star but the brain of a South African child is already retarded at the age of 2 years because of malnutrition? Before we can truly appreciate these marvels, we must be truly free.

In Southern Africa where cultural advancement or frustration depends on the whims of the racist oppressors, the people have taken up arms in order to exercise their right to reconstruct and rehabilitate the personality of the South African people; to open the doors of universal learning and culture; to gain access to the knowledge and science withheld by the white racists, knowing that in order to achieve this we must also control the material, social and political keys.

THE ARTIST AND POLITICS: THE DYNAMICS OF CONTEMPORARY AFRICAN SOCIETY

By JOSEPH OKPAKU

Your Excellencies, Honourable Delegates, Fellow Artists and gentlemen (I really ought to have said "ladies", but in the light of the Chief Delegate from Ghana, Dr. Cudjoe's brilliant articulation of what I had always thought was an unhealthy prejudice of mine, I will only have myself to blame if I did not seize this opportunity to boldly express my bias in favour of men). But be that as it may, ladies and gentlemen, I would like to beg the indulgence of His Excellency, Mr. President, Secretary-General O.A.U. and that of the O.A.U. ministers here to allow me to skip the praises heaped on this brilliant body and, instead, pay my meagre tributes to the people of Algeria and the other political people here in Algiers for having made this cultural experience possible. It is not that I seek to rob our ministers and delegates of the praise due them. Rather, it is my intention to use this choice of who to praise to introduce the few comments I wish to make at this point. To put it differently, still borrowing from Dr. Cudjoe's imagery, I wish to intimate that the honeymoon is over and it is time for politician, artist, and critic to tie their wrappers firmly and prepare for the the bout. We Africans are a wrestling people, and, gentlemen, the African spirit is always restless and frustrated if

it cannot fulfil its quota of debate and healthy argumenta-
tion. There are four restaurants here, gentlemen, and I
am sure that there is plenty of wine and beer for us to
make up to each other after we shall have debated warm-
ly and heartily.

In the past several days I have sat in the plenary
session and tried to convince myself that I was in the
right place and had not by error strayed into an international cocktail party. I fear, gentlemen, that there are
many of my fellow African writers and artists who share
this feeling of disbelief at what we have heard and then
been forced to read.

Gentlemen, until Africa comes to realise the simple
fact that the integrity of a nation lies in its ability to face
up to serious facts and do what it must, even if it means a
little loss of praise, we shall continue to be like the
archtypical prostitute who spends all her time powdering
her face and using skin bleach even though her black face
is far more beautiful. All this week, gentlemen, I, as a
young African, have felt like the eldest son of a
prostitute.

If you will pardon a little criticism, I would like to
refer you, for example, to the international publicity
announcing this festival. To put it mildly, it was not the
best. So much space was spent trying to convince readers
(or was it ourselves?) that Africa did indeed have a
culture and if they did not believe it, they should come
and see for themselves. This is the language of the
prostitute. It is simple: Africa is having a festival. If any
European wants to come, fine. If he does not, too bad.
He can stay home and watch television. For two or more
weeks *The Times* carried a half page advertisement selling African culture, but do you know that the most
important thing was absent? At no place in the whole
thing was the reader told who to call or write to if he was

interested. Africa has so many young, sophisticated highly trained professional people. Why is she so afraid of using them?

Or take the fanfare of the past week here at the symposium. Country after country spent so much time trying to convince fellow Africans that it has a culture and that it has been working very hard or that way back many centuries ago somebody somewhere did in fact start a national literature. Since it is obvious that every African in his right mind knows that there is a valid and rich African culture, is it not a pure waste of time to have devoted all that time to state the obvious? Or perhaps it was not for the African ear? In that case, gentlemen, why all the talk about imperialism and neo-colonialism? The woman who takes off her clothes and says to a man "See, am I not beautiful?" cannot turn around and accuse the man of having made her a prostitute.

All is not sunshine and roses in Africa. If it were, she would be uninteresting. Besides the fact that no nation in the world can claim to have no problems, there is no virtue in having no problems. To have no problems is not to be alive, and certainly, Africa is alive. How then can we get together here and heap praises on each other, pretending that all is well when my own Nigeria is in the midst of a painful civil war, when the Sudan is having a little action, when the mass media can whip up such hysteria that when we ought to be weeping at the death of a loved one, we are out in the streets rioting because we have picked up a fascination, by long distance, for riots and confrontations? Would it not have been better if we had spent the past several days trying to discuss how culture can progress in the midst of political turmoil?

It is not our fault that technology has made bedroom criticism impossible. But the solution is to learn how to ignore the television cameras, and say what must be said, and not to run away from the responsibility of criticising ourselves. If a man must change his clothes, gentlemen, and he cannot find a shelter, it is better that he change them in public than continue to wear the old and dirty clothes.

There are many Africans who preferred to pay their own way here instead of being on an official delegation just so that they could debate sincerely and frankly, the issue of culture which concerns their very existence. We came here to teach and be taught. We came to ask some questions and to answer others. This is a cultural festival and not the U.N. I must praise the organisers of the symposium for the choice of the theme. For when it is more appropriate that now when artists are carrying guns, when artists have taken over military propaganda, when writers and film-makers are in jail. Is not this the best time for us to discuss what all this means, where the artist has gone wrong, where the politician has gone wrong? I do not for one moment presume that there is a villain and a victim. There are many villanous artists in this world. All I am saying is that there is a serious issue and that this symposium could have offered a most unique opportunity for the meeting of the minds on such a serious topic.

This symposium promised us a dialogue on the role of culture in society and I think it is important to make good this promise here in this session. For what is unique about this symposium is that for the first time on such a large scale, the organisers have succeeded in bringing three traditional enemies together, all wetting their palms in eager anticipation of the big wrestling match. I think it will be a great shame if this match did not take place, as I am afraid it may not. These enemies are the artist, the critic and the politician. Gentlemen, it is the traditional pattern of the husband, the wife, and the mother-in-law.

Let me make the first pass by taking the prejudiced position that there is a clear distinction between the

Minister of Culture in my government and the guardians and bearers of culture. Where society is castle, the Minister of Culture is the drawbridge. He can keep the courriers within or out of the castle walls or he can allow a flow of life in and out of the castle. Like a container, he is only form, not content, and his important role can best be played only if he aims at being a good container with a good funnel and a wide spout, and not by seeking to be the content too. The latter, the courrier, the purveyor of the content of life, is the artist. His role is uniquely different, and this is what I would like to kick around, if only as a way of getting the ball rolling. We must distinguish clearly between government policy statements on culture and critical or artistic exposes on culture. I fear we have had so much of the former that this symposium has tended to sound like another meeting of the OAU, this time with a very captive and restless audience of artists. As there are many politicians and officials of culture here who will do a good job of challenging me, gentlemen allow me play the devil's advocate by expressing a few one-sided opinions.

The artist and the politician, like the Western husband and wife, are traditional enemies. They have to be because the survival of society and the healthy development of a national culture demand it. Their roles are fundamentally different, and so, I think, are their psychological disposition.

Whereas the politician is a structural engineer seeking to build the structure of society by choosing from a variety of forms and material, from the cheapest to the most expensive, from the most modest to the grandest, from the elegant to the grotesque, the artist functions most effectively in society as a critic of life and death, as a dreamer, a seer, a madman, a prophet, a bard. Unlike the politician who works with steel and concrete, the artist uses cubes, plastics and clay, in other words, he works in this air, using life as his material. The artist is a pure scientist, while the politician is most useful to society when he restricts himself to being an engineer. Like the theoretical mathematician, the artist should be free to dream far byeond the clouds without the limitations of fear or pragmatism. Then the politician may take from this treasury of fancies what is possible or desirable to construct for that society. No matter what the politician chooses to construct, the blueprints of the other fancies of the artist should always be allowed to circulate in the public libraries and galleries, in the shelves and on the living room floors. In the area of practical culture, the politician must be prepared to perform a self-negating role, an inconspicuous role. Otherwise all his good intentions for culture must come to naught. I stress this because it is the most difficult role for politicians to play. It is asking the master to put his burning (sometimes flickering) candle under a bushel. This task is perhaps the most difficult one facing the African politician today and is responsible for a good many of the difficulties facing the society. Your Excellencies, I hope you do not mind my talking of problems and difficulties, for this is the language of the artist—talk of achievements and accomplishments, of grand plans and policies constitute the language of the politician. You will understand why these two people never seem able to get together. Put differently, the artist takes pride in the modest fact that he does not know everything, whereas the politician feels compelled to at least claim to be a witch doctor capable of curing all ills. Each position is valid, but it is important to examine the distinction as it lies at the bottom of the purpose of this symposium.

Thus, whereas the politician can encourage or discourage art, whereas he can promote or persecute the artist, he himself cannot and must not take it upon himself to be the official artist, for the very nature of art invalidates the concept of official art. Art is not diplomacy, and the artist is not a diplomat. For this reason I will risk a little more specific thought. What the very nature of this symposium called for was that the politician spend all his time organising it, and then that he disappear through the back door as soon as the guests began to arrive. What has happened, however, is that the artists have stayed in the galleries and been forced to listen to politicians officiate at the artistic ritual of cultural diplomacy. While it is true that both the artist and the diplomat are showmen seeking an audience, I think it is only fair that just as the artist must take the back seat in the House of Parliament, so should the politician take the back seat in the house of culture.

I have elaborated at length on this issue because it has implications for the overall question of the role of the artist in society.

The artist and the intellectual have a much greater responsibility than they seem to realize, and they have been as guilty (if not more guilty) as the politician in being more interested in cheap publicity than serious work. It is so easy to be a writer in Africa today, we seem to think, that many of us do not even bother to read over our works before sending them to publishers. Writing is a profession, not a hobby, and to do a good work, the African writer must come to realize that it means months of pain, harsh criticism, and serious thought about society and people. I heard someone say yesterday that although she was an artist of the people (whatever she meant by that) she could not stand people. Luckily she was not African and I was able to ignore her.

Unlike the West European writer, the African writer has a serious job to do and cannot afford the decadence of avant-garde or bohemian disinterest. In England, or America the artist is a drop out. He is on the fringe; he is overwhelmed by the society in which he no longer has a say. It therefore makes sense to say that he must write as a man who no longer belongs, that he must write as a helpless voice screaming feebly in the twilight of a passing day. But this is not the case with the African writer. He is more easily likened to the East European writer, without many of his unnecessary limitations. The African writer is an important man who in general can say what he wants to say, and who is often listened to. In many cases, he actually holds important positions either in government, in the mass media, or, equally important, as a school teacher. In this vital position at a time of turbulence when the society needs all sorts of new ideas, for a continent that is in its most creative period, the writer must give at his best in thought and effort to the creation of new ideas as well as the preservation of public thought against the potential excesses of political pragmatism and artistic irresponsibility.

There is bound to be conflict, of course, and this too is healthy. In Africa we have the added situation that most of the professional artists are generally younger people and this raises another dimension of generational conflict. This is an advantage and the politicians must give up once and for all the erroneous idea that "these young men think they know too much". It is true that age is wisdom, but youth alone can refresh life and thought, and what is wisdom without the enthusiasm and flame of youthful knowledge and sensibility?

Then, there is the issue of the artist who takes a political act. Although the artist is sacred to society, I would not for one moment advocate that he be an untouchable. If an artist commits murder, he should be tried for murder. But when it comes to offences of thought and opinion, I think every government should give serious thought to the simple fact that a boiling pot explodes when a lid is put on it. I do not intend to defend any reckless action by an artist. All citizens have a responsibility to respect the law, or in breaking it, be prepared to face the consequences. However, their right to disagree with the law shall remain inviolate, this being a fundamental exercise of human intelligence. The truth, is that as long as people can say what they like openly, there is never the need to go underground. The artist will never be a threat to national security merely by playing his role as social critic.

What if, in fact, a writer is believed to have offended the national interest? In many cases, only time dictates who is right or wrong.

If only for that reason, governments should act in such a way as to give themselves a way out if they are later proved to be wrong. There is a great difference between justice and vindictiveness. The good mother does not cut her son's throat for speaking out of place. She chastises him, spanks him, and at the worst, kicks him out of the house. In all these cases she does not destroy the creativity of her son, because, good or bad, she still loves him.

The artist must not be destroyed, certainly not by the politician, because the destruction of the artist is the destruction of culture and that in turn is the destruction of society and therefore the ultimate destruction of the basis of the politician's existence.

Finally, in this new phase, we in Africa must carefully re-examine the assumptions on which we have based the definition of our intellectual theses and our practical objectives.

For example, inasmuch as a political ideology is valid only if it derives its legitimacy from the culture and thought of the society, and inasmuch as neither the socialist nor the capitalist world has had a culture identical or closely related to ours, it is rather self-evident that neither of these ideologies fully satisfies our intellectual and political needs.

Relatedly, we must also remember that in hate as in

love we are the slaves of the object of our passions. We are free only if we are indifferent.

I must confess that such words as "imperialist" and "neocolonialist" have lost all relevant meaning, whether it be ideological, intellectual or artistic.

Let us remember, ladies and gentlemen, that a nation is great NOT, in what it says it could have done were it not for this or that, but for what it does in the face of and in spite of obstacles. There is tremendous pressure on all nations, big or small. The greatness of Africa will lie in what she can do in the face of our handicaps—and I think she can do a lot if she begins to recognize the important role of free thought and criticism, and of meaningful dialogue amongst all ages. Contradiction is the fuel for cultural progress, not a united or legislated uniformity.

Finally, let us remember, Ladies and Gentlemen, especially our many African elders here, that young men, like Artists, may once in a while have a good idea. And our Africa is in such need of good and fresh ideas, that the joy of each precious idea is worth the anger and irritation of the less worthy ideas that must also be heard.

THE ARTIST AT HOME AND ABROAD

By S. J. NTIRO

I am very glad indeed to see that most African countries are here to take part in this unique gathering. I am
equally pleased to meet here creative artists, like myself,
from several African countries, some of them I have
known for years. This indeed is as it should be, the role
of the creative artists in the development of each nation's
culture is paramount. It is the creative artists as musicians, dancers, craftsmen, authors, among others who
mark the pace of cultural progress in each country. They
interpret the life of their people as faithfully as they can;
they forecast the development of their culture. They use
their imaginative power to create works of art which
increase their country's product, thus increasing their
country's wealth and stature. It is for this reason that the
creative artists deserve every support and encouragement. It is wrong to think, as some people do, that it is
only financial support that the creative artists require; far
from it. Apart from financial support creative artists need
encouragement and the assurance that their work is
appreciated. I am not talking about artists who have no
feelings for their countries' culture and are content by
making money for themselves. In fact artists of this type
are plentiful. You can see them in Paris, London and
New York where they want to make money instead of
sharing the heavy burden of developing their country's

70

culture. Artists of this kind are misfits as far as the development of African culture is concerned because our basis must be first at home and then in foreign countries.

Mr. Chairman, in Tanzania we are convinced that African culture is the total development of an African. That means the food he eats, the clothes he wears and the house he lives in. The total outlook of life makes him what he is. The way he looks at the outside world is the product of his cultural background. Here are the words of our President Julius Nyerere. "Culture is the essence and spirit of any nation. A country which lacks its own culture is no more than a collection of people without the spirit which makes them a nation. Of all the crimes of colonialism there is none worse than the attempt to make us believe we had no indigenous culture of our own; or that what we did have was worthless—something of which we should be ashamed, instead of a source of pride.

In developing our African culture we do not mean isolating ourselves from the rest of the world. If our culture is to grow healthily it should seek inspirations from other forms of culture without being swamped by those foreign forms. That is why it is vital that the actual development of the cultural and artistic activities should be done by our people and not by foreigners however knowledgeable they may claim to be of our culture.

Mr. Chairman, it is impossible to develop our African culture without political freedom. No country in the world has ever been able to develop the culture of its own people without being free to do so. Our brothers and sisters in Mozambique, Angola, Zimbabwe, South Africa and S.W. Africa are being subjected to the most inhuman conditions not because of any crimes they have committed but because of their struggle to be free. Obviously the European colonialists are not to leave them free. The Portuguese, Smith and the South African white minority regimes are co-operating successfully in suppressing the African freedom fighters. The big European powers are giving them all the help they need to make sure that the Africans will always be ruled by them in those countries. What are we doing to help them? When the O.A.U. member states agreed to break diplomatic relations with Britain over the question of Smith's U.D.I. how many fulfilled that promise? If all the member states of the O.A.U. had invaded Smith and his minority government on the day he declared U.D.I. the African continent would have been a happier place today! It is the duty of all of us member states of the O.A.U. to ensure that freedom is won. But freedom cannot be won only by resolutions; it can only be won by the gun in the bush! We all know how hard it was for freedom to be won in those African countries where Europeans had settled. It is saddening to remind ourselves that as we hold this seminar here in Algiers thousands of South African troops are pouring into Rhodesia to strengthen Smith's position. If South Africa knew that the African countries were united in their defence of the freedom fighters she would hesitate sending her troops there. Since we agree that freedom is concomitant with the development of African Culture then we must support the freedom fighters until freedom is won.

THE GREAT BATTLE
OF NEGRITUDE

NEGRITUDE: A SOBER ANALYSIS

By HENRI LOPES

As we have been called upon to speak in this symposium for the first time in the name of the Delegation from Congo-Brazzaville, may we express the joy of our people, our country and our government at being represented at this first giant demonstration of African thought, African arts—in short, African life.

It is for us a cheerful duty and a real pleasure at this time to thank all of those who organized this festival which, we feel, should usher in the rebirth of African thought, of a common Pan-African culture, just as the Panhellenic Games engendered a common Greek culture which was to leave its mark on the entire history of European thought.

Military power by itself is not enough to enable a people to assert itself. *On the contrary,* how is it possible to explain that the black people of Africa and the African diaspora have been able to survive the greatest deportation in human history, conquest, slavery, the Ku Klux Klan, aesthetic, intellectual and even religious debasement, in a word, banishment from mankind, if there were not the songs sung in the holds of slave-ships, those songs which they formerly used to support their fight against nature and to lift themselves above the sufferings inflicted by a monstrous humanity, to outface death? How is it possible to explain our survival if there were not the remembrance of tutelary and guardian masks carved by sculptors from Ife, Bandiaga or M'bouli; if there were not the remembrance of tales and myths describing the African as a strong and proud man; if there were not the ancestral dances to bring relief after the overseer's whip on the cotton plantation? In a famous statement made at the first Congress of Negro Artists and Writers, Frantz Fanon showed how storytellers emerged in the maquis of the Algerian resistance. The fact is that in moment of hope, weariness and despair, man needs dreams. These dreams are supplied by art. And the remembrance of common hopes and dreams is what is appropriately called national culture. But this cannot be allowed to petrify. It must develop with time and the transformations which men and the passage of time make in their surroundings. For those who are fighting today in Angola, Cabinda, Guinea Bissao, Mozambique, Rhodesia and South Africa, the poems of Agostino Neto, Mario de Andrade, Marcellino Dos Santos, Cesaire and Henri Krea and the sort of song which is Frantz Fanon's conclusion to his "Wretched of the Earth" are not a luxury but an inspiration.

Culture is not a collection of encyclopaedic information pertaining to such and such a region, but the organisation of knowledge enabling men to act and to behave in such a way as to work towards a better life and a fuller understanding of each other. Culture is life. It is quite wrong to claim that it turns its back on life. In this present age, when there are those who imply that a militant shows weakness if he is also a poet, musician or other kind of artist, we, the representatives of a country that has chosen to develop along socialist lines, wish, on the contrary, to proclaim loud and clear that art and culture are nourished with the most precious sap of life.

From art and culture a man can draw the strength to live and to fight for the highest ideals of mankind. I remember a comrade who, incarcerated in a prison cell for many long months without books, without paper or writing materials managed to survive. For, he told me later, he was recreating the world and Africa. But above all, he said, because the stirring texts of revolutionary writers he had read when he was a student rose slowly from the depths of his subconscious and he himself wrote verses that he sent to his wife. In this sense, it is of the highest importance that our artists should feel Africa in their bones, in the same way that Goya was inspired when painting his *Thirteenth of May* and Picasso when denouncing Guernica. This was the idea expressed by Elsa Tridet when she wrote "War, disease and famine can discourage genius but cannot kill it. If its tongue is cut out, it will speak with gestures and if its eyes are put out it will continue to feel its way. . . ."

Cesaire once said, and very rightly, when speaking of artists, that they must be "engineers of the soul". The whole truth is contained in this phrase.

This Festival and this Symposium are not just a meeting, just an excuse for festivities. They constitute a confrontation, the moment for emulation and perhaps also for an international soul-searching with a view to a fresh departure.

Here we shall be discussing, for several days, the lines along which artistic creation should proceed. This is a difficult task. A task—and we are sorry to say this—that appears impossible given so brief a period. And artistic creativity can ill abide constraints.

But if this Festival can bring home to each one of us, who are all in responsible positions, that the artist is not an amusing oddity, that he is not the amiable village idiot but a precious instrument of our own improvement, then we shall not have come here in vain. We should act in such a way that if Rabearivelo, the unknown sculptors of the Ife bronzes or the author of the Sundiata Keita were to come into this hall and ask us what we have done to help them to live and produce other work, we could give them a straight answer with no element of mockery.

To us Congolese who have chosen the Socialist path to development, culture represents an irreplaceable adjuvant for the initial effort required of us. The austerity necessary for economic independence, and the fact that the results of our efforts to develop will not be immediately apparent, imply that we must provide our people with opportunities for leisure-time enrichment at low cost. Only culture can provide these. We should mention in passing that the great task of construction which we have undertaken necessarily implies the maintenance of myths. And although artists and intellectuals in general tend to stand aside from myths and to divorce themselves from mysticism, there are nonetheless myths which our artists must propagate in their work. A festival like this should select these myths. We should mention, among others, the myths of work and of the necessity for a real Pan-African unity. This does not mean that work unconnected with the myths that we propagate should be entered on the *Pan-African Index*. Artistic terrorism must be rejected. But we must, on the other hand, develop a high level of artistic criticism armed against the alienating tendencies of certain artistic productions and at the same time impelling artists to set in motion an intellectual life blending with the life of Africa today. This must be a life serving the interests of the people, of society and of its development.

This Pan-African Cultural Festival gives us all an opportunity to look beyond race and thus to call in question the idea of ''negritude'' without any intention of starting a dispute. We met together at the Congresses of Negro Artists and Writers held in 1956 and 1959, on the keynote of our race and common sufferings, and in 1966 at the World Festival of Negro Art which had the same keynote. In 1969, we have met to celebrate our more or less close connection with the African continent and our common option and efforts to obtain entire possession of the lands, oceans and rivers of this continent. As from now we will no longer be able to define ourselves by race or by any other physical characteristic, but by geography and, above all, by our common determination which is the best basis for national and international unity.

We must overcome racial conditioning and humanise it, just as the peasant works to transform the most difficult country and to give it a covering of manioc, sweet potatoes or coffee. We must stop this headlong and illusory flight towards cultural purity. Man speaks to man, whatever the colour of his skin. Endogamous societies are only what they are because of geographical isolation. Paul Valery defines the European not by "race, language or customs but by his desires and the strength of his will-power". What is there that is Gallic about the so-called heirs of ancient Gaul? And are the Roman virtues really found among the present-day inhabitants of the Eternal City? Antonio Gramsci criticizes this tendency to say that Italy is not the heir of ancient Rome because nothing "august" is any longer to be found there.

Another geographical and cultural environment has an adverse effect on racial consciousness. Race is so greatly exalted in the U.S.A. only because of the segregation there. Langston Hughes recognised in "The Big Sea" that he belonged to America and not to Africa. We know how Richard Wright was taken aback and almost thrown into despair during his visit to the Gold Coast in 1953 because of the distance between him and his fellow-negroes. "I could not understand at all", he wrote. "I was black and they were black but my colour didn't help me". And at the first Congress in 1956 he could not say whether an American negro should give pride of place to

African negro or to American culture in spite of Senghor's exhortations to "Take the tents of Africa as his classics".

The values of "negritude" are to be found among various peoples in varying, but not immutable, connections. Worship of the dead, solidarity, union with the cosmic forces, rhythm, are not attributes of negroes alone.

The worst danger about "negritude" is that it constitutes an inhibiting force for negro writers, so far as creative activity is concerned. If it does not actually incite folklore in literature, as denounced by David Diop, it does lead to conformity of style and content, as prejudicial to cultural vitality as all other constraints, moral or other. As our poet, J. B. Tati Loutard, has written, an originality crisis is rampant today among young African writers and it is paralysing the literary vocations. In their phobia at not being able to say things differently from the Europeans or the Asiatic, they do their utmost to cultivate an agreed difference, whereas they merely have to lift the screen of race to liberate their writer's temperament. Thus, we cannot end this contribution without emphasising that it is high time African art rid itself of certain ideas which engender and foster a static conception of culture.

The African writer or painter must keep abreast of the times, must face up to them victoriously. Our culture must come out from the museums, be revived and help African man exploit and dominate his soil, his sub-soil, his rivers, his forests, his oceans, his lakes and his atmosphere.

And, African artists, do stop stressing the superficial differences which seem to single you out and which, in fact, set you apart! We do not mean the personality which distinguishes one artist from another, but the false cultural areas to which one has given the seductive names of negritude, arabism, bantuism, and which, in fact, only result in people no longer understanding one another in the end. There is an Arab proverb which says that men resemble their brothers rather than their father. We should like to add that, with the swift development of knowledge, the mentality of the 20th century is not that of the 19th century, even though the two come next to each other.

King Makoko, confronting De Brazza or the kings of the old Kingdom of the Congo, if they were to come into this room, would not understand our delegation's contribution. And yet we are Bantu just as they were. Would their "Bantu" culture help them to understand the educational needs of our youth? The rights of African women today? The organization of which our society today is in need? The economic tasks we must accomplish for our independence?

How, too, forbear from mentioning the example of Frantz Fanon who came here to fight for a people to whom his mother did not belong, who adopted him and made an African out of him without so much as asking him anything about the degree of his Arabism, who simply turned him into an African. For our artists, it is a matter of furthering a culture that it may give rise to mentalities such that a young African from Algiers should understand one from Bujumbura, and that a young woman from Bulawayo should feel akin to one from Cairo. For this reason, we should like to take advantage of this platform to denounce publicly all the institutions and all the coteries which arrogate to themselves the right to continue speaking in the name of all Africa, on topics which today are obsolete.

The African governments must oppose this and must not extend their help to such decadent academies which, even if they did know a period of glory, could not, from their exile, understand the upheavals which affect Africa and can therefore no longer speak in the name of its intelligentsia. The Symposium must launch an appeal to African artists to break their shackles and free themselves from exploitation at the hands of the merchants of African culture. Our artists must first become known in their own country and over the entire continent. And if they are not understood, then let them explain themselves to the public. From such a dialogue will be born an African cultural life, whereas African production outside the continent will yield only exotic fruit.

It is therefore desirable that from this Festival and Symposium should emerge a policy of cultural exchange among the various republics represented here. When a writer has his work published in Europe, it is because no publisher and no broadcasting time are forthcoming in Africa. Every African country has cultural agreements with the Great Powers, but how many such agreements are there between African countries, even when they are neighbours? East State on the continent should undertake frequently to accept artistic productions from other countries. African artists and men of cultural eminence should be able to travel throughout Africa to explain their work and their motives to the peoples of other African countries. The exchanges organised today by this Festival on a Pan-African basis should become a permanent feature of bilateral relations between African countries.

As we said a moment ago, even if the nature of the local genius determines that the cadence, rhythm or choice of colours be different in the Magrab, the savannah or the forest regions, this will not deter the men of our continent from a sense of fraternity nor from establishing contacts with a sense of the commonality of their problems. It is not true, honoured Delegates, that our struggles, the revolution in which we are engaged, are a passing phase. We declare, on the contrary, that the Revolution is fundamental and that the African artists should undertake to change human nature, to shape human beings free from alien influences—free and better (even if they are negroes) who will no longer endure that man should oppress man.

As President Marien Ngouabi said, "The aim of our culture is not to lull our friends with fairy stories, nor to boast of our art or civilisation—in a word, our knowledge of human sciences. It has a more important part to play, namely to awaken in the African a sentiment of striving for the national liberation of the continent. It is not even a question of proclaiming or glorifying our heroes, though this is indispensable. African culture should be the light which guides our combatants towards national liberation, because it will enable Africans to understand the necessity for them to free themselves. For when a vast continent such as ours is able to appreciate and to defend its culture, this means that it is determined to fight. Without this struggle our culture would not exist, because it would be misunderstood by the forces of evil".

TRADITIONAL CULTURE AND MODERN CIVILIZATION

By ILUNGA KABONGO

Speaking from this tribune for the first time, I should like, in the name of the Democratic Republic of the Congo, to express my warmest thanks to the people, the Government and the President of Algeria for the friendly and gracious welcome so generously offered.

On setting foot on the warm and welcoming soil of Algeria, the glorious scene of one of the most courageous and poignant struggles for national liberty, we have been struck by the unity of conditions and preoccupations which, above and beyond local diversities and regional determinations, forms the weft of the common destiny of our peoples.

Here, as at home, we find at the outset the same cultural diversity, the same effects of colonialism and the same determination to battle for political and economic independence and for cultural liberty.

Here, as at home, the path of liberty is bedewed with blood and tears but marked also by intrepid and heroic deeds.

Here Africa finds in Frantz Fanon its most telling prophet, whereas we have, in Patrice Lumumba, one of its greatest martyrs.

This is as much as to say that our hearts, in Kinshasa and in Algiers, have often beaten to the same rhythm, have felt the same emotions, have known the same sufferings and nourished the same hopes. These realities, Mr. Chairman and honoured Delegates, for the soundest foundation for culture.

"The cultural universe" as Mr. Paul Mushiete, our Cultural Minister, recently reminded us, "is one of the most indefinable, to the extent that it is the very life itself and covers both the beginning and the end of the preoccupations of man at grips with the stresses of existence".

In other words, in contradiction to the opinions of some, culture is not a mere parasite, fixing itself like an extravagant adjunct upon plants considered as fundamental; it is life, because it expresses the spirit and the thought and thus influences the conditions of our existence. In return, it receives therefrom a qualitative, determinative contribution.

There is thus a constant interaction between material production and the concrete conditions of existence on the one hand and human comportment and cultural expression on the other.

We therefore consider it necessary to draw a sharp distinction between culture and civilisation. The first has to do with spiritual qualities expressed in material and intellectual works; the second is concerned with material things themselves, the proudcts of technique and skill.

Given this distinction, we can grasp why, while modern civilization spreads its tentacles over the whole earth and even beyond, our cultures remain ethnic, national and racial, bound up as they are—despite mutual cross-pollenation—with language which is itself in the end no more than the expression of that intangible but real collective ego of a people.

In the light of the foregoing, I should like to expand briefly on two themes which seem to lie at the very heart of the considerations before this symposium: firstly, Negritude and African Culture, and secondly, traditional culture and modern civilization.

Negritude and African Culture

In our eyes this Festival is the apotheosis of an effort several decades old, undertaken by men of colour, profoundly split among themselves but aspiring to regain their self-respect, to rediscover and to live anew, without shame for the colour of their skins or the fact of being negroes.

These efforts and aspirations, at first a rarity, finally won through and impressed upon the world the rhythm of our dances, of our songs, of our sufferings.

Here then, it is proper to pay solemn homage to those who, with limited means, fought the good fight in the name of the culture of an immense proportion of the colonised peoples of Africa and the American continent.

Let us frankly acknowledge that negritude, despite its limitations and even deviations, has given to many of us the conscience of being something other than mere beasts of burden under foreign masters. Thereby negritude planted the first pickets in the direction of national libera-tion by restoring to us our identity and, quite simply, our status as human beings. For, was it not Fanon who wrote: "Man is only human if he wants to impose him-self upon another man in order that the latter shall recog-nize him. So long as he has not won the other's recogni-tion, it is the latter who remains the subject of his activities. It is upon this other, upon recognition by this other, that his human value and reality depend. It is in that other that his life is condensed".

Because it has given us back to ourselves, the Negri-tude Movement forms part and parcel of our history and can therefore by no manner or means be brushed aside, even if, at the present time, we recognize the need to transcend it.

Out of date as an historic movement, Negritude

undoubtedly is, but not so the cultural reality it has striven to valorize.

Our peoples are still in search of a common social and cultural mould within the framework of our States and this search can only start from the present-day elements such as our languages, customs, folklore, traditions and epics, in short our history. And even more, we from Congo-Kinshasa, one of the countries on the borderline between independent Africa and the part of Africa which is still colonized, on the threshold of the minority, racist regimes of southern Africa, are aware that our survival depends, as our Minister of Culture said, on the struggle we shall lead against the ever threatening attempts to de-personalize us.

The African culture we all want to shape from our common awareness of the same conditions of existence and struggle cannot therefore stem from anything but our national and regional identities, absorbed in a more lofty common denominator. The Congo with its frontiers touching those of almost a dozen African countries, quite naturally seeks this common denominator first and foremost in Central Africa, owing to the community of culture which links us to our brethren in neighbouring countries.

In coming to this great meeting in Algiers, we are constantly inspired by this same desire to find and shape cultural unity on yet a higher level, that of Africa as a whole.

In conclusion, we feel that we cannot melt into universality, African though it is, if its elements lack definition, not to say authenticity.

We are in favour of unity, we are in favour of cultural symbiosis, but these presuppose, at the outset, elements which are identified, differentiated, and adopted.

The second theme which we would like to submit for your consideration concerns the necessity for cross-fertilization between what is referred to as our "traditional" cultures and modern civilization.

There is an all too frequent tendency to treat them as opposites, thus creating false dilemmas and false choices for us. The economic development and modernization to which our countries aspire do not imply that we abandon our cultures and our ways of thinking in order to adopt those of others.

We should be all the more cautious in this connection in that we must admit that the technology of modern civilisation risks building a world of machines and weapons which will be more and more difficult for men to keep under control.

We should remember the warning uttered by Martin Luther King. He said that to the extent that our scientific power is out-distancing our moral strength, we run the risk of reaching a point where missiles are guided and men are misguided.

In other words, we must channel the contributions of modern civilisation, of which we have so great a need for our survival and development, without allowing ourselves to be dominated and absorbed by others.

In this matter, there are no ready-made formulas, no well-trodden paths. We must pioneer; we must invent.

Once again we are reminded of that poignant declaration by Fanon:

"If we want to make Africa into another Europe or America into another Europe, then let us entrust the destiny of our countries to Europeans; they will know how to do it better than even the most gifted of us.

"But if we want humanity to advance one iota, and if we want to raise it to a different level from where Europe has placed it, then we must invent, we must discover.

. . . For Europe, for ourselves, and for humanity, Comrades, we must make a new start, develop a new thought, and try to create a new man''.

These, then, are some of the ideas that our delegation would like to include in the subject matter of this Symposium.

In concluding, I very much deplore the fact that I cannot suggest a working example of the two themes which I have attempted to outline here. The kind of cultural synthesis which we have in mind resembles the image which our Congolese music, commonly called "modern Congolese music", evokes for us.

Seeped in our most authentic folklore, in the rhythms of our drums and the melodies of our era, its roots go deep into the soul of our people vibrating down to its most sensitive chords. But it is African, as its spread through Africa testifies, Negro by its American Negro strain; and yet it is of this century, by its genial adoption of the instruments of European civilisation. It is popular, traditional and modern at the same time, African and foreign, and yet profoundly marked with the stamp of our emerging personality.

It is our most fervent wish that from these sources a common language and common signs will be born and will develop as this music did, but soundly based on our respective differences; a language worthy of our times, capable of ensuring our survival, in liberty, and our humanized development.

As for us, our attitude in this concern, as in all others, remains founded on a policy of independence and co-operation. As Lieutenant-General Joseph Desire Mobutu, President of the Republic, recently pointed out:

"Our policy is based on the independence of judgment and mutual co-operation among peoples. It excludes both aggressiveness and passiveness and it must fight against any negation of that personality which is ours".

NEGRITUDE IS DEAD:
THE BURIAL

By STANISLAS ADOTEVI

Underdevelopment, as we now know, is the presence of absence in the present, the mythical character in a debased drama, named neo-colonisation which fills the stage of today's events with both actors and scenery, which robs the wakeful state of its certainty. It is a mysterious force whence issue the Delphic emanations of external exploitation, the matrix from which fetishes are endlessly turned out. It is this which makes and unmakes governments. Every African brought into its service like Caliban by Prospero's wand, is working only to accomplish its desires.

Therefore, since in Africa there is no reality except through this savage fiction, the extraordinary resilience of which Caesar spoke and which all of us wish for can only come about through the projection over Africa—the whole of Africa—of unbridled entities which, spreading to infinity, liberate new energy. These new categories, this system of unaccustomed entities, must assume the task of retranslating in detail all the excrescences with which Africa is afflicted.

In concrete terms, it will no longer do to talk of African unity; we must pursue the means. We can no longer content ourselves with abstract affirmations about African culture in general; we must elucidate scientifically what it is that makes such and such a manifestation

89

distinctly African negro, another Magrabin and a third by its origins and inspiration strictly Arab. This is the truth, eroded sometimes by the passage of time but confirmed by circumstance. All of us share the desire to bridge centuries and differences and to create a united Present.

Mr. Chairman, distinguished delegates, it is to a review of conscience that I invite you—to a casting up of accounts, and finally to a resolution.

Since we must arrive at a resolution, each one of us has a duty to regard differences in the perspective of unity.

Magrabism and Panarabism are no doubt political concepts, but it would be hard to deny that their infrastructure is cultural.

Negritude thinks of itself, no doubt, as a purely literary concept; in truth, it is today a political mysticism.

These, Gentlemen, are the problems we have earnestly to tackle.

For my part, I should like in turn, but in other terms, to take up the theme of negritude. Negritude has failed. It has failed, not in the main because a few pseudo-philosophical scribblings have attributed to it the wish to denounce a certain form of African development, but because, denying its origins to deliver us, bound hand and foot, to ethnologists and anthropologists, it has become hostile to the development of Africa. The negritude we are offered is the relegation of the negro to the slow rhythm of the fields, at the treacherous hour of neo-colonisation. As Madame Kestloot has realized a little belatedly, it is not surprising that the young no longer flock to hear her.

The approach to eternity of the negritic negro is not a metaphysical one, but political. Negritude today fixes and coagulates, for unavoidable ends, the most well-worn theories about African traditions, of which it claims to be the literary expression.

By rehashing the past and tickling a morbid sensitivity, it hopes to make us forget the present. The negritude of speeches, the negritude of today, provides, when the great distributions are made, the "good negroes". Alas for the great poetic vision!

"Do you suppose", we read, "that we can beat the Europeans at mathematics, except for a few outstanding men who would confirm that we are not a race of abstractions?" This sentence was contributed by a theoretician of negritude to the UNESCO Courier of April 1965. Re-read it; you will look in vain for poetry. What you will find is the confirmation that the zealots of negritude are not content merely to point out a difference which is, after all, understandable, but as part of this mania for upholding the concept of theoretical imperfection they endeavour consciously to oppose the black continent to a Europe which is rational and, above all, industrial.

It is easy to discern the intention behind all this mental confusion. From the unfinished concept of negritude one passes to another, very vague and very subtle, of the negro soul; and thereafter to the uncertainty of a philosophy without imperatives and without foundation whose sole title is the frenzy which, it appears, is to regenerate the world—the African world and, of course, the rest. At the end of the road we are offered African socialism which, excuse the incongruity, is merely the conclusion of a syllogism of which the premises is the lubricious negro. This comes from no theorist of negritude, but we know our Sartre. However great our liking for him, we find passages which are mere enormities. "Negritude", he wrote, "is not a state but an attitude . . . an act; but an act which ignores the world, which does not tend towards transforming the wealth of the world . . . it is a matter of existing in the midst of this world . . . of an appropriation which is not technical". From this it follows that for our negro poets (and I quote):

"Existence is the repetition year by year of the sanctified coitus . . . the human rises out of nothing like a penis in erection; creation is an immense and perpetual parturition; the world is flesh and the offspring of flesh.- . . . Thus the deepest roots of negritude are androgynous". This is sheer phantasmagoria. It is not surprising if after this the negroes are incapable of making revolution. Revolution is primarily technical and that is why Marx was the one to write the finest songs about the bourgeoisie.

But Sartre, in self-defence, came practically to another conclusion, It will suffice to read the final pages of that very fine text "Orphee Noir" to become aware of this. By keeping the sexual pedal pressed right down, Sartre drifted into delirium, which is normal. Negritude, by seeking fecundity elsewhere than in Africa, lapsed into socialism, which serves it right.

We know that African socialism derived from negritude will bring about the downfall of the warehouses.

This is the winding street of resolutions and the end of all our hopes. Negritude, by pretending that socialism already existed in traditional communities and that it would be sufficient to follow African traditions to arrive at an authentic socialism, deliberately camouflaged the truth and thus became ripe for destruction.

The first outcome of all this nonsense are the ghosts *which disturb our dreams at night:*

The purring of states which are running in neutral gear; antidiluvian demagogy; government waltzes; a cacophony of administrative interferences in stagnant economic operations; daily increasing cleavage between town and country; unemployment and impotence of the educated; lack of structural changes; incompetent civil servants, and so on.

Only frenzy and bitterness is in sight. This must change and to do this it is not sufficient to talk of negritude, for African negroes know they are negroes and that they are in the midst of the present African catastrophe. In other words we must deal with today's tasks.

This duty may be understood in accordance with the seriousness with which the following questions are tackled: How shall we modernize Africa? How shall we get rid of old structures? How shall we encourage technical culture? What importance should we attach to each stratum of our society? What place will be occupied by women and young people? How shall we resolve our ethnic problems? How shall we approach traditional religions.

For the intellectual, the worker, the shopkeeper, the peasant and for those who do not want to travel outside the country, these are the daily problems which must be solved immediately and which have nothing to do with the pink pages of ''Larousse''.*

The artificial quest for traditions is, as Fanon says, a ''mere study of exoticism''.

Negritude, hollow, vague, is inefficient as an ideology. There is no further place in Africa for literature other than that of the revolutionary combat. Negritude is dead.

A worrying thought arises at this point. I should like to combine this worry with my own worries. It lies in the same direction.

Doubtless, if we examine the events over the past ten years in Africa, and if we disgustedly consider this cavalcade of servility and begging and if we measure the extent of this hyprocrisy, we cannot prevent ourselves from calling for a revolt.

Africa has not gone and she does not seem to be ready for departure.

---

*The pages giving the meanings of classical quotations.

The false alarms, the courtelinesque ballets and the tragi-comic setting of the gigantic Luna-Park make people quick to conclude that these negroes are worth nothing and are still under the influence of their fantasies and keeping the worst surprises for the best intentions. The conclusion can be quickly drawn and it is drawn. It grieves and humiliates us and we are tempted to throw up the sponge. It could be the same for Negritude.

It is necessary to restore the natural aridity to things, to understand how I deviate from my friends, not because of the objectives or the projected end, but because of the means. To understand Negritude, we must put it back in its former neurotic context and by comparing it with the current situation, ask ourselves what the chances are of exorcising it.

At this abstract level, it is easy to see that nothing has changed. Exploitation has become more disgusting, and this continent which, except for man's looting, was not destined for misfortune, lives without an objective and with a stagnant future. We know what they say: mess, waste and disorder. This is what the great friends of these States are saying among themselves. To know this is to know the necessity of recovering in the same movement at least the Negritude programme, if not the final goal.

Without a doubt, the irrationality of under-development, and especially that of negroes, is enormous. But without going as far as taking examples from their history, it might be useful for Europeans to make the dialectic reversal advocated by Marx, which has now become a working argument. This reversal will allow us to refute certain allegations. And we have known since Montesquieu that, in political life, "All political vices are not moral vices and all moral vices are not political ones". In the same way, we will be led to think that, however vicious negroes may be, they are not completely commanded by their imagination: and that, beyond the negro's unreason there lies a reason that is not reasonable, but extraordinarily rational. All this unreason has its structure: colonial necessity whose dominion is so sure that it can not only digest the strangest eccentricities but even the stroke of fortune bringing success or failure to a coup d'etat, and which depends on an Ambassador's smile or his silence. This understanding of the structure of the exploitation of negritude should have assured him.

Its failure came about because it neither would nor could do this work for itself or for us. In any case, there can be no doubt that Negritude will never do it now, but Negritude, at the outset and merely because it did not yet have the possibility, already raised its voice in certain contexts in a way that could be heard and which some of us did hear.

In consequence, whatever may be our quite justifiable references with regard to it, and although certain aspects may seem old-fashioned and with frankly reactionary objectives, we should consider it as a primitive period necessary to the African renaissance. I would say, and I choose my words carefully, that at a time when the whole world was given over to racialism and people like Andrass and Morand were taken for vagabonds, at a time when the whole of humanity raised voice in competitive cacophony, there was a single pistol-shot in the middle of this concert—negritude. It shook a few consciences and brought a few negroes together, and this was a good thing. But I do not intend to defend negritude against its internal weaknesses and the disintegration with which it is threatened.

We should nonetheless recognise that the exaltation of our heroes can be none other than abstract. It underlines contemporary demands—poetry of the unusual and of solitude, doubtless, but at the same time political in its refusal to betray its origins. It was political before being lyrical.

I am not speaking of deviated or perverted negritude. I am speaking of our debt, and above all, our pride, in belonging to the tradition of African civilization, and in possessing values which distinguish the black world from that of the white men. In the realm of artistic creation, this attitude calls for a casting off of European models and a profession of faith in the destiny of Africa. Formulated thus, Negritude should be considered as the first moment of present day requirements; I think that it was, yesterday, one of the possible forms for the struggle for emancipation.

It is a curious struggle, I will be told, that contents itself with words when depersonalisation is rampant in Senegal and men are dying like flies in the banana-fields of the West Indies. Doubtless this is so, but one should forget, for an instant, the Negritude of the dictionary and neo-colonial imposture, and should try to understand what courage was needed to dare to protest against humiliation in the "thirties". And as regards words, I should recommend a little more thorough reading of Marx. One can read, in his "Contribution to the criticism of Hegel's Philosophy of Law", this phrase which may appear astonishing to some of you.

"It is evident", says Marx, "that the aim of criticism can in no wise replace criticism by armed force. Material force can only be countermanded by material force, but theory is also changed to a material force as soon as it penetrates the masses". I do not think, therefore, that the error arises at this level. The capital error of this older Negritude, the great sin of negritude in general was to have been, at the outset, inverted love. It was to have believed, even before its birth, in universality—when the universe was forbidden to it. The carnal ardour of black hatred should have been opposed to the cosmic insults to which none other than the black race have been subjected. But our poets, overtaken by unreason, preferred the crazy advances of love. Damas says this when he looks in vain for "a shoulder in which to hide his face and his share of reality". On behalf of us all, pigment confirms the truth that this entire negritude is morbid sterility because it never knew what harvest it would reap. And indeed, that which brings about the restructuring of the world concerns revolution, not cosmic ferment. Negritude was born dead; it was going to die and it died.

A message, however, remains. Apart from the ineffectiveness of its negation, apart from the labyrinth of mystification, Negritude was a rejection of humiliation.

Today this humiliation is still apparent and the problem posed by Negritude remains. There are the unwanted gifts intermittently showered upon us so as to ensure our continued subjection. There is the deterioration of rates of exchange, there are the prices fixed in Paris, London and elsewhere. And for one unemployed—let no more be said—there is the apetizing food to be had in foreign embassies. There is the isolation of China. There are the millions that foreign aid brings in to the countries that are supposed to be aiding us, and the moving text by Che that I will read and which says, in effect:

How can we speak of the "mutual benefits" if we have the sale, at world market prices, of raw products costing unlimited efforts and sufferings to the under-developed countries and the purchase, at world market prices, of machines produced in today's great automated factories?

If we establish this sort of relationship between the two groups of nations, we will have to agree that the Socialist countries are to a certain extent implicated in imperialist exploitation.

It will be argued that the volume of exchanges with the underdeveloped countries constitutes an insignificant percentage of Socialist countries' foreign trade. This is absolutely true, but makes no difference as to the immoral character of this exchange''.

In short, there is the spirit of Camp David. And finally, there we are—divided, crushed and pulverized. A reduced and shaken Africa, with no grasp of its future.

Africa, still anti-Aristotelian, is still in the expectation of form. But the great uphevals of the next decades will proceed from this unreasoning, formless Africa. All that is needed is unceasingly renewed action, an imposed discipline and, above all, a way of thinking which can embrace situations, discern difficulties, repulse determinism and make real the new situation enabling us to reach our goal. I would put forward the doctrine of Melanism.

One could find another name for it, but the essential thing is the cementing force and thought which, operating in the perspective of unity, reacts on particular sensibilities as do Magrabism and Arabism.

The Melanism which I would propose to you is open to all Nubia (Africa). It is not a new racialism but an identification. It is an affirmation of the plain fact that to be a negro today is still to live through the violent depredations of the slave trade.

Melanism is the acceptance of a state of war, but with arms other than prayers and negro spirituals. It is, said Machiavelli, ''an act of humanity to take up arms in the defence of a people for whom they are the only resource''.

Melanism will be the unique resource of a people who can no longer deck out its torture with trophies conquered from shame. It will be, as Cesaire says, the expression denying the whip. We must give the lie to negation by assigning positive tasks to each negro.

We are not trying to racialise problems but to understand that white people have the habit of putting all negroes into the same category and to inspire themselves with this same common historical attack and subsequent traumatism, so as to define a strategy for the present. To put it clearly, negroes should relegate their tears to antiquity. The battle has taken on a physical form, and should henceforth only have a physical expression. And, for certain American negroes, it would be illusory to think that the battle will end with the illusory conquest of civil rights. Even if they one day take over economic and social power, or if, in the meantime, they have crumbs thrown to them in the middle hierarchies, they should know that they are nothing, so long as the negroes of Africa have not yet completed the ascendancy, the tragedy of which was related by King Christopher.

All this goes to say that the essential task must fall on the negroes of Africa. And they can only carry it out by coming to agreement on the following questions: Is it true that no race has been more insulted than ours? Is not the present-day situation the perennialization of this humiliation? Is it not true that the Africans themselves (our ancestors who acquiesced in the selling of slaves and who are the present-day apologists of modern sodomy) bear the overwhelming responsibility for this fearsome cavalcade? And, as things are thus, is it worthwhile making the effort to get out of this slough of spittle, tears and blood? Finally, is there a certain and effective means of doing this? And if so, what is it?

These are the five questions that Melanism would place before the conscience of each African.

For my part, I do not think much of African socialism. It is the ideological expression of a social category which installs, in a backward country, capitalism with its backward economy. It has nothing to offer to us.

I therefore think that the only practical socialism is that propounded by Marx, completed by Lenin and applied, with a greater or lesser degree of success, by the socialist countries. This socialism is the only practical possibility—with, of course, the variations imposed by geography. But we know Lenin's dictum "Communism is the power of the Soviets plus electrification". This is not yet the case in Africa. There is also the advice given by Lenin to the 2nd Internationale. To make the great socialist leap forward one must, he said, have an active, organised proletariat and help form socialist governments. Now, what we know of our proletariats and the present international situation condemns us to defer this hope.

There remains capitalism. I will not speak of the extent of this phenomenon, but will content myself with listing its failures by means of a quotation from Meister:

"Finally one fails to wonder about the inability of liberalism to apply to new countries the principles which made possible the spectacular development of our Western countries. By its very development, capitalism impedes the development of new countries: the principle of the free circulation of capital empties these countries of their surpluses, while that of free enterprise kills the embryo of industrial development. To stick to these principles and leave their frontiers open means condemning these countries to the same stagnation as that reigning in Latin America, that typical product of neo-colonialism in the last century. It is obvious that the liberal way is a total failure in Africa.

Although during several decades Europe has been the theatre of the greatest capitalist upheavals, and although capitalism today still appears as an extraordinarily fertile model which constantly generates free energy, here, for the African, it is, to use a metaphor, an extinguished and slag-covered volcano.

We therefore are forced to look for something else. Melanism which, I admit, is somewhat irrational, aims at keeping the sore open and, by shelving the solutions so far proposed, gets rid of the inextricable estrangement and founds the state in which the future history of Africa will take on a meaning.

I have already defined Melanism. It is not just a phobia. As it cannot be compared to the "anti-racist racism" Sartre speaks of in "Orphee Noire", it is our purpose here to de-mystify the concept of race and to wrench it out of the hands of reactionary politicians who are using it to obscure the issue.

Although Sartre's objective was the same as ours—to denounce the evil that has led to the racism of the black poets—ours differs from his in that it does not limit itself to exorcising race by making it active, but aims at strengthening a people by a racial awareness, a people which perhaps is still abstract although not paradoxical, and which is probably mistaken as a result of inhibition.

There remains however, in spite of the precautions taken, something which should not be left obscure. We should repeat here what we have already said:

Firstly, we are products of white unreason: we are Negroes only for the whites. In Africa, to be a Negro, is to be as natural as the infinite stars in the night. Secondly, whatever our opinions, whether we are Christians, Muslims, Communists or reactionaries, and often at the height of battle, white necessity has been burnt to a cinder in our flesh. And thirdly, as it is our purpose to save ourselves from racism by constructing a modern state in Africa, this our purpose can only be made real by an exacerbated nationalism, the force of which, although partly resting as objective facts, also derives, according to Renouvin, from irrational elements. Consequently, we cannot reject the irrational part of such an enterprise. On the contrary, if we take the end into account, the objective pursued will give the enterprise a positive value, as has always been the case throughout history. Undoubtedly, to be able to speak of national feeling, we should, according to the well-known pattern, first have a Nation.

But who could deny that Islam has favoured nationalism? And is it possible, as Renouvin asks, to understand anything about Japanese nationalism without referring to Shintoism?

Our project therefore, far from floundering through excessiveness, may break silence in pointing to the beyond and in rejecting limits. It states the necessity for a modern state while indicating the means to attain it.

Therefore it takes its inspiration from the great nationalist upsurges of the past centuries, but with the difference that, although it may serve to create a myth, this myth should draw its truth only from its own strength: we need a myth which is not mythical but a reality shattered in the bric-a-brac of time. A myth such as the one Gramsci, who pronounced the only right and profound judgment on Machiavelli, discovered in "The Prince", which he considered as an: "Illustration of a political ideology which does not present itself as a frigid Utopia or a doctrinaire argument, but as the creation of a concrete reasoning process which operates on a dispersed and scattered people to provoke and organize their collective renaissance".

In the same way, Africa must be convinced by meditation on race. It should come to terms with its time so as to regenerate the future. In this connection, there are two objectives: the establishment of a collective Melanian will and new mental structures.

There are five prerequisites for attaining these objectives:
   (1) On the political level: the establishment of a modern state.
   (2) On the economical level: a democratic national economy.
   (3) In the field of the philosophy of history, all systems which persist in discovering cyclic returns

and which deny indefinite progress should be rejected.

(4) On the intellectual and moral level:
  (a)   in the moral field, an educational system drawing its force from a constant reference to past and present humiliations of the race and which also considers reprehensible any insane cult of the past, even when national, as well as all stupid borrowings from abroad.
  (b)   in the intellectual field, opposition to stifled traditions, an appeal for rational innovations of the various world revolutions.

(5) Lastly, on the level of personal training, we should only strive for a perpetual creation of ourselves by ourselves and for a constant creative activity based upon a sense of initiative and responsibility and only retaining elements useful for the Nation.

To sum up, pending the union of the whole of Africa, this transitional ideology aims at the establishment of a strong and prosperous national state which, inside the country, brings about the recovery of the race by vivisection; outside the country, asserts African irredentism using subversion if necessary; finally, on the economic level, takes advantage of the contradictions between and inside the power coalitions in order to found a modern industry and economy.

A hallucination? Perhaps. In any case, the methods will have to be transformed. Practical and theoretical necessities often entail the introduction of new concepts into the problem.

Before socialist recovery, must come recovery of ourselves. This is not a matter of repudiation. Tactics had to be changed. We are changing them.

In any case, these lines are addressed to the young

Africans of my generation. To the generation which, like me, will perhaps not see the promised land, but which should know that the shore exists. Melanism is after all the preliminary to socialism. Instead of disdain and condescension, each African, as is more or less the case with the Chinese today, will read in the eyes of the European the first signs of terror. Therefore, everybody should, in the sinister hour of discouragement, repeat after Fichte these sentences of restored hope: "Already one sees the new daybreak shine, it casts a glow upon the mountain tops, announcing the coming day". I want, as much as is in my power, to seize the rays of this daybreak and condense them to make a mirror which reflects its image on our desperate era, so that it may find there its true core, and perceives, through its successive transformations and developments, the anticipated form of its definitive face. No doubt this contemplation will dissolve the image of our former life and that what is dead will not definitely enter in the tomb before emitting excessive moans.

NEGRO-AFRICAN CULTURE AND POETRY——ELEMENTS OF THE SURVIVAL OF OUR CIVILIZATION

By LAMINE NIANG

From the natural incapacity of the human spirit to perpetuate itself in cruelty has dawned the era of our dreams in which emotional expression, that blessed reinforcement and springboard of redemption, supersedes the alarming vigour of the rational.

More effective than hope, it is dedicated to the restitution of man in his primordial dignity, which egotism has scattered among the shades. As a result of this dispersion, the man of yesterday, his spirits blurred, lived in a structure anything but flattering to universal consciousness. In this situation one man here and there, falling victim to the hazards of geography and of an imperfect system of defence based on his temperament, his philosophy and his religion, became the servant of another man better served by his temperament and by his faculty of subordinating his philosophy and beliefs to his needs.

What does it matter today when this concept was born? In our Savannah, when sowing time came round, did not people turn their backs on the previous balance between production and consumption? This was less of a sacrifice in that the faith imbibed in childhood moves in balance—invisibly perhaps but infallibly in balance—in which every spirit, however maleficent, receives the just and immutable reward for its thoughts and emotions. The negro was no hoarder. His flawless faith, the authenticity which emanates from his deepest consciousness has certainly retarded the march of his destiny.

And yet, his nature, as it is, has earned him eloquent expressions of sympathy and, who knows, of envy, despite the delirious cyclone of pragmatism, the feast of positivist minds. Mr. Balandier, who can claim to know us well, wrote: "No-one ever heard a Negro moaning that life is not worth living". L. Senghor supports him, writing: "Neither fear nor material preoccupations dominate the religion of the negro, though both are present, and the negro, like anyone else, is a prey to human anguish".

Our dead of yesterday have borne away their tribulations along the way of no return. The page of their trial is turned forever. May our voices echo those of us who have a bowel and a soul to pray to God, in whose image we are created that He grant these dead the solidarity and paternity for which they strove until the sublime moment when they breathed their last, massacred, for the concretisation of those sentiments without which the universal society—multinational and multiracial—would lose both sense and savour.

Our questions as regard the backcloth of the world beyond the tomb remain unanswered, but we know— those who are left—that the era of emotional expression ushered in but yesterday at the World Festival of Negro Arts, and which is with us in this symposium in Algiers, is sufficiently illuminated by the juxtaposition of past errors, of tribulations endured, lapses of memory, lack of intelligence and the echo of a certain logic which aspired to "go it alone" in the interaction between Man and Nature. Was it not Francois Mauriac who wrote: "An excess of misery brings peace". Echoing him, we would add: "An excess of errors transforms". At this stage, misery and errors enrich our field of awareness.

Since this second half of the XXth Century began mankind has been in search of new ways. He finds himself obliged to transform his will to live; and to this end he adopts new aspirations. Malraux, one of the best qualified authorities on the subject, in the course of his speech at Rabat, proclaimed: "For the first time we are witnessing the end of the great agrarian civilisations. In discovering the machine, the XXth Century pictured man as the servant of machines, not as agents of coercion but of liberation, certainly as the donors of leisure, and thus our imaginations are satisfied. What machines have made, we all know, but while the machines which transformed the word were a-building, there was created in parallel the machinery of dreams".

Thus it happens that "We are the first generation to use the machinery of dreams. For humanity which does not know how to fill its leisure time—and sport is emphatically not sufficient—looks to dreams to fill the gap. And this dream which is to fill the gap has little in common with the dreams of bygone days. . . ."

But the only weapon we possess against these despots—dreams, imagination, money, blood, sex, a heightened awareness of death—these "powers" which are those of the "demon", is Culture. Works of art outlive cities.

Today, our concern should be to recreate our culture and fit it into a universal culture, bearing in mind the fundamental transformations of thought and of the rhythm of living to which we are subjected. This is one of the great novelties of our century. But we must take care also to create a sociometric order of cultures by selective affinities, bearing in mind their respective climate and geography. For, today more than ever, there is only one civilisation and that, technological. Our African negro culture, as being one of the last to emerge from the oblivion of the past, is moving faster than all other cultures.

Universal civilisation! It encompasses everything, determines everything. It tears us out of our static universe and compels us, men, societies and cultures, to refashion the unity of mankind and the world.

Nevertheless, every society expands within its own culture, though this is transformed with time and our changing needs. To transform and adapt itself while yet retaining its character, its originality, these are the requirements of every culture which means to resist assimilation. Sumer, despite its greatness, has now passed into books; future generations will no longer read directly from its clay tablets, which wind and weather are eroding. The age of the Pharaohs has left us its pyramids and its works of art which alone remain to convey their message, in view of the almost total oblivion which enshrouds their creators. Then we have the fabulous riches of the kings of Dahomey, now credited to the account of the winds and the sands, of which only some masks remain. "The world of culture passes not by inheritance but by conquest".

But of all the components of culture, poetry best stands the test of the ages, because more than any other, it is concerned with the destiny of the spirit. And it is the spirit that we look for in the gaze of Tutankamen, in the tender piety of the Joconda and the blank gaze of the death-mask of the wizard-nester of Koutial.

Poetry transmits to us the content of the ages. In Western Africa (to speak only of what I know), in the absence of a written language, the history of our defunct empires, the structure of our ancient societies, is passed on from father to son by word of mouth without discontinuity, by our "griot" poets. These narratives, for the most part of a laudatory nature, are so intensely lyrical that they can be sung, essentially characterised as they are by improvisation and rhythm. Speaking of this poetic genre and its "ouoloffs", Badara Mbaye Kabou, Ahoune War Samb, Baye Takhi Lalo and others whose names unfortunately I cannot recall, L. Senghor said: "A poem, in the last resort, is nothing but the expression, through images and rhythm, of profound feelings. So much the better if the feelings are noble. Negro-African poetry is functional".

"But I am not exclusively thinking of this poetic genre. To pay due homage to it let me recall the saying: "The great poets were of the auditive, not of the visionary type". Poetry must therefore lead somewhere. One cannot well deny its function—the dispensation, in equal parts, of knowledge and joy. What of its use among westerners in the Mysteries and in the Canticles!

No-one denies any longer that language liberates mankind, but without the channel of poetry this liberation remains static.

The negroes of Africa are little concerned with the achievements of the past, abyssal when all is said and done. Nevertheless the Georgics, The Aeneid, The Divine Comedy and the Old Testament demand recognition as the apotheosis of poetry, rich in instruction and a source of delight which the negro will not disdain.

The poetry of Negritude is a dispenser of joy. Lorca wrote "No matter how little some people may like it, the American negro constitutes over there the most lively, and the most delicate element. Because they believe, because they hope, because they sing". And this Prince of poets might have summed up: "By reason of their emotions and their sensibility, the negroes are the poetic salt of America".

A faith uninterrupted, hope of fundamental transformations, rhythm at work, rhythm in the dance, whatever wind may blow, these are the mainsprings, these are the sap which plays its part in human liberation. These are the hinges of communication between man and Nature. These elements form an essential part of African negro culture and constitute the sap, part carnal, part spiritual, of poetry.

Our *ad hoc* poetry, called "fighting" poems, is bound to disappear, as did the Romancero Gitano which Lorca and his followers rescued from oblivion, reconstituted and adapted. But when we come to the poetry of Negritude codified on the basis of a sense of universality—nature ready to play its part along its own lines, which is the foundation of liberty—then new horizons continually open before us. But these horizons are there to be conquered and explored. Open to the whole planet, they lie under no single banner. And it is here that our compatriots must understand that in a universe in headlong motion they cannot rebuild human life on the basis of dead things. Dead things belong in museums.

New men, new poems. While there are forms of poetry which "enshroud" themselves, the poetry of negritude, enriched by the contributions of cosmic syncretism and fresh emotions every day replanted—thanks to science—has its part in the Universal. The African negro feels at home in his emotions—in all emotions. His sensibility moves him to discern joy and anguish. And we all know that "easement liberates genius".

An idea or a sentiment not expressed in words is an infant still unborn. And the ornament, the crystal, of language, is poetry. From his birth onwards, the African negro is familiar with intuitive emotions, the sole realities which survive and which are the receptacles of cosmic conscience. "Emotion is negro; reason is hellenic". Cosmic emotion is alpha and omega, the limits of the Temple, despite the radiance of the science which satisfied our ethical needs and our leisures! This is the maximal concentrate of poetry! This is the realm of African negro poetry!

Boileau exhorted the poets: "Let us work for Glory". By glory we understand the harmony between Man and Nature, Man come to terms with his limitations and more especially the glory of survival over death in the form of culture. The reign, if it ever existed, of poetry as the projection of a subjective universe is dead without appeal.

But the functional poetry of the African negro must forego its inspiration and its rhythm. It must vaunt itself to be the song of universal Nature. It would be wrong to abandon the magic of words, images and expression.

African negro homogeneity, assuming that it will one day reach the stage of tertiary requirements when the machine will no longer be an obsession, gives us no right to consider our poetry as an end in itself. For when this moment comes, other scientific discoveries will inevitably push back our horizons. Besides, the negro does not see Nature and the things of Nature as atonal, or as objects to which he can simply attribute his own sentiments. Nature and natural objects have feelings of their own. Their existence implies communion, a continuous dialogue.

In this sphere the mission of the African negro poet, with his virgin mentality now liberated, his auditive faculties and his vision, is to organise words in the form of pictures so as to evoke for the humble consumer-communicant the thoughts and the riches of the heart of a stone, confidences whispered by shadows, all the messages beamed at us. As Delacroix said: "Nature is a dictionary". To this I will add: It is for the artist and especially the poet to introduce, or re-introduce his fellow-humans into Harmony. For this purpose each poet chooses a point of impact from which to carry out this re-introduction in terms of joy, anguish, wonder, dissatisfaction, and so on. The plurality of poets can only be explained by the plurality of situations and problems. It is synonymous with the plurality of means of re-introduction.

African negro poetry is functional. This does not mean that it lacks purity, by which I mean whatever is poetical in a poem. A pure and virginal spirit radiates words, images set with sounds, elements in the scale. Now, the negro body is all movement and rhythm. As Leslie said: "Movement is the motive of every being".

Space is a great musical score in which all songs are juxtaposed. And we owe it to ourselves to borrow from other cultures and other civilisations as much as they borrow from us.

Poetry can penetrate a profane heart only if it sings. Music, as we know, lulls us, but it has its message, too. That is why, to the negro, poetry and music are inseparable. Together they form the spell which arrests us, charms us and "gentles our manners". The boatmen of the Volga, convicts chained like the slaves onboard ship, sang during their gruelling labour, just as did the humble and peaceable weaver of Sokone.

Yes indeed, because poetry, when in the form of rhythm and song, touches each one of us in the mysterious, marvellous, inviolable deepest centre of his being, whence alone, perhaps, we can penetrate the core of objects and of hearts. Poetry which reaches the highest sentient summit of this intimacy is one with the unity and harmony of the world. Here again it must be reaffirmed that the poetry of Negritude is Art. Thus it enters into the field of beauty, but a field swept clear of nothingness. The African negro has no sense for nothingness. An imagination which rests upon nothing will encounter nothing. In the inner world of the negro, everything has a soul, everything is alive and everything has rich treasures to offer the seeker. These are gifts of the One. The negro poet is not merely a visionary, for all visions have their place or their orbit on the edge of reality. When the negro thinks or acts, his vibrations are dictated by the interplay between his senses and his memory. This vibration is the alchemist's retort whence emerge words and images, the elements of reality.

Thus it is that the poet and his verses constitute a filter for those who wish to enter the harmony of the world. They open up the road on which the subjective meets the actual. In doing so, poetry does not distinguish itself from individuality; they are welded together. In such a case we have authentic poetry, not prefabricated but experienced.

This alliance between the two universes, this symbiosis, allows us to see the night, for example, not as something fearful but as a stage in the feast to which all are invited, the shadows as well as the light. The forest is no longer a realm of terrors but a place to be visited with awe in order to listen to the voices of the other world, to receive and transmit messages. The sea is not a monster. Only the insensitive and inward-looking spirit fails to communicate with it. Terror and alarm are by-products of the solitary spirit, the spirit without contacts, filled only with itself.

But this alliance, this symbiosis, is capable of reducing space to meet the needs of the spirit. "It builds up" as an African negro has said, "whole oases out of the smoke of a stale cigarette stub". And so the negro, who is not at all interested in the material universe of Chenier, feels in every fibre with "la jeune Tarentine", because a shock instantly calls forth an emotion. Yet the spiritual universe of "la jeune Tarentine", cut off before her marriage as the author was before his natural term, evokes images which are, however, far removed from the poetic usages of ancient Greece and the folklore of its Gods. In the negro mind all time is a continuum.

Here then is an account—modest, I hope—of the contribution and the impulse of African negro poetry in its own framework, adjusted to the Universe. Here, too, are the cultural elements carried forward through time and space by this "functional poetry"—elements which the white civilisations of America and Europe have borrowed in the negro forms of art and negro rhythms. Thus we can say that the content of our thinking in matters of culture rejects anything that would attach it to a subjective universe. And this way of thinking will be perfectly at home at the crossroads of fundamental transformations today as in the future.

The negro body dies; negro thought remains. It will disappear only with the world—with Harmony—to which it is moulded.

LITERATURE

ALEX LA GUMA AND THE RESPONSIBILITIES OF THE SOUTH AFRICAN WRITER

By J. M. COETZEE

With the best will in the world it is impossible to detect in the fiction of black South Africans any significant and complex talent which responds with both the vigor of the imagination and sufficient technical resources to the problems posed by conditions in South Africa.

Thus writes the critic Lewis Nkosi, summing up the conclusions of a survey of black South African writing in which he discusses Richard Rive, Bloke Modisane, Ezekiel Mphahlele, and Alex la Guma. Nkosi goes on to suggest that unless the South African writer can learn to present an imaginative transformation of mere "journalistic fact," he should, perhaps, "temporarily renounce literature" until the political problem has been solved.[1]

Whether or not this suggestion is intended merely to provoke thought, Nkosi's criticism, telling though its general thrust may be, reveals a fairly specific, and *ipso facto* debatable, conception of the role of the writer. This conception is, to Western eyes, orthodox, so orthodox that we tend not to think twice about its foundations. Yet what are these foundations? In Nkosi's view, the writer

---

[1]"Fiction by Black South Africans," reprinted in *Introduction to African Literature*, ed. Ulli Beier (Evanston: Northwestern U.P., 1967), pp. 211, 212.

begins with social "fact" and transforms it into art by a process in which the other two reagents are imagination and technique. Technique may evolve from indigenous African tradition, or, in default of that, may be taken over from the experimental line in modern European and American literature. Imagination, we gather from Nkosi's examples, is art's enabling faculty (we may ignore the circularity here: Nkosi is not writing an essay in aesthetics).

Two questions arise. The first is, in essence: what kind of literature ought the Africa of today to evolve? The immediate answer is, of course, that there can be no talk of a prescriptive "ought": Africa will evolve the literature it evolves. The question becomes more meaningful, however, if we pose it specifically in Nkosi's terms: what value does the experimental line in modern Western literature hold for Africa? No doubt the African writer, simply as craftsman, finds experimentation interesting; but does not the Western experimental line assume *and perpetuate* a rift between the writer and society at large which is a fact of life in the West but need not become a fact of life in Africa? And does homage to Western experimentalism not involve a rather simple-minded view of an absolute "technique" which, as in the myth of our science, can only progress, never regress (Nkosi uses the phrase "the lessons of the masters" (211) without irony)? If Nkosi allows that a literature based on African traditions and a literature employing Western "techniques" are equally valid choices for the African writer (211), are we not entitled to ask—and here we reach the second main question—whether there might not be a whole spectrum of valid literatures open to Africa, and to suggest that the writer should not, so to speak, choose his tradition at random, but rather choose it with some sense of the social implications of his choice?

The whole vast question of the social responsibility of the writer has, of course, peculiar complications in Africa, arising from social and linguistic fragmentation, illiteracy, etc. And in South Africa there is a further twist: because of government censorship, few black writers can expect to be read in their own country. So the question must for the present remain at a theoretical level. Yet we cannot deny that an Africa of mass communications will come into being, and that the foundations of the literature, spoken or written, of that Africa are, for good or ill, being laid by the African writer of today. Questions of theory today will be questions of practice tomorrow. Nkosi too has his eyes turned to the future when he decides that South African writing is going nowhere and suggests that writers should perhaps retire to wait for more auspicious times.

One of the few writers for whom Nkosi has praise is Alex la Guma, in whom he finds a redeeming "enthusiasm for life as it is lived" (216). I should like to turn to La Guma's best-known work, the short novel *A Walk in the Night* (1962),[1] and by examining it in some detail attempt to show that it exemplifies a conception of literature radically different from Nkosi's. The question I should ultimately like to ask is whether the direction indicated by La Guma is not a more fruitful one for the South African writer—and for South African society—than that indicated by Nkosi.

A Walk in the Night is set in Cape Town's District Six, a seedy Colored ghetto in which working-folk and gangsters grind out their existence under the eyes of armed white policemen cruising the streets. A worker named Adonis, drunk and smarting under various injustices, kills a harmless old white man. He escapes undetected, and blame is attached to Willieboy, a small-

[1] *A Walk in the Night* (Evanston: Northwestern U.P., 1968).

time thug, who is then hunted to his death by a sadistic white policeman named Raalt. Adonis, meanwhile, slips further and further into the gang-world of the slum.

The naturalistic bias of the novel is clearly spelled out. In a series of flashbacks, the dying Willieboy remembers the squalor and harshness of his childhood. He has spent all his life trying to differentiate himself from the depressed squalor of the masses: he finds his escape from anonymity in petty violence, loud clothes, liquor. Living a life peripheral to the life of society, he reacts to his discovery of the murdered white by running away: his relation to the law, he knows, can only be that of victim to persecutor. He is betrayed to the police by the garish shirt he wears. His socially conditioned character is his fate. The real killer Adonis has belonged to the working-class mainstream until this one day of his life. But now he is dismissed from his job for talking back to the white foreman and humiliated in the street by two white policemen. He goes to a bar to drown his sorrows, then returns home to take out his formless anger on the old white man. He is observed slipping away from the scene by the thugs who hang out on every street corner, and joins their organization under hinted threats of blackmail (La Guma's sinister gangland stands in sharp contrast to the romantic outlaw world of Can Themba and Bloke Modisane). Adonis's actions are in fact all reactions against the forces of *apartheid.* But even the policeman Raalt is not ultimately in control of his actions. Aside from the pathological structures imposed on his behavior by his religion of race, his thoughts are dominated by the newly discovered infidelity of his wife, which arouses in him a vindictiveness that he takes out on the people of District Six. (Indeed, the gratuitous introduction of Raalt's wife into the plot can *only* be explained as part of a scheme to display a group of characters with little control over their fate: an autonomous Raalt might have threatened this scheme by becoming a villain-hero of pure evil.)

Now, the atmosphere of doom created by the plot of *A Walk in the Night* will be familiar to any reader of South African literature, whose godparents, it would seem, are *An American Tragedy* and *Native Son*. And we are entitled to ask what purpose a literature serves which only chronicles the lives and deaths of little people, the victims of social fates too dark for them to comprehend. No doubt most people are "little," but there is much justification for the Marxist criticism that the substitution of the average for the typical which we associate with the rise of European naturalism was itself a concession of victory on the part of the European writer to the forces that brought about social fragmentation and moral depression—forces that equally well created bourgeois capitalism in Europe and the introverted violence of the District Sixes of the world. If we are justified in transferring this criticism to *A Walk in the Night*, then we can go on to suggest with some force—for reasons different from Nkosi's—that a moratorium might indeed be declared on this kind of literature of defeat until the political problem in South Africa has been solved.

But I do not believe that such criticism can justifiably be made. *A Walk in the Night*, despite its naturalist assumptions and its doom-laden atmosphere, contains embedded in it an analysis of the political weakness of Colored society in South Africa, and hence implies an explanation of the negativeness of a fiction that realistically portrays that society. To understand La Guma's analysis, we must look beyond the main line of the story to a group of three minor characters who at first sight may seem peripheral to it.

The first of them is Greene, a man with "a haggard, wine-soaked, ravaged face" (13) whom Adonis meets in a bar. Greene listens to a taxi-driver acquaintance repeat fragments of a speech he has heard at a political rally ("Heard it at a meeting on the Parade. Whites act like that because of the capitalist system"), then shuts him up: "Cut out politics. . . . Those bastards all come from Russia" (17). Later in the same conversation, Greene refuses to recognize a connection which the taxi-driver inarticulately perceives between the lynching of a black man in the United States and a fatal knife-fight in District Six. Hours later, after the bar has closed, Greene is mugged by Willieboy in a dark street (72–73). There is no hint that he even now recognizes a connection between his fate and abstract political forces.

The second of these minor characters is Joe, a home-less youth who lives off handouts and by scavenging along the seashore. Though he lives on the borderline of starvation, Joe pleads with Adonis not to give himself to the underworld. The moral force of his plea, particularly in view of his revelation of a childhood closely parallel to that of Willieboy (who is Adonis's *alter ego*), seems to argue that conscience need not die under the weight of social forces. Yet the last page of the novel seems to hint that Joe is drifting toward suicide:

> Somewhere the young man, Joe, made his way toward the sea, walking alone through the starlit darkness. In the morning he would be close to the smell of the ocean and wade through the chill, comforting water, bending close to the purling green surface and see the dark undulating fronds of seaweed, writhing and swaying in the shallows, like beckoning hands (96).

Joe is, in Afrikaans, a *strandloper,* a beachcomber, and we may remember that one of the Hottentot tribes encountered by the first Dutch colonists at the Cape was also given the name *Strandlopers.* Are we being too fanciful if we see in Joe's end the death of the last remnants of independence from the market economy?

The third of the characters is Franky Lorenzo, a young stevedore prematurely aged by "hard work and unpaid bills and sour babies" (35). He lives in the tenement in which the white man is killed, and it is his wife who finds the corpse and gives the alarm. When Raalt arrives, however, Lorenzo and his wife co-operate least of all with him: his wife does not acknowledge giving the alarm, and Lorenzo braves Raalt's threats and tries to prevent another of the tenement-dwellers from incriminating Willieboy: for a moment

> he met the constable's eyes holding them with his own, until he felt his wife tugging at his arm, pleading: "Franky, don't get into trouble, please" (62–63).

The Lorenzos refuse to co-operate not because they know Willieboy but out of a sense of solidarity with whomever the police are hunting. Franky yields to his wife not because he is afraid of Raalt but because he feels that his first responsibility is toward his family. In one sense, therefore, his family is a liability which prevents him from becoming the focus of resistance against the police. On the other hand, his children are the promise of the future whom he must guard. When his wife tells him that she is once again pregnant, he thinks, with bitterness:

> The rich people got money but they got one, two kids. . . . We haven't got even enough for one kid and we make eight, nine—one a year. Jesus (36).

But an alternative, bittersweet interpretation of the pregnancy is implied in the last sentence of the novel:

Franky Lorenzo slept on his back and snored peaceful-
ly. Beside him the woman, Grace, lay awake in the
dark, restlessly waiting for the dawn and feeling the
knot of life within her (96).

What political meaning is embodied in these three
characters? Lorenzo, potentially the focus of class
solidarity and resistance, compromises with his present
lot and steps back into the uneasy quietism of the older
generation he has prematurely joined. Joe, independent
by choice from the white capitalist economy, drifts
toward death: with him will die an altruistic morality not
determined by the social pressures that destroy Adonis's
integrity and turn him into a criminal. Greene refuses to
allow ideology to penetrate his life and so is doomed to
suffer without knowing why he suffers ("Doom'd for a
certain term to walk the night," says the epigraph). Both
Greene and Willieboy, the latter in his unreasonable fury
at the American sailors who visit a Colored brothel,
represent a cultural introvertedness which is another
reflection of the introversion of violence in the ghetto.
The future—the "dawn" of the evasive final sentence of
the novel—belongs to the next generation, but what color
that dawn will be is not prophesied.

The reading I have given *A Walk in the Night* reveals a
considerable weight of political statement. While the
main line of the plot does show men overwhelmed by
social forces they do not understand, subsidiary lines
present a critique of the Colored proletariat which
includes the following three articles: (1) it has become a
social class in a capitalist society; (2) uncertainty before
the promise of bourgeois security creates a lack of cohe-
siveness in it; (3) it lacks political awareness. *A Walk in
the Night* is a novel without a hero: this fact is of itself
the most comprehensive political statement La Guma

makes. Nevertheless, it is indicated clearly who the potential hero is: Franky Lorenzo.

La Guma is not a naturalist but a critical realist. One of the implications of his novel—that, while the novelist cannot falsify his subject by creating heroes where none as yet have arisen, he can explain why they have not arisen and point to potentialities for heroic action——seems a more courageous and valuable literary act than the silence Nkosi proposes. As for Nkosi's censure of South African writers in general for not absorbing the lessons of modern Western experimentalism, we may ask whether the prescription is not too simple. The history of literature is not a history of discovery and progress, but rather a history of changing epistemologies and modes of expression that change with them. What is the "correct" mode for a society which, self-divided, swings uneasily from the Geneva of Calvin to the Manchester of 1830 to the Los Angeles of today, in search of an identity it may never find?

PERCEPTIONS ON SOCIAL AND POLITICAL ACTORS AND PROCESSES IN AFRICAN LITERATURE

By G. C. M. MUTISO

Summary

It will be the argument of this article that in African literature the major identified actors and potential actors are the literati, the bureaucrat-professionals, the politicians and women. These groups in their interaction are always dominated by the politicians who are always contemptible. The literature strongly suggests that social and political leadership should move away from the domination of leadership by politicians to leadership by literati and bureaucrat-professionals. The literature further recognizes that the latter two groups are at this moment unsuited for social and political leadership because of two factors. One, is that their very roles cut them off (physically and ideologically?) from the masses. On the other hand, their training stresses values and a way of life which is so radically different from the lives of a great number of those they have to lead. Probably the literati and bureaucrat-professionals will only come to social leadership only when they make peace with the ''ways of the ancestor''.

African literature is defined in this article as literature from former British holdings in Africa. This is an 'artificial' distinction but given the inability of this writer to read French, Spanish, Portuguese or Arabic, the distinction had to be made. Conceivably the few available translations into English would have been included but this would have been a violation of the representativeness principle.

We shall consider the social and political actors, in the following order: the literati, the bureaucrat-professionals, women* and finally the politicians. We cover the processes in the various sections and summarize in the last section on the politicians.

The Literati

Ulli Beier has written that "It is one of the greatest ironies of history that the great quest for a new African identity comes from French West Africa and not from British West Africa. The French have destroyed far more African traditions than the British and have been far more successful in assimilating Africans to their European way of life. The British with their system of 'indirect rule' have left many traditional African institutions intact."[1]

But this is only part of the story. Whereas the literati of the former French holdings in Africa have had a clear identity in their dissent from the philosophical and sociopolitical systems of the French the literati in the former English holdings have suffered a continual crisis in quest of their identity both during and after the colonial period. The intellectuals are not sure whether to stay in the European schema or create new and opposing systems.

---

*The section on *Women* will appear in a future issue of the Journal (Ed.)

[1]Ulli Beier. In Search of African Personality: *Twentieth Century.* Vol. 165, No. 986, April, 1959, p. 345.

They are 'exiles' and therefore,

The return is tedious
And the exiled souls gather on the beach
Arguing and deciding their future
Should they return home
and face the fences the termites had eaten
And see the dunghill that has mounted on their birth-
         place?
But their journey homeward done on the sea scapes roar
Their final strokes will land them on forgotten shores
They committed the impiety of self deceit
Slashed cut and wounded their souls
And left the mangled remainder in manacles
Before the sacred altar, alongside the sacrificial cock
Whose crow woke the night sleepers at dawn

                    *   *   *

At the stars entrance the night revellers gather
To sell their chatter and inhuman sweat to the gateman
And shuffle their feet in agonies of birth
Lost souls, lost souls, lost souls that are still at the gate.[2]
    Thus the literati are caught at indecision of what to do
inspite of the fact that

                    *   *   *

        This is not a time for jesting,
        But for living as they did,
        When our forefathers had to save
        The very ethos of a race

[2]George Awooner-Williams. Exiles. *Black Orpheus* No. 13, 1963, p. 53.

> Those are the days when men must speak.
> Shout the meaning of their souls _____ .[1]

The literati are not cognizant of the fact that they as intellectual leaders of their emergent societies have to pay by individual suffering and that:

> What you suffer in your day
> Is the price you have to pay
> As you try to come to rest
> From the swaying force of change.[2]

That is to say the intellectual leadership of the emergent societies depends in the last analysis, on the integrity of the literati and not on their being swallowed in the petty world of politics, money and women as we shall later see.

There is in the colonial literature the further argument that it is only in wresting the instruments of government from the colonizer that the literati can begin to have an identity rooted in the past of society which is also primary for the identity of his society as distinct from that of the colonizer. To wit

> We have ruled ourselves before
> Though in a much more simple world
> And if your heart is sound and strong,
> You may triumph where we faltered
> And avoid the mocking pity
> Of the man who in his heart
> Curses and despises you

---

[1] Albert Kayper Mensah. The Ghosts in John Reed and Clive Wake (eds.) *A Book of African Verse*. London: Heinemann, 1964, p. 39.

[2] *Ibid.*, p. 40.

You deserve self government now,
But you must avoid its dangers

*   *   *

If you want to make it work,
Do not fall prey to daily
Fear of death, and sudden death.
Try amid the blood and passion,
To discern a fitting answer
To the cry:
"Self-governing what?
Self-governing whom?"[1]

The idea that the literati must participate in the struggle
for independence and hence the recreation of a culture—to replace the West when violence ends that
culture—appears in other works in an existential vein:

What have we to offer, we
Fruit of an unwise copulation between witches?
The whole earth both its good and ill
And all that's been usurped by magic fraud
Leaving us with only our hate;
The undying patience of the truly primitive
The solid passion of the wholly vital
And when your fine ingenuities
Have toppled you back again to rubble
We Calibans will inherit the earth.[2]

Other than fighting for their identity in the milieu of
the opposition to the colonizer, the literati have to 'quest'

[1]*Ibid.*, pp. 40–41.
[2]Nkem Nwankwo. Caliban To Miranda. *Ibadan*, No. 21, October, 1965, p.
17.

for identity in the opposition of the traditional system. I emphasize here that the quest is not because the literati are the copies of the colonizer but simply because by their knowledge of the colonizer and his ways they are not of the people, that is of the traditional culture and the occupations of the traditionalists who in the economics of the new Africa are equivalent to both Marx's and Toynbee's proletariat. Nwanodi sums the point up best. He writes:

*   *   *

We fell into the river
splashing the water
On the river weeds,
We heard the rushing of water
Smelt the offshore farmtime ashes
and heard the offshore farmtime songs
We moved with the currents
Showing kola-free teeth—

But we have poured more wine
than the Gods can drink
more than the soil can drink,
and have become outcasts
dispersing the fishes
for which the baskets are laid
and the fishermen did not like us

We turned and left the spot
but softly his voice rings:
The waters' are yours
and the water's yours
we are mere beings

beggars for your kindness
Oh! Watergod
give us, Oh give us.
your products for our care
Soon the evening will come
and we'll go home with our baskets
Let not those who sit
by the fire feel cold.

We looked at each other,
Packing our things hastily
Fearing more curses on our heads

Suddenly the drums beat
and the blowing of horns
Called on all to the open ground
as the sun
falling into the sea
threw glowing rays on all

Thus we stood shivering
from the violation of many
that judge and mock
our inviolate temper;

They spat on our terylene
and called us outcasts
We held hearts with lips;

We have wished for many things,
Thought of many seasons
More than the Gods can grant.[1]

[1]O. G. Nwanodi. *Icheke and Other Poems*, Ibadan, Mbari, 1964, pp. 28–29.

Thus the literati being pressured by the Western tradition to play a leadership role in society and being cast out by the traditional African Society because of his strange ways, finds solace sometimes in self-pity and negativism:

> I am not the hero
> of my own history
> I am the spectator
> of my own tragedy
> Disbelieving in everything
>   I believe in nothing
>   Including myself
>   Including yourself
> To stop doubting
> Is to stop thinking
>   The doubtful mind will
> Make hiatus of reason
>   Not from scepticism
> But from a divided will.[2]

Beyond the issue of lack of identity, the literati's quest for identity is sometimes hampered by the perverted values implicit in the system. There are Africans who refuse to admit the fact that an African can be 'as good as' the Whiteman. Consider this statement by Bye-loh—an old type minister about the new and competent African civil servant—

"But that John Hayford now. God why should I hate him so, when he's so useful to me? But I just can't help myself. He has all the wiles and brains of a

---

[2]T. C. Nwosu. The Unbeliever, *Nigeria Magazine*, Vol. 81, June 1964, p. 148.

Others develop nihilist philosophies like those of Sagoe—Voidancy or Sekoni—the Universal Dome—in Soyinka's *The Interpreters*.

Whiteman. But his skin being black as mine, I'm damned if I'll admit he's superior to me. The Whiteman taught me to honour the Whiteman. I see no harm in that. It is not so hard to admit a Whiteman is one's superior. When I go into a Whiteman's presence, I not only feel inferior, I *know* it's proper for him to be superior to me. That's why as a Minister I refused to have a Whiteman as my Permanent Secretary. I just couldn't have brought myself to feel I was *his* boss in *my* Ministry. And damn it all, it'd be damn awkward to catch oneself answering one's own secretary, Sir—But John Hayford now. He's no Whiteman. Yet everyone admits he's cleverer than any Whiteman in the Service. Why should that be? After all he *can't* be better than a Whiteman, cleverer—better?"[1]

The post-colonial system in which the literati are to function questions their achievement of an identity and leads to a kind of individualist spirit in the perceptions of the literati. Thus one writer can state,

> I will lie here alone,
> Forgetting experiences past,
> alone
> to say 'am born alone,'
> lie and dream of dreams to come—
> the fantasy of youth:
> Nursed in rain and sun.
>
> Now am born alone
> joys of ills and fear of health
> in the welling of reddening dawn—

[1]Raymond Sarif Easmon, *The New Patriots: A Play*. London: Longmans, 1965, p. 33.

new child of mature thoughts—
alone
to say 'am born alone'

I will wait here alone,
Sit and sip from the broken mug
and eat from mortars half burnt
by harmattan blaze.

Born at twenty-six!
It's too early—and late
to forget the things I know well
remembering only myself
lost in search for something,
something that does not exist.

But am born now to say:
'My heart's mine only'
I will walk here alone,
Seeing the scenes I see—[1]

This theme of the loneliness of the literati is shown in one of the earliest novellas. In *When Love Whispers*, written in 1947, Cyprian Ekwensi narrates the loneliness of Ike who wants to marry across tribal lines and how the parents of both sides oppose the marriage. When Ike goes to England to study law, his girlfriend—Ashoka—is seduced by one of his colleagues who refuses to marry her. Ashoka is ultimately married by the local chief who lusted after her all along. Thus Ike in pursuing law loses the human peace he would have had if he had chosen to marry in his tribe. Note that the values the literati stand for are always defeated by traditional values. For example, the local chief marries Ashoka even though she has a

[1]O. G. Nwanodi. *Icheke and Other Poems*, Ibadan: Mbari, 1964, p. 6.

child out of wedlock, whereas the man responsible refuses in the name of the uncivility of the idea! Even more striking in *depicting* this idea is Soyinka's play *The Lion and the Jewel*. Lakunle—a village teacher (representing the literati in the setting) seeks to marry Sidi but his arrogance and bombast are no match for the cunning of the traditional Chief Baroka. Sidi the village beauty gets carried away by the fame of being photographed for a magazine. Although Lakunle quotes to her almost all of the "Shorter Companion Dictionary" she is not interested much but she falls prey to Baroka when she believes the rumour he had spread that he was impotent. She goes to taunt him but he seduces her and thus she is bound to marry him.

The literati attitude towards manual work is important for us to delve into because to the extent they disdain of it, they offer aspirational values to the rest of society which oppose manual work and therefore become disfunctional towards development. William Conton writes:

> "The Sagresa school had tried to teach us a trade, but so strongly did public opinion outside the school hold the view that even a starving professional (read litcratus) was nearer to the kingdom of heaven than the most successful artisan, that none of us took these attempts seriously."[1]

Even though William Conton goes on to point out that he lost this vice abroad, there is no major African writer who has depicted any major educated character indulging in manual labor out of his own choice, or an educated person who does not aspire to a white collar job.

The African literati have guilt feelings stemming from

[1]William Conton. *The African,* New York New American Libraries: Signet Books, 1961, o. 101.

the tribal ties which they feel they must break to function as literati but for which they are expected to pay in kind. This is the case with Obi Okonkwo, the hero of Chinua Achebe's *No Longer at Ease*. The Umuofia Progressive Union feels that he is their *property* to be used as they see fit. The Secretary to the said organization,

> ". . . spoke of the great honor Obi had brought to the ancient town of Umuofia which could now join the comity of other towns in their march towards political irredentism, social equality and economic emancipation . . . The importance of having one of our sons in the vanguard of this march of progress is nothing short of axiomatic. Our people have a saying "Ours is ours, but mine is mine." Every town and village struggles at this momentous epoch in our political evolution to possess that of which it can say: "This is mine." We are happy that today we have such an invaluable possession in the person of our illustrious son and guest of honour."[2]

The tragedy in terms of identity and function of the society is that this is just one side of the coin. Obi, who one feels should know better, admits,

> "---his people had a sizable point--- They had taxed themselves mercilessly to raise eight hundred pounds to send him to England. Some of them earned no more than five pounds a month. He earned nearly fifty. They had wives and school going children; he had none. After paying the twenty pounds he would have thirty left. And very soon he would have an increment which alone was as big as some peoples' salary--- What they

[2]Chinua Achebe. *No Longer at Ease*, London: Heinemann, 1960, p. 32.

did not know was that having laboured in sweat and tears to enroll their kinsman among the shining elite, they had to keep him up there. Having made him a member of an exclusive club whose members greet one another with, 'How's the car behaving?' did they expect him to turn around and answer: 'I'm sorry, but my car is off the road. You see I couldn't pay my insurance premium.' That would be letting the side down in a way that was unthinkable.''[1]

The question is whether the literati allow themselves to become absorbed by the traditionalist by keeping the traditional obligations or do they wonder and muse and perhaps break away like Egbo in Soyinka's *The Interpreters?*

"Perfunctory doles towards the Union of Osei Descendants . . . messages between the old man and himself . . . all these had built up ties surreptitiously . . . delegations too, to feel him out, sent by Egbo Onosa as he knew quite well—destiny, they said, you were destined . . . all these and much more . . . his own overwhelming need to retain that link with some out-of-the-rut existence . . . illicit pleasure at the thought that a kingdom awaited him whenever he wanted it. . . . And he only plunged again into the ancient, psychic life of still sediments, muttering, how long will the jealous dead remain among us!''[2]

Some of the literati sometime do not even have the self doubt of what their identity, and therefore role in society,

[1]*Ibid.,* p. 98
[2]Wole Soyinka. *The Interpreters,* London: Andre Deutsch, 1965, pp. 119–120.

is. Rather, they jump into the world, acquire the trappings of wealth by all devious means even though at one point they had pangs of conscience—although this, as in the following case does not stem from within the society but from without. Odili in Chinua Achebe's *A Man of the People* is a case in point. After buying a car he states:

"I could not help thinking also of the quick transformations that were such a feature of our country, and in particular of the changes of attitude in my ownself. I had gone to the University with the clear intention of coming out again after three years as a full member of the privileged class whose symbol was the car. So much did I think of it in fact that as early as my second year, I had gone and taken out a driver's licence and even made a mental note of the make of car I would buy. . . . But in my final year I had passed through what I might call a period of intellectual crisis brought on partly by my radical Irish lecturer in history and partly by someone who five years earlier had been, by all accounts, a fire-eating president of our Students' Union. He was now an ice-cream-eating Permanent Secretary in the Ministry of Labour and Production and had not only become one of the wealthiest and most corrupt landlords in Bori but was reported in the Press as saying that trade-union leaders should be put in detention. He had become for us a classic example of the corroding effect of privilege. . . . Many of us vowed then never to be corrupted by bourgeois privileges of which the car was the most visible symbol in our country. And now here I was in this marvellous little affair eating the hills like yam—as Edna would have said. I hoped I was safe; for a man who avoids danger for years and then gets killed in the end has wasted his care."[1]

Not only has Odili bought a car but the party of intellectuals, ironically called Common People's Party, which he joined not because he had a social conscience but because the corrupt Minister Nanga had seduced his girlfriend, gets bribes from other political parties so as not to fight them. The leader of the 'intellectual' party ironically asks Odili:

"Now you tell me how you propose to fight such a dirty war without soiling your hands a little."[2]

Freddie, a character in Cyprian Ekwensi's *Jagua Nana* who is "virtuous" in the sense that he transcends tribal and national differences to marry a girl from without his nation, falls when he categorically states: "I wan' money quick—quick; an' politics is de only hope."[3]

Even where the literati join in the government, they are dominated by the politicians in what they do—even where they have the interest of the country at heart. They are victims of the structure of their societies which puts more value on a politician and politics than on the literati and intellectual leadership. Consider the case presented by Achebe in *A Man of the People.* There is a coffee price slump. Because a political party's electorate is mainly coffee farmers this is a crisis.

"The Minister of Finance at the time was a first rate economist with a Ph.D. in Public Finance. He present-ed to the Cabinet a complete plan for dealing with the

---

[1]Chinua Achebe. A Man of the People, London: Heinemann, 1966, pp. 122–23.

[2]*Ibid.*, p. 142.

[3]Cyprian Ekwensi. *Jagua Nana*, London: Hutchinson, 1963, p. 137.

situation. The Prime Minister said, 'No' to the plan. He was not going to risk losing the election by cutting down the price paid to coffee planters at the critical moment: the National Bank should be instructed to print fifteen million pounds. Two-thirds of the Cabinet supported the Minister. The next morning the Prime Minister sacked them and in the evening he broadcast to the nation. He said the dismissed Ministers were conspirators and traitors who had teamed up with foreign saboteurs to destroy the new nation . . . *The Daily Chronicle,* an official organ of the P.O.P. had pointed out in an editorial that the Miscreant Gang, as the dismissed ministers were now called, were all university people and highly educated professional men. (I have preserved a cutting of the editorial).

"Let us now and for all extract from our body-politic as a dentist extracts a stinking tooth all those decadent stooges versed in textbook economics and aping the Whiteman's mannerisms and way of speaking. We are proud to be Africans. Our true leaders are not those intoxicated with their Oxford, Cambridge or Harvard degrees but those who speak the language of the people. Away with the damnable and expensive university education which only alienates an African from his rich and ancient culture and puts him above his people."[1]

Inbuilt in the systems being evolved is this fantastic bias against the literati. Perhaps the writers to some extent are to blame for not working hard enough to propagate the ideas and roles of the literati in society. Consider the fact that of all the books and plays written only one deals with University life per se. This is *Toads*

[1]Chinua Achebe. *A Man of the People*, London: Heinemann, 1966, pp. 3–4.

For Supper by U. Chikwuemeke Ike (London: Harvill, 1965). This novel details the life of an undergraduate and it is very short on social concerns or on elucidation of the role of the university in shaping ideas to develop African society. The only thing which worries the undergraduates is their next meal and whether they—of all things—can foxtrot! Perhaps this is normal since we find Soyinka satirizing the Professor in African Universities. Their only concern is whether those at their parties follow the Victorian notions of compulsory retiring of their women upstairs, gossip on how many pregnancies the college obstretrician has dug up and another professor's declaration that he never takes prostitutes home—only to his garage![1] Perhaps the conclusion should be that African Universities fail to be agents of change.

The only novel which specifically seeks to deal with the hardship and dangers of intellectual leadership is *The Voice* by Gabriel Okara (London: Andre Deutsch, 1964). Okolo, the hero—the name means voice—searches after 'it' but "the Elders, not wanting the people to hear 'it' "[2] stop him. He is banished by Chief Izongo who is advised to do so by a B.A.; M.A.; Ph.D., that is to say a corrupt member of the literati. The writer makes it clear though that the Elders and the chief are acting in a corrupt and therefore non-traditional way since "Our fathers insides always contained things straight. They did straight things. Our insides were also clean and we did the straight thing until the new time came. We can still sweep the dirt out of our house every morning."[3]

Having gone through all the tribulations and the side arguments for the under-developed situation with the primacy of state authority and how if he kept quiet he

---

[1]Wole Soyinka. *The Interpreters*, pp. 143–148.
[2]Gabriel Okara, The Voice. p. 25.
[3]*Ibid.*, pp. 47–48.

would make it by acquiring cars, women and booze, Okolo holds out a dim prospect for himself and maybe for the literati in the future by stating that:

"If the masses haven't got *it*, he will create *it* in their insides. He will plant *it*, make *it* grow inspite of Izongo's destroying words. He will uproot the fear in their insides and plant *it*. He will all these do if only, . . . if only what?"[1]

There the question hangs. Perhaps it is the only realistic summary of the role of African literati other than T. C. Nwosu's "B. B." To wit,

> Twenty pounds for a modest flat
> That breeds relations like a rat.
> Fifteen pounds for the loan of a car
> That signals poverty weeping from afar.
> Ten pounds to the H. P. agent
> For the telly won on monthly rent.
> Six pounds to the overbearing creditor
> Who indulges such a chronic debtor.
> Five pounds for the weekend booze
> And the girls for the usual cruise.
> Two pounds ten for the ticking parasites
> That visit more often than bed bug bites.
> One pound ten on football pools
> Won more often by the best of fools.
> Pause and think on this subject
> Of monthly income and monthly budget.
> You only need to take a quick glance
> To see both will never balance.[2]

[1] *Ibid.*, p. 104.
[2] T. C. Nwosu. B. B. Ibadan, No. 24, June, 1967, p. 40.

This being the major social datum of the literati perhaps it is no wonder that they are corrupted by money which in a way solves their identity problem, not as most of the writers would like, but by allying themselves with the politicians and thereby getting the status and status roles not open to them as literati *qua* literati.

The Bureaucrat-Professionals

The central fact in the depiction of professionals or bureaucrats is that they are mistrusted and are maneuvered by the politicians. Chief Nanga—our man of the people—bluntly tells his colleague in corruption, Hon. T. C. Kobino, "You know very well T. C. that you cannot trust these our boys. That is why I always say that I prefer to deal with Europeans."[1]

Lombe is 'stuck' because the Ministry will never let him rise higher since they have to maintain "efficiency and integrity" provided of course by foreigners![2]

Udo Akpan, a District Officer in colonial setting, is frustrated in his administrative duties, eradication of cocoa disease by cutting them, by Beja-Beja, a semi-literate politician who agitates:

"What we in Ipaja want the government to do for us is not to cut down our cocoa trees. Government need not do this to demonstrate to us the power of the White man. We already know that."[3]

Sekoni, an engineer, refuses to continue, " ' . . . signing vouchers and llletters and bbbicycle allowances' " (Then,) Pandemonium, except for the practiced chairman, calm and full of instant calculations. 'Just wait outside a moment, please Mr. Sekoni.'

---

[1]Chinua Achebe. *A Man of the People*, p. 47.

[2]David Rubadiri. *No Bride Price*, Nairobi: East African Publishing House, 1967, pp. 16–17.

[3]T. M. Aluko, *One Man One Matchet*, London: Heinemann, 1964, p. 8.

'Is he mad?'

'O mo tani?'

'Why do we employ these too-knows?'

'No, no, no,' and the chairman soothed them. 'He obviously needs a transfer. He is one of the keen ones.'

And to Ijioha Sekoni went, 'where you may work with your hands until your back blisters' and Sekoni built a small experimental power station. And the Chairman chuckled and said,

'I knew he was our man. Get me the expat. expert.' Hot from his last lucrative 'evaluation' came the expatriate expert. Expatriate, therefore impartial.

'Constitute yourself into a one-man commission of enquiry and probe the construction of our power station at Ijioha which was built without estimates approved expenditure.'

'Is it unsafe for operation,' and he winked a truly expert expat expert wink.

'That's the safest idea. You put it in technical language.'

And the expatriate expert came to Ijioha, saw and condemned.

And the chairman read the report and said, 'That expert never fails me; salivating on the epithets, a wasteful expenditure, highly dangerous conditions, unsuitable materials, unsafe for operation.

'Bring me the Write-off-file,' chortled the Chairman.

And the project was written off while parliament at question time resounded to 'the escapade of the mad engineer.'

'Interdict him shall we? Bring me form S2/7 Interdiction of Senior Civil Servants and Confidential File Sekoni Chief Engineer-in-charge Ijioha.'

And the Chairman—for his subsidiary company registered in the name of his two-month-old niece had been the sole contractor for Project Ijioha—cleaned out a few thousand in immediate compensation and filed claims for a few thousand more.

'I always say it, the Write-Offs pay better than fulfilled contracts.' And to Sekoni, 'The expert says that was junk, Engineer, junk.'

And Sekoni bewildered, repeating, 'J-j-j-junk? J-j-j-j-junk?''[1]

Worse are the facts that Sekoni did not know he was being manipulated by the politician and also that the villagers would tell him that 'electricity was a government thing' and when it got ready it would provide it for them. He has been used by the politician for the latter's ends, and furthermore, the politician has manipulated the illiterate rural masses against the professional and well meaning bureaucrat.[2]

Even though the writers admire and praise the bureaucrats and professionals there is a major identity and functional problem of this 'class.' This is the failure of the bureaucrats and professionals to know the 'ways of the ancestors' and when and how to introduce Western ideas into settings where they are not as readily acceptable. Consider the teacher in Aluko's *One Man, One Wife*. He tries to dispute ghosts and the inherent superiority of the White man, stating:

''What the Whiteman can do, we too can do. But we must first go to school''[3]

To this Joshua—a Christian Church Elder disserts, stating:

''Teacher you are black, I am black. Don't let us lie to

[1]Whole Soyinka. *The Interpreters*, pp. 27–28.
[2]*Ibid.*, passim
[3]T. M. Aluko. *One Man, One Wife*, p. 38.

each other. Even Christianity cannot explain certain mysterious things in this country. Even the Whiteman's magic cannot explain these things. Teacher there are ghosts."[1]

In this exchange one professional playing the role of innovator—purveyor of new values—runs into a semi-innovator who is willing to question even the fundamental identity of the teacher. For the teacher not to believe in ghosts is to lose the identification with the people and therefore ability to initiate change. The same failure is expressed by Grandma Gbemi when she utters the following incantation against lawyers and doctors:

" 'Lawyer! Lawyer!' Grandma Gbemi cried in distress. 'Shonponna m'lord forbid that I should ever have anything to do with sound and send them to gaol. They are as bad as the doctors who cut open people's stomachs."[2]

Udo Akpan and his doctor and lawyer friends are similarly rejected in *One Man, One Wife.*

The people mistrust the professionals in part by virtue of the nature of the professions. A doctor does not just cut people but does so in pursuit of the demands of the profession. This is not to argue that some professionals are not mistrusted and rejected by the people because they 'mis-practice' their professions. One lawyer, Chris, is rejected because he is a 'shyster' in T. M. Aluko's *Kinsman and Foreman.*[3] Benjamin-Benjamin an educated 'shyster' is not only rejected but also killed because he 'mispractices' his education. Opposite him is Udo

[1] *Ibid.*, p. 38.

[2] *Ibid.*, p. 153.

[3] T. M. Aluko. *Kinsman and Foreman,* London: Heinemann, 1966. See also Chief Isongo's advisor who is B.A., M.A., Ph.D. in Gabriel Okara's *The Voice.* London: Andre Deutsch, 1964, and Gadson, Senior Assistant Secretary to the Ministry of Consolation in Cyprian Ekwensi's *Iska,* London: Hutchinson, 1966.

Akpan, the new African D.O. who states that his
" ' . . . appointment as a District Officer is an experiment. And I want to do everything to make the
experiment succeed in the interest of the blackman.' "[1]
He explains to Stanfield, the English Officer he is replac-
ing, that,

> " 'Before you (British) came to this country with Pax
> Britannica, a citizen of proved anti-community activi-
> ties like Benjamin-Benjamin was easily disposed of.
> He just vanished . . . After we in the Administration
> had failed to rid ourselves of the curse that was Ben-
> jamin-Benjamin, an Ipaja man who had not heard of
> British sense of fair play and justice, and in any case
> had no use for it, got rid of the common enemy. He
> did it in a moment. We had failed to do it in two
> years . . . After Olowo had shot his enemy he did
> not want to live. He turned his own gun on himself.
> But we did not allow him to die . . . we concentrated
> on him the best medical attention in the country. And
> after all this care and attention . . . we are going to
> hang him by the neck till he be dead!' "[2]

Udo Akpan thereby points out the two crucial problems of the colonial bureaucrat-professional. On one
hand he had to prove to the White man that he was
worthy of his position and on the other, he was operated
by two conflicting codes in a social setting where he was
rejected by the colonizer and by his own people. He had
to challenge both systems. Thus Udo Akpan is sympathetic to the elimination of Beja-Beja and he is willing to
restructure the role of the bureaucrat in society from the
traditional British conceptualization. He states categorically:

---

[1] T. M. Aluko. *One Man, One Matchet*, p. 30.
[2] *Ibid.*, pp. 187–188.

"The British Civil Servant does not have to engage in politics because there are literally hundreds of thousands of fellow Britons who are outside the Civil Service and who are available to engage in politics both at the national and the local governmental levels. The Civil servant can therefore sit at his desk to carry out his own assignment, that of implementing policy decisions. . . . But here in this country the situation is sadly different. The best brains of this country are with a few exceptions all in the Civil Service. Can this country with its limited resources in educated manpower afford to have their mouths padlocked in the Civil Service while second-rate and sometimes semiliterate men are saddled with the very important duty of legislating and taking executive decisions for the state? Can we not have a state of affairs where the civil-servant can make his views known publicly on matters on which he is by qualification and experience competent to express his views?' "[1]

We have already pointed out that the politician, who usually is less qualified than the bureaucrat-professional, dominates the post-independence political and social situation, and the bureaucrat-professional is co-opted as an ally by the politician because of economic and prestige purposes. The articulated preference of social and political leadership by intellectual-bureaucrat-professional is a value stressed by the writers but they point out clearly this is not the case yet. There are many reasons. One is the non-discriminating nature of the population in perceiving being educated as being equivalent to rejecting the 'ways of the ancestor' and also equating all educated with those few corrupt educated. Thus those who are

[1] *Ibid.*, pp. 193–194.

educated are rejected because the Beja-Beja's are rejected.[1]

The other major reason is the bias in the societies in favor of the politician. The politician 'brought' independence and therefore he has control of power and status roles. Usually the professional stayed out of the nationalist movement because the colonial order would have victimized him.[2] He never acquired from the public the credit of ridding them of the Whiteman like the politician. The politician also by controlling power and status positions can manipulate the system to pay him to the extent that in purely economic terms he can 'buy' the bureaucrat-professionals to his camp or at least the bureaucrat-professional has to pay the politician homage if the former wants economic security. Finally the bureaucrat-professional suffers from lack of identity and economic security in his career. Lombe will never rise up to the top of the Civil Service because foreigners are preferred by the insecure politicians at the top.[3] The Minister finishes Lombe off because he would not yield a girlfriend to the Minister![4]

Dan Kaybi is a victim of lack of identity of another sort. He is a young civil servant, who wants to marry across tribal lines. The parents on both sides disapprove. However his Permanent Secretary approves—he regards this relic tradition as irrelevant, as also Kaybi does. However, as Kaybi celebrates the authorization by the Permanent Secretary—which insures his professional progress at least—he is knifed trying to stop a fight between the youths of his tribe and those of his wife's tribe.[5]

[1]*Ibid.*, p. 196.
[2]Lenrie Peters. *The Second Round*, London: Heinemann, 1964, passim.
[3]David Rubadiri. *No Bride Price*, passim.
[4]*Ibid.*, pp. 93–94.
[5]Cyprian Ekwensi. *Iska*, London: Hutchinson, 1966, passim.

John Hayford is paid the 'highest' compliment by his idiotic Minister who states that: " 'He has all the wiles and brains of a Whiteman,' "[1] yet we know that as a brilliant professional he cannot be very comfortable working with an idiotic Minister who is a shuffling frothing jelly in the presence of a White person.

Obi Okonkwo succumbs to the economic pressures and accepts a bribe. Although he falls, what one should recognize is the pressure put on him by the Civil Service to maintain the standards of the colonial bureaucracy in terms of cars, dress and ritual and also his own people's pressure as one who had a White man's job. All this together with the personal loss of his mother and girlfriend make him a supreme cynic.[2]

The army can be included in the bureaucrat-professional class but unfortunately not many writers have concerned themselves with the military. As a matter of fact no novel is written with this violence-control-arm of the government playing a central role. This, one predicts, will not be the case in the future since there have in the recent past been 'enough' coup d'etats to require analysis by the writers. We should note that Chinua Achebe in *A Man of the People* does not see the army as central in the political process. It simply "obliged us by staging a coup at that point and locking up every member of Government. The rampaging bands of election thugs had caused so much unrest that our young army officers seized the opportunity to take over."[3]

We should note that Achebe just stresses the obliging nature of the Army in the coup d'etat and further that it was the young officers, suggesting that the old order was

---

[1] R. Sarif Easmon. *New Patriots*, p. 33.

[2] Chinua Achebe. *No Longer at Ease,* New York: Obelensky, 1961, pp. 1–5 and passim.

[3] Chinua Achebe. *A Man of the People*, p. 165.

tied with the old army, that is to say there is opposition between those who stemmed from the colonial set-up in political, civil service and military careers and the new, the young who are creation of the post-colonial and independence period.

The other treatment of the army is in David Rubadiri's *No Bride Price.* Here there are several key ideas. First there is a civilian organization which works to bring the army government to power. This organization embraces the low and alienated educated who are closed off from work and live on the bar-cocktail party route with the seamier side of the top echelon of business and diplomacy.[1] This seems to point out that the educated who cannot get into the system will ally with the army to throw unenlightened bureaucrats and politicians out of public life. More interesting is the idea Rubadiri puts forward when he argues that Gombe, the father of independence in this particular country, that is to say the one who played the dominant political role in the ending of the colonial situation, headed an underground organization which allied with the army to bring the coup. He argues that the 'father of the nation' had quit the government because it became corrupt and his interest in the new order is good government.[2] This suggests the idea that probably the only way to get 'good', that is to say non-corrupt, government, is to use the young educated and the military. The military leader puts his case for the coup the following way:

"This is General Masauko of the National Army. I have today removed from power the government. This was made necessary for the good of the nation. Over the past three years much harm has been caused by the

[1] David Rubadiri. *No Bride Price,* p. 46
[2] *Ibid.,* pp. 167–169.

people you elected to rule you. Not only has there been corruption, murder and injustice but their policies and love of power had forced them to use all means to destroy the people. A whole generation of young people has been turned into monsters, trained to be destroyers of lives and destroyers of our formerly simple and great people. Foreign killers from abroad for reasons of their own took on the responsibility of performing those tasks and the nation now will have to live through a generation of citizens whose values no longer exist but simply function blindly for the ambitions of a handful of people to whom the only achievement was power and the retention of power."[1]

The ideas expressed here are of interest to us because they point to the army basically as the saviour from corruption and the rejection of the dominance of politics and politicians. We should note that Lombe—the civil servant is rehabilitated into the new order: Thus suggesting that the future may see more and more an alliance of a very political bureaucracy, intellectuals (looking to the African past for the major values of society) and the military who by their very definition are professionals. This seems to be confirmed by the spate of coups and attempted coups since 1960 all over the continent.

The Politicians and the
Political Process

> Ism to ism for ism is ism
> Of ism and isms on absolute-ism
> To demonstrate the tree of life
> Is sprung from broken peat

[1]*Ibid.*, p. 156.

And we the rotted bark, spurned
When the tree swells its pot
The mucus that is snorted out
When Kongi's new race blows.
And more. . . .[1]

The 'politician' is relatively new in the African culture. He is older than the pure literatus but younger than the bureaucrat in the former British holdings, because the British with their emphasis on the civil service stressed the bureaucrat at the expense of the other categories. The colonial politician came to flower around the fifties as an agitator for independence.

". . . like all politicians, often (came) to power by giving reign to precisely those urges and inclinations which people of good breeding the world over try to keep in check—the inclination to draw the decision and scorn of others upon one's rival for example; and the urge to acquire as much personal power and wealth as possible. . . .

Unfortunately as the colonies advance(d) toward self-government, the African politicians with whom the British Officials came into contact, and are inevitably compared, have usually been much less well prepared from their careers. Politics is unfortunately still widely regarded as a profession something less than honourable in Africa . . ."[2]

The colonial politician was primarily an agitator and to the extent that there was not a dearth of things to agitate for he never really learned how to put a program, how to articulate it and how to become accountable to the people. Furthermore he never worried on whether he was to be instructed by the people and act as their agent or just

[1]Wole Soyinka. *Kongi's Harvest,* London O.U.P. 1967, p. 1.

[2]William Conton. *The African,* New York: New American Library Signet Books, 1964, p. 178.

do as he pleased. This is to say the issue of accountability never arose because of the very nature of the colonial social system. In a system where the payoff for agitation was high—which is what all the slogans for independence were—there was no room for introducing the principle of accountability either by the politician or the people. This is why the traditionalist Chief Ozuomba can state

"Can't you see that these mushrooming politicians, who are nothing but a bunch of Europeans in black skins, are determined to prostitute our culture, our pride, our dignity."[1]

He is speaking of the fact that the politician plays an 'outsider' role to the traditional set-up and that his values are animated mostly by personal considerations or calculations of utility and not on how he fits into the society.

In the independence period the politician is generally depicted as the one person who above all exploits the people and therefore the crucial hurdle towards cultural identity, national unification is above all his failure to live to a higher cultural value rather than just believe in money—materialism. The politician blocks rational decision-making in the whole of society and thus blocks development.

In the novel *Jagua Nana* we find the following statements by Jagua the prostitute—

" 'No Freddie. You got education. You got culture. You're a gentleman an' proud. Politics be game for dogs. And in dis Lagos, is a rough game. De roughest game in de whole worl'. Is smelly an' dirty an' you too clean an' sweet.' "[2]

[1]Obi Egbuna. *Wind Versus Polygamy*, London: Faber and Faber, 1964, p. 38.

[2]Cyprian Ekwensi. *Jagua Nana*, p. 137.

In the play *The New Patriots*, a Chief Justice gives the following estimate of what politicians are:

". . . the politicians themselves need no training or apprenticeship in their craft; *they* gravitate into politics like rats into a sewer and swim around quite naturally in the filth."[1]

In the novel *A Man of the People* we are informed that those in power—

". . . a handful of us—the smart and the lucky and hardly ever the best—had scrambled for the one shelter our former rulers left and had taken it over and barricaded themselves in. And from within they sought to persuade the rest through numerous loudspeakers that the first phase of the struggle had been won and that the next phase—the extension of our house—was even more important and called for new and original tactics; it required that all arguments should cease and the whole people speak with one voice and that any more dissent and argument outside the door of the shelter would subvert and bring down the whole house."[2]

In the quest of 'building the one house' the politician accepts only the self as master designer and builder with the help of money. Jagua asks Uncle Taiwo where the money he spends came from—Uncle Taiwo, the suave politician with a Pontiac, answers

" 'Is party money. I give dem de money like dat, so them kin taste what we goin to do for them, if they vote us into power.' "[3] We are further told, "Uncle Taiwo for

[1]Cyprian Ekwensi. *Jagua Nana*, p. 137.
[2]Chinua Achebe. *A Man of the People*, p. 42.
[3]Cyprian Ekwensi. *Jagua Nana*, p. 138.

all his kindness was coarse, believing only in the power of money."[1]

Momoh Seisay—a member of a government—enlightens us further on values the politician aspires to. He states, " . . . . 'Oh, Lord, what a beautiful and simple system of government a dictatorship is. That's what we need in this country. Leader of opposition—lock him up. Gag your trade union leaders with gold or fear. As for the press which thinks abuse of Government is the only freedom of speech, either control it absolutely, or hold the bribe of a Government job like a carrot in front of those donkeys who call themselves newspaper editors.'"[2]

Such tactics are applied against the intellectuals with a finesse which would astound Machiavelli. Consider the case of Sagoe—a journalist returned from the United States. He goes for an interview for a paper. The interviewing board, like all other boards in the country, we are told, is the enclave of the politicians on a downward skid. Their compatriots cushion their fall by appointing them to these government boards. Anyhow, when we walk into the room the only question asked is

" 'Why do you want this job:'
'I don't know,' Sagoe said.
The carcass of the Managing Director swelled, spurted greasy globules of the skin in extreme stages of putrefication and burst out in an unintelligible stream through the ruptured throat, 'Do you think we have come here to tolerate your cocky impudence. You small boy, you come here begging for a job. . . .'
'I have not come to beg.'
'Don't talk when I am talking otherwise just get out.

[1]*Ibid.*, p. 142.
[2]Sarif Easmon. *The New Patriots*, p. 25.

We want the kind of person who is going to respect his superior not conceited boys of your type. Suppose you are not begging, who is interested in that? Your letters are begging my Friend, go sit down. . . . Please go from my sight. . . . These small fries they all think they are popularly in demand, just because they have a degree.' "[1]

No interpretation of the thinking of this person and his values is necessary. Perhaps the next area is to point out the perceptions of the politicians and the other categories with regard to the parties, the electoral process and the techniques.

Since the politicians perceive their public duty as basically that of acquisition and perpetuation of power, it logically follows that they cultivate only "primitive loyalty,"[2] that is loyalty of the clan and the tribe and not of a party or of overriding political or social programs. Thus our man of the people, Nanga, seeks to recruit Odili into his entourage –

" 'By the way, Odili, I think you are wasting your talent here (teaching in a village). I want you to come to the Capital and take up a strategic post in the Civil Service. We shouldn't leave everything to the highland tribes. My secretary is from there; our people must press for their fair share of the national cake.' "[3]

There is further suggestion that it is not only the view of the political process but rather of the majority of the mass. Odili—the literatus in *A Man of the People*—states

" 'My father's attitude to my political activity intrigued me a lot . . . He took the view (without expressing it in so many words) that the mainspring of political

---

[1]Wole Soyinka. *The Interpreters*, p. 78–79.
[2]Chinua Achebe. *Man of the People*, p. 8.
[3]*Ibid.*, p. 13.

action was personal gain, a view which I might say was much more in line with the general feeling in the country than the high-minded thinking of fellows like Max and I.' ''[1]

Parties per se mean nothing.

"Nearly everybody was a member of the Party, but nobody could say with accuracy when the Party was born: to most people, especially the younger generation, the Party had always been there, a rallying center of action. It changed names, leaders came and went, but the Party remained."[2] An amorphous thing which took all shapes at different times for different things to win elections, it is not the party that is primary but the money, as we have pointed out, the conviction of "a large clan (who) make up nearly half of the electorate"[3] and above all it exists to know how to delude the public. For example, when people demand the paving of a road, Ekunyah the perfect politician explains the technique—

" "The road will cost several thousand pounds. But wait . . . tell them I shall build the road . . . hire about a hundred drums of tar. Line them along the road . . . Then hire several loads of sand and heap the sand at suitable intervals along the road. An impression must be given that the roadwork is starting any moment now. Most important of all, bring this road development scheme to the notice of the newspapers. Don't forget to report in the newspaper the contribution I have made to the Church Organ Fund. . . . Think what it will mean when all the women in the Church whisper it around that Ewia

[1]Chinua Achebe. *A Man of the People*, p. 128.

[2]James Ngugi. *A Grain of Wheat*, London: Heinemann, 1967, p. 13.

[3]James Ene Henshaw. *Medicine for Love*, London: University of London Press, 1964, p. 43.

Akunyah has paid a hundred and twenty pounds towards the Church's new organ fund. . . . How many beggars have we in this constituency?. . . . What percentage of the total electorate?. . . If all the beggars were to vote against me in a block, would it make a difference to the results?' ''[1]

Since the answer is "no", the beggar is sent away without any dole.

Another important aspect of parties is that not only do they exacerbate the tribal animosities but even their very existence disrupts the family and the tribe. This is the lament of Ocol's wife—Lawino:

> I do not understand
> The new political parties
> They dress differently,
> They dress in robes
> Like the Christian diviner—priests
> But Ocol treats his brother
> As if they are not relatives.—[2]

whose husband and brother-in-law fight each other from two different political party bases. It is ironical that the ability of the political parties to bring unity, development and the new culture is questioned by the traditionalist Lawino. She wonders—

> The new parties have split the homestead
> As the battle axe splits the skull!

*   *   *

[1]*Ibid.*, pp.44, 45, 46.
[2]Okot p'Bltek. *Song of Lawino*, Nairobi: East African Publishing House, 1967, p. 181.

> Is this the unity of
> Is this the Peace
> That Independence brings?[1]

Then on the motivations for joining of parties—

> The stomach seems to be
> A powerful force
> For joining the political parties,
> Especially when the purse
> In the trouser pocket
> Carries only the coins
> With holes in the middle
> And no purple notes
> Have ever been folded in it
> And especially for those who
> Have never tasted honey from childhood,
> And those who grew up
> Fatherless or motherless
> And those with no sure jobs.[2]

Thus we are told from a modern praise song that the motivation for the various parties is what one can get for his stomach and that basically the riff-raff and the outcasts are the ones who most seriously take part in "political activity". This takes us to another point—the role of the "wild ones."

The "wild ones" are the thugs or Youth Wingers attached to every politician. They are under his pay to sing his praise,[3] to act as errand boys like running to buy

---

[1] Okot p'Bitek. *Song of Lawino*, p. 182–183.

[2] *Ibid*, p. 190.

[3] Wole Soyinka. *Kongi's Harvest*, Passim, *The Road*, passim, James Ene Henshaw, *Medicine for Love*, passim. Cyprian Ekwensi, *Beautiful Feathers*, passim.

sweets and soda for the "humble citizens",[1] and above all to fight, maim and even kill the opposition. The thug element in the parties is so strong that they do not only hold the parties hostage, in several countries they have led to takeovers of governments. Achebe points out that the rival gang fighting ultimately led to an overthrow of the government in his *A Man of the People.*

"The people had nothing to do with the fall of our government. What happened was simply that unruly mobs and private armies having tasted blood and power during the election had got out of hand and ruined their masters and employers. And they had no public reason whatever for doing it."[2]

What of the fabled people as actors in the political process? They are simply apathetic and cynical. They argue that they have to take what falls to them. To wit,

"Honourable Chief Nanga is my brother and he is what Whiteman call V.I.P. . . . Me na P.I.V. . . . Poor Innocent Victim . . . Yes me na P.I.V. . . . A bottle of beer de cost only five shillings. Chief Honourable Nanga has the money—as of today."[3] All social concern about corruption and the wild ones mean nothing to this guy who is thirsting after only a beer. Thus when

" . . . Political commentators (say) that it was the supreme cynicism (of the politicians) that inflamed the people and brought down the Government, . . . that is sheer poppycock. The people themselves, as we have seen, had become even more cynical than their leaders and were apathetic in the bargain. 'Let them eat,' was the people's opinion, 'after all when the Whitemen used to do all the eating did we commit

---

[1] Wilson K. Mativo. Our True Speaker, *East African Journal,* January, 1968, p. 52.

[2] Chinya Achebe. *A Man of the People,* p. 162.

[3] *Ibid.,* p. 108.

suicide? Of course not. And where is the all-powerful Whiteman of today? He came, he ate and he went. But we are still around. The important thing then is to stay alive; if you do you will outlive our present annoyance. The great thing as the old people have told us is reminiscence; and only those who survive can have it. Besides if you survive, who knows it may be your turn to eat tomorrow. Your son may bring home your share . . ."[1]

This points out the very strong determinism—past oriented—which we will return to in the section on social change. It further suggests that the populace do not *really* understand the stakes involved in pitting this kind of orientation to public wealth. Perhaps our traditionalist woman Lawino is right when she points out that women do not yodel and ululate in political rallies because they like what is said or understand but rather that

> They shout and make ululations
> Because they are tired
> Tired of the useless talk
> Tired of the insults
> And the lies of
> The Speakers.
> They shout and raise their hands
> Not because they understand,
> But because they do not understand
> The many foreign words.[2]

The politician is always damned by the intellectuals and the African writers in particular. The condemnation

---

[1] *Ibid.*, pp. 161–162.
[2] Okot p'Bitek. *Song of Lawino*, p. 193.

dates from the early fifties when Dr. R. E. G. Armattoe broke with Nkrumah over the running of Ghana when the latter became Prime Minister. Armattoe wrote in *Servant-Kings*

> Leave them alone,
> Leave them to be
> Men lost to shame
> To honor lost!
> Servant Kinglets,
> Riding to war
> Against their own
> Watched by their foes
> Who urge them on,
> And laugh at them! . . .[1]

In *They Said,* he pinpointed the criticism of a fellow-intellectual turned politician, and therefore corrupted, in the following words,

> They said
> You may take donkeys to water
> But you can't make them drink,
> You may teach monkeys to chatter
> But you can't make them sing;
> You may soak a coke in water
> But you can't make it sink;
> You call him the Prime Minister
> And would that make him think
> They asked.[2]

[1] R. E. G. Armattoe. *Deep Down the Blackman's Mind,* Ilfracombe: Stockwell, 1954, p. 23.
[2] *Ibid.,* p. 101.

This criticism of all politicians has continued in African literature. In the play *Kongi's Harvest* such criticism is illustrated by the exchange between the Organizing Secretary of Kongi's Party and the Third and Fourth Aweri's—Kongi's Official Disputants—(a kinder word, stooges).

> *"Organizing Secretary.* All we want is some way of persuading King Danlola to bring the new yam to Kongi with his own hands . . . Kongi desires that the King perform all his customary spiritual functions, only this time that he perform them to him, our Leader. Kongi must preside as the Spirit of Harvest, in pursuance of the Five Year Development Plan.
>
> *Fourth.* An inevitable stage in the process of power reversionism. . . .
>
> *Organizing Secretary.* And the key word, Kongi insists, must be—Harmony. We need that to counter the effect of the bomb-throwing. Which is one of the reasons why the culprits of that outrage will be hanged tomorrow.
>
> *Fourth.* An exercise in scientific exorcism—I approve.
>
> *Organizing Secretary.* Every Ismite must do his Mite. . . . Ismite . is . Might. . . .
>
> *Fourth.* It needs a live person to make even a symbolic act of capitulation.
>
> *Third.* Especially when harmony is the ultimate goal.
>
> *Fourth.* I think I see something of the Leader's vision of this harmony. To replace the old superstitious festival by a state ceremony governed by the principle of Enlightened Ritualism. It is therefore essential that the Oba Danola his highest opponent appear in full antiquated splendour surrounded by his Aweri conclave of Elders who, beyond the outward trappings of

pomp and ceremony and a regular supply of snuff, have no other interest in the running of the state. . . . The period of isolated saws and wisdom is over, superseded by a more systematic formulation of comprehensive philosophies—*our* function, for the benefit of those who still do not know it. . . . And Danlola, the retrogressive autocrat, will with his own hands present the Leader with the New Yam, thereby acknowledging the supremacy of the State over his former areas of authority, spiritual and secular. From then on, the State will adopt towards him and to all similar institutions the policy of glamourised fossilism.''[1]

Thus, through satire the writer points out the incongruity of the new political leaders who are inhuman, totalitarian and essentially egomaniacs as opposed to the figure of the traditional leader Oba Danlola who is human in the play.

Other characterizations of Ministers are just as biting. Consider the Minister of Consolation in Cyprian Ekwensi's *Beautiful Feathers*. He heads a ministry which ''was founded as a *sympathetic* gesture, a kind of Universal Aunt,''[2] as the Perennial Secretary—who is white and stays only as a personal stooge tells us! *'Our True Speaker'* Mr. Malu is another politician. Matiuo writes of how he swoops down into the rural areas, finds a meeting by his rival in progress—gets his thugs to break the rival's car, buy sweets and soda and drives away just as soon with a convoy of bodyguards to live in the city until the next election.[3]

It is not just that writers depict their hatred of the

---

[1]Wole Soyinka, *Kongi's Harvest*, pp. 20, 22–24.

[2]Cyprian Ekwensi. *Beautiful Feathers*, p. 78. Italics mine.

[3]Wilson K. Mativo. 'Our True Speaker; *East African Journal*, January, 1968, pp. 49–52.

politician, they put value words in the mouths of other professional groups—Kachigwe has this exchange in *No Easy Task* about the politician Dube:

" 'Do you admire his brains?'

'Me,' he said it as if I had asked him to love a snake. 'He is a politician, and politicians are a tribe of their own. I am a journalist, not a politician.' "[3]

To argue that politicians are a tribe of their own is in the African context to define them as outside society——pariah to all others in their values and their interests. Thus when Gikonyo wants to buy land from a departing European, but is refused a loan by a Member of Parliament, who then goes on to buy the same farm we know that the Member of Parliament is looking after the interests of his own tribe.[4]

We can therefore understand the feeling of alienation by all other non-political tribes when George Awoonor-Williams writes,

"And our songs are dying on our lips
Standing at hell-gate you watch those who seek admission
Still the familiar faces that watched and gave you up
As the one who had let the side down
"Come on, old boy, you cannot dress like that"
And tears well in my eyes for them
Those who want to be seen in the best company
Have abjured the magic of being themselves
And in the new land we have found
The water is drying from the towd
Our songs are dead and we sell them dead to the other side

[3]Aubrey Kachigwe. *No Easy Task*, London: Heinemann, 1965, p. 88.
[4]James Ngugi. *A Grain of Wheat*, London: Heinemann, 1967, pp. 191–192.

Reaching for the stars we stop at the house of moon
And pause to relearn the wisdom of our fathers.[1]

We can understand that the politicians are a new tribe and by their own creation in new lands. They co-opt some professionals to be like them but they are rejected by all other sectors as the purveyors of modernity since their modernity is at the expense of all other people. We can understand that politics dominates and therefore politicians have the highest pay-off. Other sectors of society acquiesce to them but this acquiescence by the public is preached against by *all* the writers. Achebe through Odili, however, puts it best in explaining the coup and the people's reaction. He muses:

" 'Koko had taken enough for the owner to see,' said my father to me . . . My father's words struck me because they were the very same words the villagers of Anata had spoken of Josiseh, the abominated trader. Only in their case the words had meaning. The owner was the village and the village had a mind; it could say no to sacrilege. But in the affairs of the village became powerless. Max was avenged not by the people's collective will but by one solitary woman who loved him. Had his spirit waited for the people to demand redress it would have been waiting still, in the rain and out in the sun. But he was lucky . . . (because he) inspired someone to come forward and shoot (his) murderer in the chest—asking to be paid.' "[2]

The hope therefore lies with the people led by the intellectuals, professionals and bureaucrats. No one tells us how they are to win over the struggle for power from the politicians though.

[1]George Awoonor-Williams. 'We Have Found a New Land.' *Rediscovery and Other Poems*, Ibadan: Mbari, 1964, p. 10.
[2]Chinua Achebe. *A Man of the People, p. 167.*

ALGERIAN POETRY:
POETIC VALUES, MOHAMMED
DIB AND KATEB YACINE

By ERIC SELLIN

Some critics claim that there is little poetry of basic merit written in French today by Algerians and that what has been written has been too narrowly devoted to celebration of the Algerian independence effort and the attendant martyrdom. It is true that there has been a limited output, but this is understandable if we consider that, unlike the case with folk art, a high degree of education is generally a prerequisite to the practice of the writer's craft. Algeria still has a staggering percentage of illiteracy and, since French is but one of the linguistic options open to the young writer, it is clear that Algeria is relatively rich in Francophone poetry.[1] The best Algerian novels and poems may be placed without shame beside

---

[1]The future of Francophone writing in Algeria is uncertain. In 1956, Kateb Yacine said in an interview: "La langue francaise appartient á un passé encore trop récent, été et sa diffusion n'a pas été assez large (80% d'analphabètes apres 130 ans de colonisation) pour qu'on puisse la considérer autrement que comme *langue d'avenir*, appelée sans aucun doute, à jouer un rôle de première importance dans la formation de notre culture nationale" (Geneviève Serreau, "Situation de l'écrivain algérien: Interview de Kateb Yacine," *Les Lettres Nouvelles*, No. 40 (juillet-août 1956), 107). Despite the government's efforts to promote Arabic as the official and cultural language, French remains inextricably entwined with the Algerian identity. Even the man in the street, when speaking Arabic, constantly inserts whole sentences in French into his speech. However, one cannot tell how successful the Arabization of today's children will be in obliterating French; it is possible that Algerian literature of French expression will one day be a period piece, as it were.

those of, say, Switzerland or Belgium, and a masterpiece like Kateb Yacine's *Nedjma* is of such stature as to loom glorious in the literature of any country in the world.

Almost one and a half million Algerians died in the war for independence and one can only guess at how many potential or budding writers perished, not to mention the mature talent of Mouloud Feraoun.

The militancy of the poetry written in the 'fifties and 'sixties may well have tended to create a *poesie de circonstance*, but the authenticity of the events behind the poems sometimes pierces the convention. In any case, the recent efforts are superior to the so-called Algerian poetry of the 'twenties (when "Algerian poetry" meant verse written by Europeans living in Algeria). A typical poem of that period may be taken at random from Robert Randau's anthology, *De treize poètes algériens*, published in 1920. Here, replete with all the weaknesses of latter-day Romantico-Parnassianism, is the beginning of a poem by Edmond Gojon entitled "L'il":

Ainsi, je t'ai suivie à travers ces ruelles,
O toi qui ne montrais qu'un oeil profond et noir,
Puits de félicité, souk d'ombre où j'ai pu voir
L'Orient miroiter devant des mers cruelles.

Tu reserras le voile empli de ton odeur,
J'imaginais ton corps souple et nu sous ce voile,
Mais ton oeil triste et beau comme un lever d'étoile
Me ramenait sans cesse à tant de profondeur!

O prunelle sans âge, ô regard qui provoque . . . etc[1]

To this grotesque cyclopean ode one will certainly prefer any heartfelt lament from the war period; it is easily overshadowed by many of the recent poems writ-

[1]*De treize poètes algériens*, edited by R. Randau (Algiers: Association des Écrivains Algériens, 1920), pp. 83–84.

ten by amateurs who have surpassed themselves, spurred on to an extraordinary music by the impact of the events of 1954–62 and the lingering struggle for national identity.[1]

As so often happens in times inhospitable to the egoistic introspections required in the poetic process, the novel has, for the moment, emerged as the genre of distinction in Francophone letters in Algeria. We may cite as leading novelists: Kateb Yacine, Mohammed Dib, Mouloud Feraoun, Mouloud Mammeri, Malek Haddad, Marguerite Taos, and Assia Djebar. It is not strange that among these novelists we also find the leading poets. Indeed, the foremost Algerian writer, Kateb Yacine, reaches poetic heights in whatever genre he touches, be it nominally novel, play, or poem. His genius, like Goya's, persists despite the horrors of war and the exigencies of politics and is merely colored by them, not crippled by them.

Algerian poetry, then, has tended to be militant during the last twenty years. The three principal sources of inspiration for that poetry have been the war for independence itself, the work of such political kindred spirits as Eluard,[2] and the great, repetitious bulk of

[1]Composed in 1953, a good example of the awakening national conscience is found in the interesting lament by Ismael Ait Djafer entitled "Complainte des mendiants arabes de la Casbah et de la petite Yasmina tuée par son père" (See *Les Temps Modernes*, No. 98 (janvier 1954), 1227–52.

[2]A great many Algerian poems seem to be directly derived from Eluard's "Liberté" (See Jean Dejeux, *La Poesie Algérienne de 1830 à nos jours* (Paris and the Hague: Mouton, 1963), pp. 74–76. A flagrant example is "Liberté" by Nadia Guendouz which begins:

Liberté	Liberté
Tes lettres en feu	Je t'offre mes mains
Sont gravées	à encercler
Dans mon coeur, mon ame	Liberté . . .

and ends, after continuing in the same vein for two pages, with the words: "Liberté / de naître, de mourir / pour toi mon amie / ma patrie liberté" (Nadia Guendouz, *Amal* (Algiers: Société Nationale d'Edition et de Diffusion, n.d., pp. 46–48).

militant poems which tended to be self-perpetuating, becoming a veritable convention for the post-*moudjahidine* generation of poets.

This militant poetry is now on the wane since many memories are short and the extraordinary human drama of the war is no longer present to inspire directly and political reconstruction tends to provide a somewhat slo-gan-minded muse. Even poetry written when the war was in progress or fresh in the mind of the poet is—like Raleigh's selfmade epitaph—less poignant to us today for its poetic truths than for its human interest, less forceful for its poetic impact than for its contextual brutality. Are we moved by the text? Or are we moved by the remembrance of the tragic events which took place between 1954 and 1962 during which well over 10% of the Algerian population was killed in one of the century's most fierce and brutal wars? We are moved by authentici-ty, as one should be, but it is necessary in any approach to a poetry conceived in the midst of momentous events to retain proper focus on the differences between histori-cal, personal, or political authenticity and poetic authen-ticity. Often historical or personal authenticity touches in us pools of emotion which become troubled and whose blurred reflections we, in our narcissistic interrogations, misconstrue as poetic or artistic feelings. Sometimes poets try to translate their reactions to momentous human authenticity into texts which they then assume will, ipso facto, have poetic authenticity. This misunderstanding naturally leads to poetic failure. In recent years, two young American poets have tried to retell in poetry the agonies of Scott's fateful expedition to the South Pole and the heart-rending ironics of the letters written home by doomed German soldiers at Stalingrad. In both cases I assume that the poets mistook their powerful personal emotional reactions to the dramas in question for feelings of creative impulse. However, creative impulse implies a gap and a need for and move toward "closure," as they say in psychological parlance, and I would suggest that these men had experienced the moment of fulfillment or "closure" in their reactions to the original dramas and, therefore, approached the composition of their poems not in the heat of poetic need but sated with emotional fulfillment. In any case, their paraphrases of Scott's diary and the Stalingrad letters are lifeless texts compared to the original documents. It seems to me that such is the case with most of the Algerian militant poetry. Overwhelmed by the immensity of the war's horrors, many poets have recoiled and given off faint signals, codes whose meanings reflect the author's human response and, no doubt, trigger human responses in those who are equally familiar with the references and associations. These semaphores may be factual indices of brutality—as in a poem in which the author flashes the name of a place where atrocities took place[1]—but they may at the same time have no or very little poetic force and it seems to me very important to keep this distinction in mind. Inevitably, then, one will get a less authentic account of the Algerian events through extant poems than through the tragically human and somehow definitive account of those events as set down in Mouloud Feraoun's *Journal: 1955–62.*[2]

I should like to illustrate my point about the confusion between powerful content and poetic impact with a con-

---

[1]For example, the reference to Palestro in the following passage from "Algerie" by Nadia Guendouz:

Aujourd'hui sur les tombes	Les gorges de la mort
d'hier	Palestro
Le blé a poussé	Les graines noires
Les veines qui ont arrosé	Qui ont pris vos vies . . . (Amal, p.20).

[2]Paris: Seuil, 1962. Feraoun was assassinated on May 15, 1962, in the Algiers suburb of El Biar by the OAS and the final pages of the diary are painfully moving.

verse example. One prolific critic of Algerian literature considers non-militant poems ''serene'':

> *Il faut dire toutefois que la poésie algérienne contem-*
> *poraine d'expression francaise ne comporte pas que*
> *des oeuvres engageés. Des auteurs ont publié ou publi-*
> *ent en meme temps des oeuvres plus sereines.*[1]

Ombre gardienne, by Mohammed Dib, is then cited as a prime example of this so-called ''serene'' poetry. Now, there is more *poetic* dynamite in *Ombre gardienne* than in any of the militant poetry with strictly *narrative* or contextual impact or violence! What is forceful in the latter are the facts which could be as well or better handled in prose; what is forceful in the former could only occur in poetry—indeed, *is* the poetry! The cosmic fulgurations of many of the short pieces in *Ombre gardienne* are ''tortured'' and ''anguished'' and anything but serene. Compare, for example, a good topical poem by Hocine Bouzaher entitled ''L'Imparfait et le present'' in which the facts and the personal drama are the meaningful components:

> *A Alger*
> *Près de l'Université*
> *Au coeur du quartier interdit*
> *Il y a un café*
> *Tout petit*
> *Rue de Tanger*
>
> *Nous nous y retrouvions après les cours*
> *Il y a longtemps de cela*
> *Et nous parlions à voix basse*

---

[1]Déjeux, Poésie algérienne, p. 64.

Un jour de novembre
Nous nous serrames la main et
Nous partîmes

Allaoua n'est pas revenu
Et moi j'écris dans ce même café de la rue de Tanger
L'imparfait est terrible mais
Plus terrible encore est le présent
Pour qui se souvient
Allaoua avait do sang dans la bouche
Allaoua avait des balles dans les flancs
Allaoua avait des yeux rieurs
Allaoua était mort

Avant ce poème[1]

to the suite by Dib called "Eléments" in which the mystical poetic images are the meaningful components as one will readily see from the following section:

Silence si fort des jambes,
Silence d'épines vertes
Et des bras autour du cou,

Ma femme contre la faim
Qu'on ne peut déraciner,
Les paupières fermées chante.

Il neige encore. L'étoile
Qui tue le jour sur son corps
Est en cendres, tout en cendres

Et crie prés de moi, légère
Bouche ni pâle ni rouge,
Sirène de sang qui dort.[2]

[1] *Espoir et Parole*, edited by D. Barrat (Paris: Seghers, 1963), pp. 160–61.
[2] *Ombre gardienne* (Paris: Gallimard, 1961), p. 30.

When one has sifted out the impelling but topical *cris de coeur* inspired by the war and the political and social injustices involved therein, as well as the works by genuine writers who somehow have failed to create a poetry with staying power—even good poets like Jean Amrouche and Malek Haddad—the two Algerians who remain as undeniably major genitors of a poetic impact are Mohammed Dib and Kateb Yacine.

Mohammed Dib[1] is best known as a novelist and short story writer, but his output of poetry, despite its lack of bulk, as well as the poetic quality of some of his prose, clearly indicates that he constitutes with Kateb Yacine the mainstream of serious Algerian—and Maghreb—poetry of French expression. This assertion will not surprise those who have read Dib's later novels which are often less concerned with narrative and historical fact than with exploring dimensions of time, and which tend to reflect the underlying currents of a period or a character rather than the sequential events or acts, or physical or psychological analysis of man.[2] Dib is less flamboyantly poetic in his novels than Kateb Yacine, but Dib's prose is as concerned with suites and interrelationships of images or moods—a la poetry—as with narration and characterization—a la prose.

Mohammed Dib's only collection of poems to date, *Ombre gardienne,* is divided essentially into two sorts of poem: that in *terza rima* or sonnet form predominates in the last half of the book, and the shorter mystical lyrics-

---

[1]Mohammed Dib was born in Tlemcen, near Morocco, on July 21, 1920. He studied at Tlemcen and Oujda and held many different jobs (rug-maker, teacher, accountant, critic, journalist) before becoming a writer. He is the author of seven novels, two collections of short stories, and one book of poems, *Ombre gardienne*. He lives in France.

[2]And yet, the curious kinship of two such unlike books as Dib's elusive *Un Eté africain* and Frantz Fanon's socio-historical *L'An V de la révolution algérienne* bears witness to the fact that the poetic or creative focus need not be devoid of historical perception.

—some of which are also in *terza rima*—which occupy the first half. The sonnets and tercets are essentially narrative and traditional and, in my opinion, reveal the skill but not the talent of Dib. The mind is drawn back again and again, however, to the fascinating texts of the sections entitled "Ombre gardienne," "Eléments," and "Méridienne" which are generally metrical constructions of six, seven, eight, or nine syllables and are technically as polished as the sonnets and tercets, but so conceived as to subordinate the form to the image, not vice versa.

The images in "Ombre gardienne," "Eléments," and "Mèridienne" are compelling, hallucinatory, and creatively ambiguous. Coleridge averred that while he envisioned his "Kubla Khan" in a drugged sleep, "the images rose up before him as *things,* with a parallel production of the correspondent expressions . . ." and Dib's images seem to rise before us in intolerable urgency as *things,* but things which our minds cannot grasp and which must be intuited in the poem. Tolerance for ambiguity, a sign of both creativity and madness, is required of the reader of Dib's poems and later novels and, in this respect, Dib belongs to the brood of Char, Bonnefoy, and other modern neo-Heraclitean paradoxicalists. During a discussion regarding the proper translation of one of Dib's extraordinary images:

> *Nés d'antiques calcaires*
> *Et des feux de la mer,*
> *Ses ramiers pour la mort*
> *Resplendissent étranges.*[1]

a colleague said that he was aware of the grammatical inversion and the syntax didn't bother him, but that he

[1]*Ombre gardienne*, p. 19.

could not understand what it *meant* to have "ring-doves shine forth strangely in behalf of death." He missed the point—and not for want of intelligence—and I could see that any attempt to explain was useless. What he really needed was not to seek elimination of ambiguity, but to expand his tolerance for it. As A. C. Ward has put it: "the 'meaning' of poetry is in itself and is self-communicating to those who are fit for, i.e., receptive or attuned to, poetry," a statement he further refines by footnote: " 'Meaning' in relation to poetry is an inapposite intellectual word. The exact phrase would be 'the *poetry* of poetry is in itself . . .' "[1]

The cosmic images of Dib's poems are brief, brilliant fulgurations. The word-pictures do not demand logical explanation but defy it, striking like pickaxes in the flint of the mind. The *things* which rise before our mind's eye are phantom or mythic. The poems appear to be drawn from the same reservoir of inspiration that fed the poetic novel *Qui se souvient de la mer.* This novel, published in 1962, paints a mural of horror which is purposely free of realistic blood and gristle. In a "Postface" to *Qui se souvient de la mer,* Dib admits that he has tried to create a legendary, timeless commentary on the Algerian war in the style of Picasso's *Guernica*—but in words. Even had he not told us of his indebtedness to Picasso, the frequent references to the Minotaurs in the streets (French troops? Forces of evil? The universal war machine? Or, perhaps, even Minotaurs?) and to the strange proliferating city would suggest the kinship. The novel—if, indeed, it is a novel and not a prose poem—hovers tantalizingly between the logically and historically explicable and the hallucinatory world of the illogical and the unknown. The legendary, millenial quality of the poem-novel is

[1]A. C. Ward, *English Literature: Chaucer to Bernard Shaw,* 2nd Printing (London: Longmans, 1960), p. 537.

communicated by the author's abrupt transitions to the image of the sea which is a mother image and a life-death image throughout:

> *Aussitôt l'ancienne vie, perdue déja dans le sable, commença à se retirer de notre maison, et la douceur, la fraîcheur de la mer ne purent affleurer. Sauf à de très rares instants, la mer, plus ferme que le basalte, n'entrouvrit plus les yeux que pour voir rire son enfant, son propre mystère.*
> *Nafissa, elle, se gardait de dire quoi que ce fût. Gagnée par la douleur de l'homme? Non, patiente, attendant. Persuadée que son moment viendrait tôt ou tard, qu'il lui faudrait soigner, guérir, bercer. La mer n'est pas triste lorsqu'elle attend la nuit, comme on le croit: déjà, des étoiles bougent en elle.*[1]

The ageless backdrop to the prose-poem is the sea whence man came: "La mer embrassait ainsi les pieds de l'homme jadis, se souvenant encore dù temps où elle le portait,"[2] and the theme of the four elements is the common denominator of most of the scenes or "états d'âme" of the novel which deal repeatedly with water, space, earth, stone, stars, and flames. Turning to the brief poems in the first half of *Ombre gardienne*, we encounter the same vocabulary used so often in *Qui se souvient de la mer:* "orée," "minotaure," "ombre," "silence," "étoile," "sang," "pierre," etc. Indeed, the first poem in "Eléments" contains a description of a place reminiscent of the strange, dehumanized town of *Guernica* or *Qui se souvient de la mer:*

---

[1]Dib, *Qui se souvient de la mer* (Paris: Seuil, 1962), p. 21.
[2]*Qui se souvient*, p. 19.

> *Et la voix d'un minotaure las*
> *Depuis longtemps égare la plainte*
> *D'une ville plus vide, plus sourde.*[1]

Dib invents a fantastic environment of daily miracles. The place he invents in his poetic prose, and the poems which are basically marginalia to that prose, is new to us, but he makes it our natural habitat. As Yves Bonnefoy has said, "Le vrai lieu est donné par le hasard, mais au vrai lieu le hasard perdra son caractère d'énigme,"[2] but Dib does not leave things to chance. He deliberately places us in a series of images and a syntax which are disruptive and disquieting; yet, at the same time, he reassures us of the fundamental integrity of his poetic world by steeping it in the eternal elements and the familiar primordial objects of the universe. Dib repeatedly returns, at moments of maximum disorientation, to the immutables of sea, stone, and star, the latter providing a special fascination for him. A good example is found in the short story entitled "La Destination." The story is, it seems to me, symboic of Algeria's arduous journey to independence and the hazards and hopes encountered along the way. Composed in a highly-fragmented and poetic style, the story recounts the adventures of a young man, Chadly, who is led by a guide from the mountains through enemy lines down into a free zone:

> —*Tu es libre à partir d'ici.*
> *Il eut une sorte de déchirement de la gorge.*
> —*Tu peux continuer seul.*
> *Chadly devina qu'ils étaient sortis de la zone de ratissage que son guide devait lui faire traverser.*
> —*Quoi: c'est fini?*
> *Fini. A partir d'ici, tu es* indépendant.[3]

[1] *Ombre gardienne*, p. 29.
[2] Yves Bonnefoy, *L'Improbable* (Paris: Mercure de France, 1959), p. 181.
[3] Dib, *Le Talisman* (Paris: Seuil, 1966), p. 56. Dib's emphasis.

Chadly staggers in a near-hallucinatory state through the countryside toward his village. He is exhausted and lies down in a field to sleep. He looks up at the night and experiences an optical phenomenon well-known to star-watchers in which the eyes' adjustment makes the stars seem to blossom in space and rain down on the gazer; but even in this image a paradox or anachronism is used to make the image creatively equivocal, mystical:

> *Encore marcher? Pour aller ou?*
> *Il n'en eut plus la force. Il quitta la route,*
> *pénétra dans un pré où il s'étendit au fond d'un creux.*
> *Il éprouva la douceur de la terre.*
> *Il contempla les etoiles, leur envoya un clin d'oeil.*
> *Toutes quittèrent le ciel pour s'abattre en pluie.*
> *L'averse incandescente n'était pas arrivée sur son corps qu'il dormait.*[1]

Chadly wakes up at dawn and arrives at his native village which is empty, the doors and windows walled up in every house. He in vain cries out the names of his mother and his wife and beats the wall of his home till his fists are bloody. On the brink of breakdown, Chadly reels out of the town into the countryside whose description reflects Chadly's mental state in a distortion of vision reminiscent of the procedure in Van Gogh's depiction of the cypresses of Arles:

> *Il crut qu'autour de lui le pays avait été remplacé par un autre. Éclipsés les lieux qui avaient fait partie de sa vie, éclipsés ou retournés à un monde indéchiffrable. Il dévala des pentes. Il battit une campagne où, folle ecume, les oliviers seuls secouaient parfois leur torpeur. Ils se réveillaient, s'agitaient un peu, puis*

[1] *Talisman*, pp. 58–59.

reprenaient leur guet. La lumiére crayeuse corrodait les yeux. Il erra longtemps. Il traqua son propre fantome. Il tâtonna, se perdit.[1]

Chadly falls to the ground. He goes through an emotional paroxysm or catharsis and, recovering his mental equilibrium, sets out on the road by which he had come. The conciliatory, stabilizing role of the elements, nature, and particularly the stars—whose complicity has been implied by Chadly's "clin d'oeil" mentioned above—is confirmed in the last words of the story:

Il avançait, il étudiait l'opacité de la terre. Loin de celles qu'il avait abandonnées derrière lui, ces hauteurs remuaient. Rompu par le bruit de ses pas, leur silence bourdonnait. Infinie, leur respiration ébranlait la nuit. Et des étoiles différentes lui faisaient signe.[2]

The cosmic interaction between poet and star is found in other prose works by Dib as well. Here is an example from *Qui se souvient de la mer* which will also demonstrate the poetic quality of that novel:

L'étoile tombe en cendres qui rongent la nuit et ne laissent indemnes que nos fonctions biologiques. Nous continuons de la sorte à vivre sous son ombre, entre ses mains de plus en plus expertes dans la cruauté. Ainsi, vagues, branle-bas, sifflements, depuis un moment, c'est elle. Et comme si c'était mon propre corps, je devine combien la ville soumise à ses manipulations se raidit, se tend, pendant que les murs, soit changent de position à quelques secondes d'intervalle, par reptations ou torsions brutales, soit attendent et

[1] *Talisman*, pp. 61–62.
[2] *Talisman*, p. 63.

*guettent. Il se propage aussi des exploisions épaisses:
mais sont-ce des explosions? Plutôt des dieux de
pierre tombes quelque part, dehors, frappés. Des ap-
pels, une course, et la rumeur se brise net; silence.
Silence qui dure longtemps. Seuls errent au monde un
reclus et son ombre qui cherchent la mer.*[1]

Such passages in the poetic prose do much to
reinforce, if not logically interpret, the mystic utterances
of *Ombre gardienne*. The magic place is made less
enigmatic to us by the longer exposure experienced
through prose, but once accustomed to the environment
we tolerate more readily the following random images
from *Ombre gardienne* and understand better the inspiration behind them:

> *Une étoile qui chante à l'orée
> Du monde et rutile comme un mort
> Vient fouiller la terre quand je dors.*[2]

> *Lorsque je m'éveillai
> Une étoile attentive
> Infiniment pâlie
> Chantait sous une averse.*[3]

> *Il neige encore. L'étoile
> Qui tue le jour sur son corps
> Est en cendres, tout en cendres. . . .*[4]

The prose also gives us an inkling of the multifarious
meaning of ''ombre.'' Given the symbolic interpretation
of the sea and the elements in most of Dib's references,

[1]*Qui se souvient*, p. 40.
[2]*Ombre gardienne*, p. 33.
[3]*Ombre gardienne*, p. 34.
[4]*Ombre gardienne*, p. 30.

we can, through "rub-off" of imagistic interaction, impute to the "shadow" or "shade" a number of interpretations, but is seems to me that "ombre," as used in Dib's collection and in the poetic prose, is either modal or abstractly substantive and that the word is descriptive of four philosophical attitudes, moments, or processes which are basic to Dib's *ars poetica*.

1. Paradox and contradiction:

Mon désir
Autour d'une terre d'ombre[1]

2. The idea of flux, Becoming, or metamorphosis: "Seuls errent au monde un reclus et son ombre qui cherchent la mer,"[2] or:

Vous venez de l'ombre,
Vous buvez tout le jour,
Cactus du ventre et menthe.[3]

3. An idea of the shadow as a genetic and apocalyptic force representing the moments of birth and destruction, critical moments of cosmic interaction, and the underlying, timeless dimension of eternity:

Ces ombres rapaces et folles,
La mer qui remue un jour vide
Entend-elle parfois leurs cris![4]

4. A personification or agent—predator, guardian, or

---

[1]*Ombre gardienne*, p. 40.
[2]*Qui se souvient*, p. 40.
[3]*Ombre gardienne*, p. 40.
[4]*Qui se souvient*, p. 39.

victim—in the life struggle, as in the title ''Ombre gardienne'' or:

Aveuglantes proies et ombres ni prises ni lâchées d'un printemps désolé qui tournez autour de moi, ces mains, ces yeux, ces lèvres, toute leur vie de pourpre se souviendront de vous.[1]

The theme of the shadow is almost without exception used in a metaphysical context and generally in one of the above categories, all of which, it should be remembered, are basic to a mystical view of creation, being, and the Word, constituting a noble tradition from the antithetical *ad'dâd* and the pre-Socratic philosophers to the medieval cabalists and the twentienth-century hermetic or cosmic poets (the surrealists, Ungaretti, Trakl, Char, and others). The various themes are evoked fragmentarily in the poems by the slightest shard, but those familiar with the shapes and the wheel of Dib's art will be able to reconstruct the entire vase. One section of *Qui se souvient de la mer*, in which the poetic prose breaks into a more conventional verse form, combines all the characteristics I have mentioned:

Tout à coup, la belle étoile s'éteint, mais son chant ne s'arrête pas, lui; il dit distinctement:

Pourquoi détresse viennent-elles
Toutes ces figures de pierre
Crier à l'envi sur la mer?

Pourquoi font-elles brusquement
Le monde se tourner ailleurs,
S'embraser d'une noire absence

[1] *Qui se souvient*, p. 52.

Et vite ensuite gargouiller
Dans un reflux d'eau, d'air, de feu,
Un seul murmure de lumiére?

Ces ombres rapaces et folles,
La mer qui remue un jour vide
Entend-elle parfois leurs cris?[1]

Another author who is no less concerned with the star motif is Kateb Yacine.[2] As he has stated in the *prière d'insérer* of *Le Polygone étoile*, "Le lecteur, de longue date, était averti que *Nedjma, le Cercle des représailles, le Polygone étoile,* les poemes à paraître en un prochain volume, sont une seule oeuvre de longue haleine, toujours en gestation." He elaborates in the same place: "Les pages qu'on va lire sont en chantier depuis dix ans. C'était à l'origine un poème écrit en 1947, 'Nedjma ou le poème ou le couteau,' publié dans la même année *(sic)* au *Mercure de France,* embryon d'une tragédie (1948) que je crus perdue mains retrouvai quatre ans plus tard a la revue *Esprit,* où elle parut, 'Le cadavre encércle' 1954, avant d'aboutir à la forme romanesque, 'Nedjma' 1956."

---

[1]*Qui se souvient,* pp. 38–39. Dib's emphasis.

[2]His real name is Yacine Kateb, but he adopted the reversed form as it appeared on his school bench; and, of course, names are frequently given in reverse order in Algeria, e.g. in street names. Yacine was born on August 26, 1929, at Constantine. After early instruction at Koranic school, Yacine studied in French-language schools and pursued his secondary education at Sétif. When he was fifteen, he took part in the May 8, 1945, demonstration which turned into a massacre resulting in thousands of deaths in Sétif and Guelma. Yacine was jailed and his mother became mentally deranged after the massacre. An early collection of poems, *Soliloques,* appeared in Bône in 1946. The novel, *Nedjma,* published by Editions du Sueil in 1956, established Yacine's international literary reputation which he has consolidated with subsequent poems, plays (*Le Cercle des représailles,* 1959), and prose (*Le Polygone étoilé,* 1966). For many years now, Yacine has lived in France.

The focal point of this ever-evolving work is the person-spirit-icon-object Nedjma. Nedjma is the name of an ethereal, haunting girl, but the word also means "star," and as such is used not so much cosmically as anologically, "Nedjma" symbolizing for Yacine everything from the star of Algerian nationalism and the ambiguous hybrid cultural makeup of the new Algerian to ancestral worship. The polygon is intimately related to the star in overlapping definition as well as by Yacine's intimate association of the two abstractions. In the following section from the play, *Les Ancêtres redoublent de férocité*, the polygon is first presented as a symbol of theoretical scientific truth or a theorem in the geometry of pure thought (Some mathematicians claim that a curve is the sum of an infinite number of straight lines and that a circle is thus really a polygon.) and then as the basic symbol of the cosmos:

CORYPHEE: *Ils vont tout droit au polygone.*
CHOEUR: *Au polygone?*
CORYPHEE: *Oui, c'est là qu'on fusille.*
CHOEUR: *Polygone, polygone, polygone. . .*
CORYPHEE: *Ils ont tout mesuré. Ils passent leur temps à prendre des mesures contre nous. Le polygone, en géométrie, ça veut tout dire . . .*
CHOEUR: *Il y a, au même endroit, là où on fusille, un camp de concentration . . .*
MUSTAPHA (masqué, se détachant du choeur): *C'est vrai. J'y étais, il y a dix ans.*
CORYPHEE: *Nous sommes riches en polygones. . . .*
CHOEUR: *Sans compter les cimetières.*
CORYPHEE: *Pour ne parler que des terrains vagues. Quant à la prison, c'est un luxe, en prévision de la paix.*
CHOEUR: *Polygone, polygone, polygone. . . .*

CORYPHEE (doctoral): *Tout territoire est un poly-gone. Tous les pays sont des polygones inscrits dans la sphère terrestre.*[1]

Yacine wrote two works entitled *Nedjma:* an early poem and his major novel; furthermore, the title of *Le Polygone étoilé* alerts the reader to his resumption of the star theme, and it is clear that this work is assembled in part from the cuttings from *Nedjma.* Thus there are similarities between Dib and Yacine inasmuch as they both appear to have made considerable imaginative use of their editorial prunings and both intermingle and cross-pollinate several traditional literary genres. Fur-thermore, Yacine is, like Dib, extremely interested in forging new creative explorations and expressions of time and perception.

In a preliminary note to *Nedjma,* Yacine's editors describe the spatial effects of time in the novel as being largely the result of a circular conception of time which they allege to be a fundament of the Arabic ontology:

Le rythme et la construction du récit, s'ils doivent quelque chose à certaines expériences romanesques occidentales—ce que nous ne contestons pas—résul-tent surtout d'une attitude purement arabe de l'homme face au temps. La pensée européenne se meut dans une durée lineaire; *la pensée arabe évolue dans une durée* circulaire *où chaque détour est un* retour, *confondant l'avenir et le passé dans l'éternité de l'instant. Cette confusion des temps, que les obser-vateurs hâtifs imputent au goût de l'équivoque, et où il faut voir d'abord le signe d'un génie de la synthése, correspond à un trait si constant du caractére, à une*

[1]In *Le Cercle des représailles* (Paris: Seuil, 1959), p. 126.

orientation si naturelle de la pensée que la grammaire
arabe, elle-même, en est marquée.[1]

Many critics have challenged this passage, both as a
description of "le penser arabe" and as a description of
Yacine's creative process. One critic claims that these
assertions tend to negate the universal appeal of the novel
"en lui attribuant les dimensions d'un roman exotique"
and suggests ironically that, on the basis of the editors'
argument, "il serait du droit des Arabes de revendiquer
comme émanation de leur pensée, l'oeuvre de Proust, par
exemple."[2] The debate involves an insoluble question
which, like life after death, is subject to no definitive
answer or interpretation, but it seems to me that ·the
editorial generalities prefacing *Nedjma* contain two highly questionable assumptions which, if accepted by the
reader, lead to a special—indeed, exotic—understanding
of *Nedjma* and Yacine's *Weltanschauung.* Firstly, there
is no reason to assume that all men's thoughts do not
move in the same direction and dimension. Various cultures have differed in their attempts to explain and lend
order or dimension to the phenomenon of perception, but
it is absurd to speak of thought "moving" or having
"futurity" which is, of course, only a grammatical or
conceptual eventuality based on present speculations derived from an aggregate of past experiences. Pure
thought exists only in the present and will do so for any
writer investigating it whether his name be Faulkner,
Yacine, Robbe-Grillet, Butor, or Dib. Secondly, the
editors scornfully brush aside the idea of imputing the
time-space development of *Nedjma* to a "predilection for
the equivocal." They do not hesitate to bring Arabic

---

[1]Yacine, *Nedjma* (Paris: Seuil, 1956), p. 6. Editors' emphasis.
[2]Mohamed-Salah Dembri, "A propos de la *Nedjma* de Kateb Yacine,"
An-ñasr (Constantine), le 20 mai, 1967, p. 7.

grammar into their own shaky argument; yet one can build a compelling defense for the idea that Arabic thought and language are antithetical in origin and are based in part on the *ad'dad,* or word which means mutually itself and its opposite.[1] It seems to me that this innate lingua-ontological quality would, then, belong, if not to Proust, at least to every deeply Arabic writer sharing the same philosophical patrimony and would thus be basic to the conception of time held by Yacine, but also by Dib and others. Therefore, I would ascribe the treatment of time by both poets to an amalgam of their Arabo-Oriental cultural patrimony; assimilation of the scientific-philosophical discoveries of Einstein, the surrealists, the existentialists, and others; and an awareness of the stylistic innovations of the experimental "nouveau roman" of the 1950's and, perhaps, the novels of William Faulkner.[2]

I shall not dwell further on these poets' imaginative use of time as it is less conspicuous in the poems than in the novels; they differ considerably in their use of imagery and matter. Dib's poetic imagination, it will be recalled, revolves around the elements, and the objects

---

[1]The number of authentic *ad'dad* is disputed (See "Ad'dâd" in *L'Encyclopédie de l'Islam*) but the phenomenon is acknowledged, and we may, therefore, place Arabic language and ordering of thought in the same tradition as the pre-Socratic philosophers. For a full consideration of this matter, see: Jacques Berques and Jean-Paul Charnay, *L'Ambivalence dans la culture arabe* (Paris: Editions Anthropos, 1967); see also Carl Abel and Sigmund Freud on this matter.

[2]Critics—including the editors of *Nedjma*—often mention Faulkner as the single greatest literary influence on Yacine, an influence the latter has long denied, although his protest has grown fainter as he resigns himself to this repeatedly imposed alliance. An unpublished D.E.S. dissertation by Hocine Menasseri, entitled "Kateb's *Nedjma* and Faulkner's *The Sound and the Fury*" (University of Algiers, 1968), draws parallels between these two works. Menasseri is careful not to suggest a direct influence, but the very fact of bringing these works together in a study of this length implies influence. Otherwise why not, indeed, a comparison to Proust? A parallel study of Robbe-Grillet and Yacine or Dib would be more pertinent, I think.

he evokes normally function symbolically as peepholes into eternity. His ambiguity is cosmic and *directly* illuminating; and tolerance of ambiguity and suspension of reason are requisites to comprehension of his work:

> [*L'étoile*] *crie prés de moi, légère*
> *Bouche ni pâle ni rouge,*
> *Sirène de sang qui dort.*[1]

Yacine's poetic imagination revolves around the shiftings of tense and the objects he evokes usually function symbolically as indices of other things or concepts. His ambiguity is linguistic or compositional and seems to demand rationalization; careful analysis and use of logic are requisites to appreciation—even if they do not lead to full comprehension or resolution of the ambiguity:

> . . . *du sang farouchement accumulé par les chefs de file et les nomades séparés de leur caravane, réfugiés dans ces villes du littoral où les rescapés se reconnaissent et s'associent, s'emparent du commerce et la bureaucrotie avec une patience séculaire, et ne se marient qu'entre eux, chaque famille maintenant ses fils et ses filles inexorablement accouplés, comme un attelage égyptien portant les armes et les principes évanouis d'un ancêtre, un de ces nobles vagabonds séparés de leur caravane au cours de ces périples que rapportent les géographes arabes, et qui, du Moyen-Orient puis de l'Asie, passe à l'Afrique du Nord, la terre du soleil couchant qui vit naître, stérile et fatale, Nedjma notre perte, la mauvaise étoile de notre clan.*[2]

[1]*Ombre gardienne*, p. 30
[2]*Nedjma*, p. 188.

As in Dib's case, it is impossible to separate Yacine's poetry from the writing in other genres. The novels contain long passages of inspired prose-poetry and even break into free verse at times, especially in *Le Polygone étoilé;* and the plays collected in the volume entitled *Le Cercle des représailles* are composed largely in free verse and maintain an inspired lyric momentum. Yacine's earliest published poems are "introuvables" as the poet no doubt prefers since they were apparently amateurish. The poetry of greatest interest to us is found in "Nedjma ou le poème ou le couteau," "Le Fondateur," sections of *Le Polygone étoilé*, and the plays, especially *Les Ancêtres redoublent de férocité de ferocite* and *Le Vautour.*

There is a great deal of repetition in Yacine's work whose focal point to date is the novel *Nedjma;* what he seems to provide in his overall work is a definition of life force marked by what we might call a regional mentality. The ever-evolving, ever-revised palimpsest of Yacine's "moveable work of art" is a fitting structure for or approach to the subject matter. The various characters, locations, tribes, and acts dear to Yacine recur here and there in all the works, regardless of genre, with capricious inevitability, as it were, much as the primal life force erupts from time to time in man and family as Yacine perceives them.

The universal life forces dwell in an enormous room where timelessness reigns and where he who listens and observes can discover clues to that chaos. The one thing which does lend a sense of direction and dimension to the time-space void is the succession of ancestors whose presence is at once linear and accumulative and all-encompassing. Yacine attempts to reconcile the two cultural forces of North African and French identity—which are embodied in Nedjma and which tear at Yacine's soul—in a negation of time in which the true self will be, as it were, a sacred bastard. In a parallel with sub-Saharan animism, the poet would seek sublimation of self, whence fulfillment of self, through communion with the universal ancestral force. This force and the obstacles standing between it and the poet give rise to a whole personal iconography ranging from the star to the vulture. In *Les Ancêtres redoublent de férocité*, a Chorus of Ancestors sings in the darkness:

Nous, Comité Central des Ancêtres,
Nous sommes parfois tentés de parler à la terre,
De dire à nos enfants: courage
Prenez place dans les vaisseaux de la mort
Venez rejoindre à votre tour l'armada ancestrale
Qui n'est pas loin d'avoir conquis
Et le temps et l'espace
Mais les vivants ne savent ni vivre ni mourir
N'ont pas une pensée pour les Ancêtres
Toujours présents à leur chevet!
Pourtant celui qui écoute ne peut manquer d'entendre;
Celui qui ne craint pas d'observer le vide
Verra grandir le point noir qui le hante:
En désespoir de cause, nous avons élu le vautour
Comme le mâle insoupçonné porteur de nos messages
Oui, le vautour, et son passage est un arrêt de mort
Et il survole votre agonie
Dans sa méditation lointaine et sans repos. . . .[1]

In Yacine's poetry, there is a sense of suspended or latent violence, an unstable repose implied by the ambiguity of Nedjma's origin, the idea of virginal promiscuity, and by paradoxical statements like ''C'est une absurde/Nécessite/D'isoler une morte si vive,''[2]

---

[1] *Cercle des représailles*, p. 149.
[2] *Le Vautour*, in *Cercle des représailles*, p. 165.

"Fleur de poussiere,"[1] "Dois-je egorger la rose ou con-
sentir à sa profanation?"[2] or "méditation lointaine et
sans repos."[3] Thus, passages in which no specific
violence occurs often suggest an ominous tension and
forebode overt violence; as in the surreal moment in
Nedjma when the narrator witnesses Nedjma's bath—a
scene in which the triangular location of the narrator, the
sleeping Negro, who later witnesses the bath, and Nedjma, whose bath water reaches along the ground toward
the Negro but whose portrait is seen from the point of
view of the narrator, are all in controlled, momentary,
agonizing equipoise. When we subsequently learn that a
shooting has occurred in the tent, we are not surprised,
having understood by prior suggestion that violence must
follow any fission of that scene's unity.

Murder, rape, and brutality in Yacine's work seem to
be hieratic rituals played out in cataclysmic obeissance to
the ancestors' code of honor or vaguely sensed bidding.
Crimes are gestures or signals acted out in keeping with a
grander design, the volcanic outbreaks of an underground cauldron whose molten presence—even when
invisible—we are not allowed to forget for a moment.
Thus, whether the poet describes a firing squad in the
1950's or a symbolic rape in a primordial cave, he is
tapping the force of that subterranean cauldron. In a very
general sense, Yacine's work is a unique hybrid of high-
ly-skilled use of the French language and the North
African *mystique* whose sullen force may be symbolized
by that underground reservoir.

Objects and persons in Yacine's poems and poetic
prose and drama are highly stylized predators or victims
in the eternal, brutal life struggle, set in their proper
place in a natural order of things. Words in Yacine's

[1] Yacine, *Le Polygone étoilé* (Paris: Seuil, 1966), p. 162.
[2] *Cercle des représailles*, p. 150.
[3] *Cercle des représailles*, p. 149.

poems, therefore, are highly "verbal," suggesting a millennia-old ritual, functioning almost as hieroglyphs. Words like virgin, rose, vulture, blood, wing, veil, bed, river, and shadow become multivalent and loaded with the many-faceted—polygonal—meanings they acquire in Yacine's creative universe.

Due to the revision method of composition that Yacine has adopted in the creation of his overall work, there is a certain monotony about his poetry, but this is perhaps inevitable in a work devoting itself to the exploration of a *uni*-verse and its primordial types.

The ancestors, and "cette flaque de durée"[1] into which they seek to plunge the living, represent not only a millenial force but also the depravity and insantity which results from clannishness and incest. In *Nedjma,* all hope and all cumulative turpitude is represented by the Keblout clan. Furthermore, ancestral clans and all they stand for are represented by the founding-father image, "le fondateur." He is a symbol of tradition in a world of uncertainty, but he is also the caricature of man's aggregate strengths and weaknesses. The capricious behavior of the "fondateur" has the force and absurdity of action which comes with the abuse of power. He wanders the desert and the hills like a deposed but mythic king:

> *Sorti de l'eau, il plonge dans la forêt. Ni soldat ni proprietaire, quel est ce spectre sans mémoire dont les enfants se perdent en questions? Etait-ce un ogre prolifique, un ogre qui mangea ses fils âinés, mais préserva peut-être le dernier. (. . . .) A cette heure-ci, le fondateur quitte ses rejetons. Il revient à sa condition de spectre. Ainsi est ce métier, devenu profond par inaction forcée en cette vase préhistorique où de vénéneux horizons, profondément enfouis, rejaillis-*

[1] *Polygone étoilé,* p. 10.

sent. Il n'a plus de tabatiére. Il se revoit caracolant dans l'odeur de la poudre. Est-il possible de revenir aux nobles formes du combat? En même temps qu'il médite, il pése, d'un regard, les fruits de la saison. Il croque un poivron.[1]

Before the man born of this tradition there looms the threat that he will be the last of the decadent family whose decline Yacine likens to a gradual shipwreck:

Je suis le fils unique, issu du treiziéme mâle et du quatorzieme,[2] *par mon père et ma mère. Ce mariage consanguin sera sans doute le dernier: un lent naufrage. Et j'ai beau me débattre, inondé par la racine.*[3]

Like a demented Roman emperor or a Cenci or a Sardanapalus bent on destroying himself, his descendants, and his belongings, the "fondateur" is a leveler of time and place and leaves behind the legacy of the collective stupor of all preceding founding fathers:

Le fondateur. Nous n'osons plus déterrer ses trésors. Despote. Liquidateur de notre armée natale, il nous aura laissé le subtil héritage de ses dettes, la stupeur: l'éternelle nouveauté de vivre par milliers confondus, sans grande science et forts de ce royaume hypothétique.[4]

That Yacine is impervious to the traditional distinction of genre and that the theme of the founding father is a common denominator in his work is clear throughout his

---

[1]*Polygone étoilé*, pp. 13–14.
[2]This ambiguous paternity is reminiscent of Nedjma's mysterious origin.
[3]*Polygone étoilé*, p. 16.
[4]*Polygone étoilé*, pp. 16–17.

writing, but especially in the curious reprise of the poem entitled "Le Fondateur" in the ostensibly prose section opening *Le Polygone étoilé*. "Le Fondateur," one of Yacine's major texts, appeared in *Les Lettres Nouvelles* in 1956 as a prose poem in thirteen sections.[1] It was published under the running head "Poesie" and the text later selected as one of the best poems of the year in the anthology, *Les Poèmes de l'année*, published by Pierre Seghers. This text is repeated almost verbatim in *Le Polygone étoilé* (Pp. 14–17) as part of a long prose paragraph: the divisions have been suppressed and there is no indication that with the words "Le fondateur. Il a laissé quatorze mâles . . ." we are beginning a text which might be thought of as a self-sufficient or self-justifying creative entity. Indeed, the founding father is referred to as "le fondateur de la Fraction" in this text, and the vocabulary of fractions and division is appropriate to Yacine's artistic point of view and creative process—common denominators and partial representation in which the idea of the whole is implied rather than stated, since its statement as a whole (e.g.   ) would no longer be fractional. He builds an entire system of aesthetics on the idea of fragmentation, reprise, fraction, and repetition. In the earliest draft of the Nedjma texts, "Nedjma ou le poème ou le couteau," Yacine provides an oblique key to his point of view and his *ars poetica:* "Coupez mes rêves tels les serpents ou bien portez-moi dans le sommeil de Nedjma je ne puis supporter cette solitude!"[1] The two principal threads—besides the evident omnipresent theme of time itself—which recur in the work and which bind the fragments together are the figures of Nedjma and the elder or the founding father, and both are ambiguous, paradoxical. Nedjma is elusive and contradictory: she is real-imaginative, chaste-

[1]Yacine, "Le Fondateur," *Les Lettres Nouvelles*, No. 40 (juillet-août 1956), 9–11.

promiscuous, one-multiple, corporeal-ethereal. The founding father is reliable but degenerate: he is hope-failure, fertility-sterility, strength-weakness, longevity-illness, grandeur-pusillanimity, construction-destruction, morality-turpitude. Both Nedjma and the founding father contain in themselves their opposites and, in their opposite, the kernel of themselves as with the interplay of opposites in the yin-yang symbol of Tao. The themes and their duality are found from the beginning in Yacine's poetry. In "Nedjma ou le poème ou le couteau," written in 1947, he describes the principal subjects of his poetic quest, the ineffable charm of Nedjma:

> Lorsque je perdis l'andalouse je ne pus rien dire
> j'agonisais sous son souffle il me fallut le temps de la
> nommer
> Les palmiers pleuraient sur ma tête j'aurais pu oublier
> l'enfant pour le feuillage
> Mais Nedjma dormait restait immortelle et je pouvais
> toucher ses seins déconcertants. . . .[2]

and the metaphorically-evoked grotesqueness of the unsavory but powerful ancestor: "Nedjma tira sur la bride je sellai un dromadaire musclé comme un ancêtre."[3]

There are many similarities between the works of Yacine and Dib, among them their kindred recourse to objects in nature. There is a difference in their manipulation of these objects, however, as well as in the light in which they display them. As we have already demonstrated, there is a cosmic aura surrounding Dib's plants, minerals, and stars. They are springboards to the great

[1]Yacine, "Nedjma ou le poéme ou le couteau," *Mercure de France*, Tome 302, No. 1013 (ier janvier 1948), 71.
[2]"Nedjma ou le poéme," 71.
[3]"Nedjma ou le poéme," 71.

eternal abstractions of night, space, and enlightenment. In Yacine's work, the natural objects are springboards to an abstraction, too, but the abstraction is that of mother Algeria and, more generally, the universal mother Earth. Dib, in his contemplation of the stars, makes us see beyond into the lofty abstraction of the cosmic void; Yacine's stars—when they are not symbols—are the traveling companions of nomads, they are Earth-oriented, and their cosmic shower returns our vision to Earth, to the desert and the oasis, and to man:

> *Les nomades nous guettent leurs cris crèvent nos mots ainsi que des bulles*
> *Nous ne verrons plus les palmiers poussés vers la grêle tendre des étoiles. . . .*[1]

The earth to which Yacine's inspiration is rooted is, to a large extent, the hauntingly beautiful landscape of Algeria, but it also functions in his work as an element at once universal and tangible in whose undeniable existence we are constantly and physically confronted with both the relative timelessness of near-infinity and the immediate evidence of the passage of time, the changing seasons, and the daily decay of erosion and advancing history.

Yacine and Dib are, in my opinion, the leading Francophone writers of North Africa. They are so because of their ability to be men of their own age and their emerging nation's Third World identity without sacrificing to literary or political fashion their natural interest in the philosophical truths of the ages. To describe either poet's work, we may conclude with the following words from Whitman's preface to *Leaves of Grass:* "If he breathes into any thing that was before thought small it dilates with the grandeur and life of the universe."

[1]"Nedjma ou le poème," 70.

ON IDENTIFYING A STANDARD OF AFRICAN LITERARY CRITICISM: CHARACTERIZATION IN THE NOVEL

By RAND BISHOP

At the 1964 meeting of the African Studies Association, Professor Robert P. Armstrong gave a paper entitled "African Literature and European Critics." Professor Armstrong argued for the principle of cultural relativity in the field of literary criticism, as opposed to an absolutism based on a Western set of literary universals (the irony is intended). He referred to Jean-Paul Sartre's essay, "Black Orpheus,"[1] in saying that "this literature [African literature in French] arises directly from a uniquely African and—particularly—uniquely lived experience," and concluded his paper by saying that

What is required is a frank admission on the part of critics that we are here working with a new literature that will shape its own forms, dictate its own diction,

[1] "Orphée Noir," in *Anthologie de la nouvelle poésie nègre et malgache de langue française*, ed. Léopold Sédar Senghor (Paris: Presses Universitaries de France, 1948, 1969), pp. IX-XLIV. See also English translations: *Black Orpheus*, trans. S. W. Allen (Paris: Présence Africaine, 1963; and "Black Orpheus," trans. John MacCombie, *Massachusetts Review*, VI, 1 (Autumn-Winter 1964–65), 13–52.

199

express its own values. What is needed, both from here and from Africa is a determined exploration, by the most highly trained people, of the nature of this new literature.

My intention here is to get us perhaps a leg up on Professor Armstrong's ladder of "determined exploration of the nature of this literature," while hoping not to offer yet another of those "special types of criticism" which Chinua Achebe says "have been designed for us by people whose knowledge of us is very limited."[1]

The debate which has developed around the criticism of African literature—who does it and how, according to what standards—has been very stimulating and exciting. In its worse moments it has been acrimonious; it has never been dull. Central to this debate has been the question of critical standards and their application, and Professor Armstrong's call for a relativistic criticism has been strongly seconded by some Western and several African critics. One of the most provacative statements on the matter is that by Joseph Okpaku, who says that

Critical standards derive from aesthetics. Aesthetics are culture dependent. Therefore critical standards must derive from culture.[2]

Whether or not one accepts this syllogism, it is quite clear that several African critics do accept it. This became clear in the debate that occurred in the African literature discussion of the 1968 meeting of the African Studies Association, in Los Angeles. At this meeting Professor Charles R. Larson presented a paper entitled

---

[1]Chinua Achebe, "Where Angels Fear to Tread," *Nigeria Magazine*, No. 75 (Dec. 1962), p. 61.

[2]Joseph Okpaku, "Culture and Criticism: African Critical Standards for African Literature and the Arts," *Journal of the New African Literature and the Arts*, No. 3 (Spring 1967), p. 1.

"Whither the African Novel?"[1] in which he spoke of several recent literary works as "half novels" and lamented the fact that

> With few exceptions, the African novel in English has tended to be situational; and the African writer, so concerned with recording what happened to his society in its confrontation with the West, has failed to create believable characters who live outside of the situations in which they are involved.[2]

He went on more explicitly to say

> When I glance over the dozens of African novels in English which have been published thus far, there are few real human beings, genuine characters who stand out in any remarkable way. Most of them are poorly drawn, flat, incidental to what the author too frequently believes is his monumental message. There are few characters who are in any sense universal: confronting the problems which all of us must confront if we are to be people at all.[3]

The tone of the paper aside (which I think contributed to the heatedness of the argument that followed), Professor Larson had introduced the word "universal" into the discussion and it proceeded to dominate the rest of the afternoon. It was suggested at some point that perhaps characterization in the novel might not be a universal standard because of the possibility that it might not be an African standard. And if it was not African then it followed, in the minds of those who took this position, that it certainly could not be universal.

---

[1] Published subsequently in *CLA Journal*, XIII, 2 (Dec. 1969).
[2] *Ibid.*, 148.
[3] *Ibid.*, 149.

The debate progressed, leaving the question unanswered in my mind: Is characterization in the novel, in fact, an African critical standard? And even more to the point, how could one proceed to determine whether it was or not? It was at this point that the difficulty between the African and the non-African critics became clearer to me. I do not think the African critics at this meeting were objecting to Professor Larson's use of characterization in his evaluations of African novels; rather I believe they were objecting to (1) his assumption that Western standards are universal without (2) bothering first to determine whether these standards are acceptable to and, more to the point, actually used by Africans. They were objecting in essence to what might be described as literary colonialism. Now I have no doubt, that Professor Larson did not intend his remarks as such, yet they carried in them—I shall say *seemed* to carry in them—the ring of critical *fiat*. Only once in his paper did Professor Larson qualify himself, and thus signal his audience that he was a Westerner dealing with a non- Western literature. He says

(Students have argued with me that the place of the African in his society is different than it is in the West and that this has led to a different kind of treatment of characters in African novels. This may be true in part, but this does not prevent a man from thinking or expressing his emotions.)
I realize that I am generalizing—making extremely broad categorizations at that. One of the things I have often pondered—and I believe that this is true of anyone who is studying the literature of another culture—is whether I simply have a tendency to identify with African characters who *act* Western. (original emphasis).

So far so good. But Professor Larson then goes on immediately to weaken his demurral by saying,

> I am reminded, however, that a significant number of French African novelists have done a superior job with characterization and relating characters, skillfull, to the world in which they are involved. This is true also of the African playwright who writes in English, but the African novelist has too often subordinated character to situation, character to quasi-polemic.[1]

Whether French-speaking African novelists exhibit a talent for characterization is one question (a question, incidentally, that is very likely to occur to a Western critic); the more relevant question here is what African *critics* think of characterization and, further, what the Western critic does with what the African critic says. That is the question Professor Larson does not ask. He seems, instead, either to be putting forth his Western critical standards as universals, or, even more fallaciously, inducing African critical standards from the literary works themselves. The fallacy in the latter approach seems fairly obvious: Professor Larson sees characterization in francophone African novels because he is looking for it, which is the same reason he doesn't see it in some other novels. It does not follow naturally or logically that the African novelist intends, nor that the African critic will concern himself with, the same elements that happen to make up Professor Larson's critical construct. Therefore, the statement that "a significant number of French African novelists have done a superior job with characterization" is meaningful only in telling us something about Professor Larson; it offers little or no insight into the way Africans view their literature.

[1]*Ibid.*

But not only does Professor Larson weaken his demurral, and confuse the question of standards; before he has finished he has assumed a knowledge of the literature of still another culture. He says,

> The African writer could learn a great deal about the craft of fiction by studying the canons of writings by contemporary black American practitioners of the novel. By reading Richard Wright, Ralph Ellison, and William Melvin Kelley, he could learn where to begin connecting the human condition to revolutionary times which are always indisputably rooted to people and places.[1]

The question is, does Professor Larson really know the canons of African and/or contemporary black American literature? He may very well know them—I suspect he is as sensitive to them as most white Western critics—but I think the important thing here, from the point of view of an African critic, is that he has not demonstrated that he knows them, nor, more significantly, that he even cares to know whether or how they might differ from the canons of his own literature (since, as he seems to say, the canons of all literatures are universal). It is precisely the demonstration of this concern that is lacking in the African/Western critical dialogue—the demonstration that the Western critics is aware of the *problematic* nature of criticizing African literature, and his apparent unwillingness to deal directly with this issue. The dialogue has suffered, in other words, because we are attempting to take the second step before completing—or hardly beginning—the first.

Professor Larson has, quite correctly in my opinion,

[1]*Ibid.*, 152.

pointed out the value of approaching African literature through the methods of comparative literature.[1] It is unfortunate he did not apply those methods while arriving at his evaluations of some African "half novels" in another place. A comparative approach to those works might have led him instead to a cultural explanation of how and why the characterization in them differed from Western characterization, or else a discussion of why the characterization fails *in Western terms,* coupled with an inquiry into whether the failure is also a failure in terms of the African literary aesthetic. The statement he seems to make, however—that these novels fail in Western and *therefore* in universal terms—is unacceptable to most African critics, and, I should think, to most Western students of comparative literature.

Let us examine, then, whether Professor Larson's application of characterization as a critical standard is in fact valid within the realm of African literary criticism. (Of course it is valid within his own critical construct. The problem at hand is not one of changing one's own critical framework; it is a question of recognizing the limits of that framework). But how to discover whether a critical standard is indeed African or not?

Joseph Okpaku has suggested one possibility by answering his question, "What then are these critical standards?" in the following manner:

> The logical place to go in search of them is the African aesthetic. In particular, we should examine our traditional artistic forms as well as genuine (not "studied") contemporary African tastes and attitudes towards the various art forms. . . . The next place to search for

---

[1]"African Literature and Comparative Literature," *Yearbook of Comparative and General Literature,* No. 18 (1969), pp. 70–74.

these standards would be an examination of those common aspects of life most frequently dramatized in the arts. This would include love, life, hate, honor, duty, death, destruction, pride, prejudice, friendship, fear, violence, birth and reality amongst others. Different cultures not only have different conceptions of these but have different attitudes to them. Not only that, they give them different emphases. All these different conceptions, attitudes, emphases, tastes and preferences constitute the basis on which to build criticism. This is where the search for African critical standards must begin.[1]

When Mr. Okpaku says "African critical standards" it sounds as though he may be hypothesizing a pre-existing aesthetic content in the term that must be discovered in order to determine the standards. However, I prefer to consider the term "African" as political and geographical (limiting it to "Black" and ("Sub-Saharan"); that is, that any criticism by a Black Sub-Saharan African is "African," at least politically and geographically, in the hopes of then proceeding analytically and hopefully somewhat empirically toward an understanding of the aesthetic meaning of the term. I am not at all certain I understand what Mr. Okpaku means by "aesthetic," but I am quite certain I disagree that it is "the logical place to go" in search of critical standards. It seems to me more feasible to try and induce an African aesthetic from the eventual isolating and identifying of critical standards, rather than to deduce the standards from the aesthetic. And while I agree that "critical standards derive from aesthetics," I do not think this fact must determine the methodology of the search for those standards.

I agree that a study of traditional art forms will be

[1]Okpaku, p. 5.

useful in determining their impact upon more "modern" forms. It is generally acknowledged that the oral tradition is having an important influence upon much of modern African writing, but there have been all too few attempts to determine what this influence is.[1]

But I completely disagree with Mr. Okpaku that critical standards will be found through an examination of those "common aspects of life . . . love, life, hate, honor, duty," etc. It is clear that African love differs in its details from Western love, as indeed Mr. Okpaku explains in his essay. Africans, he points out, do not kiss. Likewise, African honor will differ in its particulars from Western honor, African duty from Western duty, etc. etc. And the value put upon these will also differ, as Mr. Okpaku has rightly said. But I would suggest that these differences and different emphases fall more properly within the domain of the anthropologist than that of the literary critic. The critic, on the other hand, has the obligation to see that these qualities are presented accurately in *artistic* terms. He has a duty to complain loudly and articulately if he thinks, for example, that African honor is being misrepresented; that is, if an African is acting somehow, as a Western critic might put it, "out of character." But I do not see the evaluation of the literary rendering of African love, African honor, African duty, etc. etc. as constituting a long list of *separate* critical standards. Rather they form a single critical standard —which I see as the African dictum that the African writer must not give a false or misleading picture of what might be called "African regalia." I do not know whether Mr. Okpaku sees this protection of African regalia as

[1]But see E. N. Obiechina, "Transition from Oral to Literary Tradition," *Présence Africaine*, No. 63 (3e trimestre 1967), pp. 140–161; and "Amos Tutuola and the Oral Tradition," *Présence Africaine*, No. 65 (1er trimestre 1968), pp. 85–106.

the *sole* function of the African critic. I agree it is an important one, though by no means the only one.

In my opinion, however, the most logical place to look for African critical standards is in " contemporary African tastes and attitudes towards the various art forms." I think an examination of African taste—as opposed to the things tasted, such as love, hate, honor, duty, etc.—will suggest critical standards. The elements of African culture will reveal much about African culture, but the attitudes towards how these elements are handled literarily will tell us much more, I submit, about African literature and the critical standards Africans use in evaluating it. It is this latter examination, the examination of African taste, that will facilitate our understanding of the canons of African literature.

It has been tacitly assumed that African critical standards for modern African literature have not existed, or, if they existed, that they were unknown. Yet Africans have been writing literary criticism of modern African literature in increasing volume ever since the inception of *Présence Africaine* late in 1947, some twenty-four years ago. And it seems to me that an analysis of this body of criticism will very likely reveal African critical standards that have actually been in existence, and in use, for some time. This criticism has taken the form both of theory and application, from Senghor's ruminations on the African cosmology to the practical reviewing of single books. The theorizing is itself very revealing, but the practical criticism, tied as it is to concrete examples available to all, provides the most interesting and useful insights into what the African critical standards are. Theory is a reflection of taste once removed; practical criticism *is* taste —taste in action.

The question, then, in this instance, is whether African critics actually use characterization as a critical standard in arriving at their evaluations of African novels.[1] To answer this question requires, quite simply, a survey of the body of African literary criticism. I have attempted to do this on a more general level elsewhere.[2] But on the specific question of characterization it develops that there are, indeed, several instances wherein African critics have judged African novels, at least in part, by a standard of characterization.

Perhaps the most serious discussion of characterization in the African novel is to be found in the pages of *Transition* magazine during 1965. Obiajunwa Wali opened a lively debate when he suggested the African novelist's difficulty in creating character out of a society in which the individual is "tyrannized" by the communal design of that society. Wali said,

In a certain technical sense, then, we say that the character in traditional African society does not exist, yet the African novelist in order to make his craft possible is forced to hammer out characters from this social block which are amorphous in many ways.[3]

[1] The point might be made equally validly by examining African criticism of non-African novels, except that the question of an added constraint—the constraint to consciously use Western standards in evaluating Western novels, insofar as that is possible for an African—might come into play, thus rendering the criticism suspect for our purposes here. Ali Mazrui coins the useful phrase "aesthetic dualism" in his article, "Aesthetic Dualism and Creative Literature in East Africa," *Cambridge Review* (23 Oct. 1970), pp. 11–17, 20.

It seems fair to assume that the African critic, if he is to exhibit African critical standards at all, will be most likely to do so in evaluating African literature. Whether he applies those standards to non-African literatures seems a matter of personal psychology too complex to consider here. The examples used, then, are taken entirely from African critical evaluations of African novels.

[2] *African Critics and African Literature: A Study of Critical Standards, 1947–1966.* Ph.D. diss., Michigan State University, 1970.

[3] Obiajunwa Wali, "The Individual and the Novel in Africa," *Transition*, No. 18 (1965), p. 32.

Wali also notes the other side of the difficulty—the novel form itself—saying,

> The greatest challenge for the African novelist then is the question of character in so far as character lies at the centre of the structure of the traditional form of the novel, and in so far as the African writer, looking for themes and settings distinctively African, becomes involved in traditional African society.[1]

Regardless of the difficult problem he has raised, it seems reasonable to conclude that Professor Wali sees character as an important element in the African novel. Moreover, rejoinders by Austin Shelton (an American critic), B. I. Chukwukere and Wali himself, though they do not deal with the concept of characterization as such, exhibit a tacit acknowledgement of its importance in their dissection of Obi Okonkwo, the central character in Chinua Achebe's *No Longer At Ease* (London: Heinemann, 1960)[2]

However, the place of characterization in African literary criticism by no means rests on this teapot tempest alone. The manifestation of it is more often to be found in practical criticism—in reviews. The earliest example of this seems to be in a mid-1950's review of Peter Abraham's *A Wreath for Udomo* (London: Faber & Faber, 1956), which another African writer, Cyprian Ekwensi, said he liked because

> The Africans, not fully realised in the first part of the book, suddenly come into their own. . . . One feels a genuine involvement in the fates of the actors of this

---

[1] *Ibid.*, p. 33.

[2] See Austin J. Shelton, "Ewo!" *Transition*, No. 20 (1965) pp. 7–9; Letter from Wali, in the same issue, p. 10; and B. Ibe Chukwukere, "That 'Wet-Eared New Graduate. . . .' ," *Transition*, No. 23 (1965), pp. 7–8.

fevered drama and each one comes to an end at once
unexpected   and   dramatic   but   thoroughly   in
character.[1]

In comparing Robert Wellesley Cole's *Kossoh Town Boy*
(Cambridge, England: Cambridge University Press,
1960) and Camara Laye's *The Dark Child* (trans. James
Kirkup, Ernest Jones, and Elaine Gottlieb. London: Col-
lins, 1955) Mr. K. A. B. Jones-Quartey preferred the
former because

> *Kossoh Town Boy* is in fact a remarkable achievement
> in correlation. The development of the story and the
> progression of thought and language match almost
> exactly the development of the hero from childhood to
> the relative maturity of age—seventeen. Camara
> Laye, to make a comparison or two, is simple and
> beautiful throughout *The Dark Child*, with no very
> great psychological or literary inflections up or down,
> as book and boy get older.[2]

Alfred Hutchinson reviewed T. M. Aluko's *One Man,
One Matchet* (London: Heinemann, 1964) very favora-
bly, in part because

> the main strength of *One Man, One Matchet* lies not
> so much in the magnificent characterization. There is a
> fascinating interplay of character and motivation. The
> characters are drawn with warmth and sympathy and
> at no point does the author try to manipulate them for
> his own ends.[3]

[1]*West African Review* (June 1956), p. 603.
[2]"A Sierra Leone Surgeon," *Universitas*, IV, 4 (Dec. 1960), 121.
[3]"Quality and Less," *The New African*, IV, 5 (July 1965), 114.

Obi Egbuna wrote that *Toads for Supper* (London: Harvill, 1965), by Chukwuemeka Ike, was "the most engaging West African novel I have read in recent years. . . The characters, whether Ibo or Yoruba, student or porter, male or female, intellectual or intelligent are real, living, convincing."[1] Alex Chudi Okeke, writing in an Nsukka newspaper, *The Record*, says of *Weep Not, Child* (London: Heinemann, 1964) that

> James Ngugi, like most proficient writers, has succeeded a great deal in his character delineation in as much as he has endowed his characters with flesh and blood so that they live before the reader. They have human feelings and reactions to situations and circumstances surrounding them. However, it is only Ngotho and Njoroge who have full, elaborate characters while others lack personalities and lineaments and therefore, become representative rather than individual characters.[2]

Not to ignore the African critics writing in French, Olympe Bhely-Quenum said of Achebe's *Le Monde S'Effondre (Things Fall Apart)* (trans. Michel Ligny. Paris: *Presence Africaine*, 1966),

> on admirera d'autre part le portrait d'Ezinma, la fille d'Okonkwo, à laquelle ce père de famille se sent très attaché parce qu'elle a du caratère . . . il y a aussi Ekwefi . . . son portrait est aussi réussi que celui de sa fille et de la terrible prêtresse chielo. . . .[3]

---

[1]"With No Pinch of Salt," *The New African*, IV, 9 (Nov. 1965), 213.

[2]"Ngugi Recounts the Ills of Colonialism," *The Record* (Nsukka) (Oct. 15, 1966), p. 4.

[3]*L'Afrique Actuelle*, No. 18 (mai 1967), p. 49.

'Kunle Akinsemoyin liked Ferdinand Oyono's *Houseboy* (trans. John Reed. London: Heinemann, 1966) because, among other things, "For me, Toundi lives and symbolizes the avenging spirit of Africa that must be appeased before Africans and Europeans could live at peace in Africa".'[1]

And Chris L. Wanjala approved of John Munonye's novel, *Obi* (London: Heinemann, 1967) in part because "In Joe and Anna the author has strong characters who symbolize an attempt to merge the old and the new values of life in Nigeria."[2]

But characterization receives comment not only when it succeeds. In fact, its validity as an African critical standard is increased just as much when the critic applies it negatively. Donatus Nwoga says of Onuora Nzekwu's *Blade Among the Boys:* (London: Hutchinson, 1962),

Unfortunately, Nzekwu does not show in this novel the imaginative ability that could have turned this important situation into the powerful drama that it ought to have been. Patrick as a person is lost in his surroundings. He is seen from the outside. We get just a faint idea of his rudimentary reactions to his surroundings, his thoughts, his feelings. The mainspring of his life is hidden from us. Patrick's mother actually emerges as the only fully realized person in the novel. . . .[3]

Of Wole Soyinka's novel, *The Interpreters* (London: Deutsch, 1965), Nwoga says that

[1]*Nigeria Magazine,* No. 96 (Dec. 1968), p. 51.
[2]"The Old and the New Do Not March," *Busara,* III, 1 (1970), 59.
[3]"Ibo Village Life," *West Africa* (July 28, 1962), p. 827.

the characters are too much unlike us, they have too much of the artist's temperament for us to follow with complete sympathy and understanding the problems, thought and attitudes that they depict.[1]

John Nagenda deals at some length with the characterization in *Weep Not, Child:*

Mr. Ngugi narrates the misfortunes in which people are caught, in a reporting, almost cataloguing manner which strangely enough for all its blood and thunder lacks any breath of real life. Part of the trouble lies in his characterization. I feel that all his characters are a continuation of his beliefs and desires and that he manipulates them at the end of a string throughout. It is as if his thoughts and words took human shape and became now a Ngotho, now a Njoroge and so on. And the result is a sterile and unmoving reproduction of many James Ngugis. And the result of this is that we feel not a flicker of spontaneous sympathy for his characters, whatever their misfortunes. Now this is a tragedy for the whole work, because Mr. Ngugi has staked all on his characters. We are meant to experience the whole drama through them. To be successful he would have had (if you will excuse the high falutin') to dip his pen into the Well of Life and his characters would have appeared directly from the Well, and they would have had a separate existence from him, the author. This would have been good writing.[2]

I. N. C. Aniebo is equally explicit in his review of Chukwuemeka Ike's *Toads for Supper:*

[1] *Ibadan*, No. 22 (June 1966), p. 63.
[2] *Makerere Journal*, No. 10 (Nov. 1964), p. 70.

There is ample evidence of his, Ike's, understanding, sympathy and insight into undergraduate life in Nigeria even though his description of it is not as deep as I would have wished. It is this lack of depth that has made those parts of the novel dealing with life in the University less convincing and very much like storytelling for children. Consequently his characterization in these areas leaves a great deal to be desired. . . .

In his next novel, I sincerely hope Mr. Ike will tell us more about his main characters. A catalogue of actions and action-thoughts do not bring a character to life, neither do they win the sympathy of the readers. He should try to create an atmosphere that would give a ring of authenticity to his characters.[1]

And Shiraz Dossa, writing in the student magazine, *Nexus,* says of *The Promised Land* (Nairobi: East African Publishing House, 1967) that

. . . the main weakness lies in the fact that Grace Ogot's short story technique has been extended into a novel which does not achieve a depth of character and complexity that a full length meaningful novel demands. In an attempt to present "a fantasy" she has in fact sacrificed consistency and complexity of character.[2]

Let us examine next what Mr. Okpaku, the critic who explicitly calls for African standards, has to say concerning Chinua Achebe's *A Man of the People* (London: Heinemann, 1966):

---

[1]"The Straight and the Whorled," *Nigeria Magazine,* No. 86 (Sept. 1965), p. 219.

[2]"A Web of Spells," *Nexus,* I, 2 (Aug. 1967), 47.

Odili's inability to live up to his masculine responsibility by failing to go to Elsie's aid when she calls out to him at the height of Nanga's barbarous and unbridled passions . . . is very unconvincing. No Nigerian, especially one bold enough to spit in the Chief's face the next morning, and considering his great sensual will at that crucial moment, would have failed to attempt to rescue his girlfriend from an amoral brute whose intentions he has suspected all evening. By the same token, one is not convinced when he now charges that Elsie is a prostitute, since it is more plausible to believe that she was overpowered by Nanga (raped, maybe). Building the rest of the plot and action on this frail base, giving Odili only puerile vengeance for motivation, results in a structural weakness, which is the major shortcoming of this otherwise well written novel. More structural unity can be derived by considering Chief Nanga, and not Odili, as the central figure, since Odili seems too weak and shallow to effectively serve in this role.[1]

Amin Kassam reviewed Okello Oculi's novel, *Prostitute* (Nairobi: East African Publishing House, 1968) unfavorably because,

I cannot help wondering if Oculi actually intended his prostitute to be a person—she is more a type, a spokesman for her kind. The only time she comes alive for me are in her description of her love affair with Bisi and in the last chapter when she thinks nostalgically of her former friends.[2]

---

[1] "A Novel for the People," *Journal of the New African Literature and the Arts*, No. 2 (Fall 1966), p. 77.
[2] *Busara*, II, 2 (1969), 59–60.

One might go back, finally, to 1962 and cite any number of passages from Ezekiel Mphahele's *The African Image* (New York: Praeger, 1962). In his chapter entitled "The White Man's Image of the non-White in Fiction" Mphahlele indentifies his critical taste with another critic's:

> E. M. Forster says in his *Aspects of the Novel* that when a novelist wants to strike with direct force, it is convenient for him to use "flat" characters; characters who can easily be labelled and therefore managed. Alan Paton's characters are nearly all flat. We can almost hear them groan under the load of the author's monumental sermon. . . . (p. 131)

But if there is any doubt that Mphahlele condones this "direct force" in Paton's *Cry, the Beloved Country* (New York: Scribners, 1948), he goes on to say

> Paton makes the most of his setting. Without it he would not have a story. . . . Paton might have attempted to study the characters of people in a process of change. . . . As it is, we get ready made characters, because he wants with a swift stroke to convey a message. We merely hear about the deterioration of Absalom's morals. . . . We do not actually see Absalom's demoralization in process. We do not even know what he thinks about himself and the social order he finds himself in . . . Human nature is falsified because there are bad characters as against good ones—in two distinct groups. . . . Paton is much more progressive than Sarah Gertrude Millin and there is a warmth in him which the latter doesn't have. But both of them present flat characters who are a mechanical instrument for the execution of plot and

the communication of a clearly defined message. Olive Schreiner and William Plomer, on the other hand, regard non-Europeans as an organic part of the setting (pp. 132–133).

Of another white African writer he says

It is a pity that a writer of Elspeth Huxley's system could not employ her wealth of anthropological material about the Kiyuku to create memorable characters in her earlier novel. The characters in *Red Strangers* are very much like pre-historic man to whom so many things happened without stirring in him a will that he could impose on the scheme of things and defeat its course. In *A Thing to Love,* on the contrary, there is a clear focus on character. (p. 151)

Nevertheless, Mphahlele has reservations toward her second novel as well:

Raphaelo has immense possibilities as a character. But I think Mrs. Huxley concentrates too much attention on plot and stereotypes to build him up and allow him to develop. (p. 153)

Mphahlele's point in the succeeding chapter, "The Black Man's Literary Image of Himself," is that, compared to the white African writer he has just discussed, the black African writer is more successful at developing black African characters as an "organic part of the setting." But apparently they too have had difficulty with characterization. He says,

Perhaps [Sol T.] Plaatje was too much of a historian, journalist and politician to visualize character independently of the historical events in which people were involved. (p. 176)

Of *Wild Conquest* (London: Faber & Faber, 1951) Mphahlele says

. . . Mr. [Peter] Abrahams fails to control the character of his witchdoctor because he tries to make him bigger than he really is. (p. 179)

And of Mako in Abraham's *The Path of Thunder* (New York: Harper, 1948. London: Faber & Faber, 1952) he says.

It is an underdog speaking about the underdog. But it is just this kind of protest which limits the emotional and intellectual range of characterization. (p. 180)

If characterization is not the only literary standard Mphahlele uses, it is certainly a primary one. That it is applied as well by a large number of other Africans is perhaps a reflection of Mphahlele's position as one of the leading African critics of the day. If would be difficult to say what influence his book has had on subsequent criticism, but the numerous examples I have offered above would suggest that his influence certainly has not been a negative one.

It is possible, I suppose, that the use of characterization by African critics is indicative of what Mr. Okpaku would call "studied" African taste. It would be nice to know what Mr. Okpaku means by "studiedness" and who is to be the judge of it. I assume he means by "studied" those critical values and tastes developed by Africans in the West, or at least outside of Africa. He may have a point—I don't know. Certainly many (though by no means all) of the critics I have quoted have spent some time in the West, either travelling or working or pursuing their education. And it is quite likely that their collective aesthetic has become to some extent Westernized, and perhaps even to the point of being in some cases more Western than African.[1] The pertinent question here is: Are we to define "African" by what *is*, or by what *should be*? I am being descriptive; perhaps others prefer to be prescriptive. I would simply point out here the sensitivities brought into play when Professor Larson is prescriptive, as opposed to Mr. Okpaku's being so. Whether Mr. Okpaku is pleased or displeased with the state of African literary criticism is a point on which we have not yet been enlightened. Yet I think critics ought to be at least somewhat cognizant of the tradition they have helped to create and to consider its future direction—and this is particularly true at this point in time in Africa. But the African critic must also be aware, I think, that he is creating a tradition as fast as that tradition is being defined. As Jean-Paul Sartre has said of Negritude, "you make it and it makes you."[2]

But to return to Professor Larson's paper. It turns out, then, that Professor Larson was using what is in fact an African critical stanuård. The salient point here, however, is that he was not aware—or did not seem aware—of using an African standard; he seems to be using a Western, "universal" standard which then becomes, logically, somehow, in his mind, African. I am not so concerned here with arguing for or against universal standards; only the methodology by which one describes a universal. Even if one accepts the possibility of universal standards it would seem that one is yet a long way from describing them. Does one say, *a priori*, that char-

---

[1]See, e.g., Ali Mazrui, *op. cit.*, note 12.

[2]*Black Orpheus*, trans. S. W. Allen (Paris: Presence Africaine, 1963), p.59.

acterization is a universal and then go on to prove it? Or does one hypothesize that universals exist and then go about learning specifically what they are? The latter approach is clearly what our African colleagues are demanding of the Westerner approaching African literature.·

But there is another aspect of the African/Western dialogue to consider. What do we call this critical standard—in this case, characterization—after we have identified it? Is it African? Western? Universal? Characterization is certainly an important standard by which Western critics judge Western novels; and I suspect Professor Larson was using his own (Western) standard in arriving at his evaluation of African novels. However, this cannot mean, by definition, that characterization is an *un-African* standard. And yet neither do I think it is inherently or exclusively Western. Characterization as a critical standard is not the sole property of the West. It is merely *a standard*—a standard which happened to have been chosen, some time past, by the West. But certainly the fact that the West chose this particular standard before the advent of modern African literature does not make it exclusively Western, to be loaned out only to the loyal and obedient. Nor does it seem very intelligent to claim that, since the novel is a Western form, conceived, nurtured and—so the argument must run—"perfected" in its present state by Westerners in the West, so the ground rules for any future development of it must come from the West. To carry this specious thought to its logical conclusion would mean that some great-great-great grandchild of Mr. Richardson would today be legislating furiously to stamp out the pernicious and worldwide aberrations threatening the purity of the Derbyshire novel! No, the African critic is free to choose his own standards and, in choosing, will thus incorporate them into an African tradition. But the critical standard he chooses may be one that has also been chosen by another literary tradition; it is made African by virtue of its being appropriated by Africans. I do not think there need be any immediately recognizable "Africanness" about the standard for it to become African, just as the converse is true for any other literary tradition.

I suspect that if one surveyed the literary criticism of India, one might find characterization there as well. Is it then Indian? I suspect the sanest answer to that insane question is that it is Western, African, Indian—all of these with the exception of "universal." Our African colleagues seem to be saying—and I quite agree—that it is *not* universal, at least not yet, because no one they know of has surveyed the world's literary criticism (nor are they likely to, I should think) in order to describe the parameters of this "universality." Hence we may *never know* if characterization if a "universal" or not. The question is: *Does it matter?* I hardly think so. The important thing to remember is that the African concept of characterization is no more Western than the Western concept of it is African. They may be very similar concepts, but more important to remember is that they have been chosen by different critical traditions.

Having identified, I hope with some degree of accuracy, one standard of African literary criticism that has been used with some regularity over the past fifteen years, I hasten to point out that my finding imposes nothing on anyone. By identifying past and present critical standards, one is by no means prescribing those of the future. This may be done by African critics, or the criticism may develop entirely freely. I am convinced, however, that a better undersanding of what these standards have been in the past can be of use both to the African and the Westerner; to the African in providing an overview of the critical tradition he is developing, and to the Westerner in making clearer how this tradition differs from his own.

Finally, I hope these thoughts will contribute to the dialogue between Western and African critics which Chinua Achebe thinks is possible "with frankness on either side."[1]

---

[1] "Where Angels Fear to Tread," p. 61.

THREE AFRICAN POETS:
A CRITICAL REVIEW

By B. EZUMA IGWE

Masizi Kunene, *Zulu Poems* (New York: Africana Publishing Corporation, 1970). Kofi Awoonor, *Night of My Blood* (New York: Doubleday & Company, Inc., 1971). J. P. Clark, *a Reed in the Tide: A Selection of Poems* (London: Longman, 1971).

For long, criticism of writing by Africans has been of two types. The first approach seeks, whether by design or not, to look at this body of writing from the point of view of western aesthetic assumptions. It has quickly categorised works in prose into the established forms—short story, the folk tale, the novel, etc. As for poetry, it is seen as a personal utterance (with all its rhetorical implications), expressing human experience, exploring the nature of reality, and employing certain devices and strategies of thought that are pertinent to the particular form adopted. Even the few Africans who point out that Western aesthetics cannot justifiably be imposed on African work fail to dissociate their modes of critical thought from the same assumptions about art which Western influenced critics have made. Thus, we cannot say that the poet's voice "comes through in the best of his lines—a beat which, coupled with the simplicity of the diction, captures the mood and slow pace of African contemplative speech" and still claim to be non-Western critics. In the first place, the notion of the beat in lines and the simplicity of diction is a recognition of the verbal communicative devices specifically employed in well-defined contexts and for defined purposes in a particular linguistic setting. Hence, in the second place, the idea of the mood and slow pace of African contemplative speech is sheer nonsense, because there are thousands of African linguistic groups and for each the verbal devices of communication vary. And the suggestion that "we have to use the foreigner's techniques and art forms to enrich our art, to release it and thus make it available to more of our people" is one that fails not only to grasp the deepest link between language and literature but also the nature of the very best writing from Africa. Literature could be the embodiment of belief or thought, but most importantly, it is the embodiment of language. What the good writer from Africa has done is see the foreign language as an encyclopedia of linguistic symbols which his imagination organises from principles based on the linguistic techniques and strategies of thought inherent in his first language.

There is no denying that this is difficult to accomplish, and the attempt to grapple with it in terms of thematic criticism has not been too successful. In merely recognising the pattern of contrast that informs a lot of writing from Africa, that is the conflict of old and new, the traditional ethos and the colonial structure, the village father and the new, emergent son who inherits the city, etc., one has simply set up an irresolvable moral dilemma both for the artist and his audience. The result is a stasis, bordering on ennui, which does nothing but kill art. And yet it is so important to make the point that African literature is alive, and quite significantly, exists on terms totally independent of any other tradition but the African one, and cries to be examined on these terms. The best of our literature appeal to a tradition that is un-Christian and un-Western. They do not incorporate the myth of Christ, or of the Fall; neither are they bound hand and foot to the myth of rationalism. But when we get away from these constructs of Western man's belief and more into the realm of the imagination, we can begin to perceive analogies (psychic and archetypal) between African literature and any other literature. Paradoxically, it is only when the former is viewed this way that it is most meaningful. And it is on this level that one can look at the works of these three very distinguished poets.

What recurrs in their poems is what Northrope Frye in another context has called the myth of concern. The concern arises out of the wish of every human society to protect and preserve those structures it considers important for its own survival. It also seeks to perpetuate the continuity of those structures. The evolution of Western tradition and art has seen the artist on both sides of the struggle about concern: Sometimes he is on the side of conservatism, seeking to preserve the known edifices of society—even when they are merely conceptual. At other times, he takes up the banner of the opposite myth (that of freedom). Because the history of most African nations took a similar turn from the nineteenth century onwards, a particular kind of concern has been generated, and the artist has responded with a thrust for tradition. The urgency of the concern is expressed by the artist's feeling that the fact of man's very being is so threatened that it is possible to conceive of his spiritual extinction, *at a point in future time.*

This whole notion these poets have handled in similar and, sometimes, different ways. In all three there is a sense of an alien myth superimposed on society, resulting in both a clouding of the traditional society's myth of itself and the inception of another myth—Western man's conception of history and evolution. This is a monumental clash, but notice how deftly Masizi Kunene puts it into harness:

A man enters and marks down our generation
And tells us how suddenly summer has come
And makes us sing though our hearts are bleeding

Knowing how because of us,
We who are the locusts with broken wings,
Our shadows shelter the earth from the sun

The dominant metaphor in J. P. Clark's "Flight Across Africa" is that of cow-slaughter. The poet looks at the body of Africa as it

                    lies
Slaughtered, the splintered green plantain
About her. Still the coaches and trucks
Pummel the body, their tracks
Or scars, sharp lines against the skies . . .

The progressivist myth of new Africa has slaughtered the tradition that has been man's experience. The old ritualistic sacrifice has been perverted into mere vulgar brutality. The poet in Kofi Awooner's "The Anvil and the Hammer" is

Caught between the anvil and the hammer
In the forging house of a new life . . .

The tradition that embodies man's most meaningful experience, the "trappings of the past" which normally connect man to the golden age of the ancestors have been vulgarised, being now "laced with the flimsy glories of paved streets". Therefore, on behalf of his audience, on behalf of a threatened cultural group, the poet prays for spiritual anchor:

> Sew the old days for us, our fathers,
> That we can wear them under our new garment,
> After we have washed ourselves in
> The whirlpool of the many rivers' estuary . . .

For Kofi Awoonor, the myth of a lost past is expressive of the lack of spiritual freedom for the poet and his audience. In "I heard a bird Cry", the protagonist is haunted by visions of spiritual aridity and moral decrepitude reminiscent of the theme of an earlier poem "In my sick bed". As the symbolic tree dries out in the desert, the poet laments that "The singing voice which the gods gave me has become the desert wind," and there is a metaphysical compulsion underlying his destiny:

> I shall leave you
> So that I can go to perform the rites for my gods
> My father's gods I left behind
> Seven moons ago

The motif of the journey that pervades a lot of his poems is used to portray the spiritual journey not of one person into himself but to restore "the fallen walls of my father's house". Only when the past is grasped this way can man talk of the present. No significance can be attached to the latter because it is a profanation of the old ways that have been central to man's moral and spiritual survival. Against the vision of dogs

> Tramping precious things underfoot
> And stray hyenas carry their loot
> To the cleared patch in the forest,

the poet postulates a climatic one at the end of "Salvation":

When discoverers land on far off shores
And the others who took the big boats return
We shall find our salvation here on the shore, asleep.

The ritual ceremony which cleanses the sojourner and makes him worthy of his find is significantly the same that radically restores for a people a sense of their past as part of their present moment. It also makes them aware of their past as history. But knowledge of that past is not based on the evolutionist myth of progress or the Heraclitean succession of time. The history of man does not record his knowledge of the objective world. For most African peoples the exact times and dates are not important. Time is defined in terms of man's experience of it, and the myths that draw his attention to it. In the central poem, "Night of My Blood", the poet recreates the myth of Ewe history. The journey from what is now Dahomey to their present home in south-eastern Ghana becomes more than a reminiscence of man's activity in a temporal order. It is rather an imaginative journey through a collective experience of refinement by fire—the process that prepares the people for inheriting the land of their dreams. Thus, the poet apprehends the past as part of the present moment and subtly suggests that it is only when the present is seen this way can it become part of any conception of an "other" world. Otherwise, man is left only with a sense of a temporal future which offers him no hope of spiritual anchor and no means of deciding the manner of his being. Man remains inept, as the poet raises important questions of concern:

Shall we jump and clutch at the stars
Singing hosannas
Shall we sing the flesh feeling songs
Of goose-pimples,

> Or shall we sing the new songs
> That are on the lips of the street boys?

Against the inhuman and life-denying Western myth of concern that has been thrust on the people of South Africa, Kunene constructs a structure of imaginative belief. For him, the situation of his people is archetypical. Whereas Jewish history rests very much on the myths of prophecy and revelation, the South Africans, who archetypically represent oppressed and persecuted man, see themselves in terms of different imaginative postulates. Hence, the tortured agony of man, because it arises out of the most abject injustice (which is part of the objective world), must, almost with the compelling necessity of natural law, be counterpointed by an era that promises social freedom and imaginative release. The new era is an expression not of a purpose that has roots in an 'other' world but of a natural wish—that of the right to exist. Throughout the poems, one does not get the sense of lament that is everywhere in Awoonor. Rather, there is a firm, authentic voice of belief—quite simply, that the sons of the soil will inherit the land because natural processes will move toward that direction. Thus, most of the poems are informed by one structural principle —*anagnorisis*. They move from a situation of a mind in pain, or in doubt, or from the destruction and death that inexorably dogs a morally arid temporal order to a vision of a future that is its exact opposite:

> The end of the cycle is the beginning of the cycle
> Years come carrying firewood on their heads
> And meet the day alight with ferocious flames
> Burning your breasts in their firmness

Time moves as a wheel of fire, burning out all the base matter that characterises an impure age, and thus prepar-

ing the way for the sojourners to pass through to the land
of their dreams, the ultimate vindication of man's existence:

Beautiful one, stretch the umbrella of the sun
And allow us to pass in your parades
Singing in the afternoon with the blades of grass
Which sleep as we sleep and fertilise the earth.
It is then that our flesh will merge
Into the beautiful one, making our legends beautiful.

This is not pantheism, but the natural consummation in
collective experience.

What is most interesting about Kunene's poetry is the
way the myth of concern is subtly worked into a thought
pattern. Whereas in Clark and Awoonor the concern is so
passionately stated to the point of obtrusiveness, in Kunene the reader and the protagonist must, one feels, leave
the broken images of an immoral ethos (usually suggested at the beginning of poems) for the almost paradisiac
one at the end of the poem. The *anagnorisis* therefore,
for both the poet and the audience he is addressing,
becomes above all a psychic and metaphysical necessity.

Pepper Clark writes a slightly different kind of poetry.
A lot of the poems in this collection are "international-
ist", and in some of them there is a disturbing sense of
verbal exuberance. This may not necessarily be a weakness because he of the three poets is most self-conscious-
ly aware of his role as an artist, and a particular kind of
artist at that. He writes the kind of poetry that puts him in
the tradition of Western-oriented humanism. Thus, his
subjects are chosen from all over the place, and his forms
are as varied. Above all, he is conscious of writing in the
tradition of the English language. (How this must affect
his poetry is the subject of another paper). His is a highly
personal poetry, dealing with issues that form the

subjects of one man's speculative and imaginative mind: "Fulani Cattle" asks what the secret of living is. In "Abiku" the poet does not raise any moral questions but merely expresses the importance of man's healthy instincts for his survival, man's constant concern as an aspect of his very existence, and man's attempt to cope with process. "Girl Bathing" is a powerfully-realised composite image: The protagonist is at once a sea goddess, a symbol of plenitude and fertility, and the objectification of the poet's aesthetic quest. The subtlety of the relationship between the poet and the apprehended object lies in the way the former has worked into the scene another composite image—that is, the log as a male (and the phallus), as poet, as observer, as the traditional quester. Still, the finest of Clark's poems are those that deal with African subjects. In these he demonstrates his ability to draw upon, and express forcefully, a tradition that he knows very well. The delicacy and interplay of images evoked in "Night Rain" come from an experience authentically felt.

In "Agbor Dancer" the poet successfully recreates a state of being that is midway between stasis and motion in time. The dancer is "caught in the throb of a drum". This unity between the instrument and the performer is part of the thematic statement that emerges from the structure of the poem: Rhythm is being. It is also expressive of instincts that are alive, of the final union between the world of objects and a conceptualised one, and between the initiates in a cultural tradition. The poem moves from a contrast between the old African oral tradition and the new written one, between ecstacy and sensual ineptitude, from the apprehended image to the explicit statement of concern:

> Could I, early sequester'd from my tribe,
> Free a lead-tether'd scribe

> I should answer her communal call
> Lose myself in her warm caress
> Intervolving earth, sky and flesh.

The anagnoristic vision everywhere in Clark is an erotic-mystical union between the protagonist and his wished-for spiritual order.

The loss of faith in the present temporal order has given rise to their postulation of an order that is based on different ethical principles, an order that combines the past, present, and future into a timeless whole.

The summation of their achievement as poets lies in the very definite sense, that emerges from their works, of a poetic that can be defined only in terms that are African. Whereas the poetry of the West has lost it, the poets from Africa have been enabled by the turn of history to fulfill the role of speakers for the community. In the tradition of most African societies, the community takes precedence over the individual. But the latter may raise a cry on behalf of the former whenever its structure is threatened. The figure that filled this role was the 'senex' or the priest. But he is a dying figure now. Besides, another myth of concern (modernism, technology) has been imposed against which he is hardly equipped to fight. Moreover, the tradition has taken a radical turn toward the literary. Therefore the mantle has fallen on the poet. Our guise is not the artistic mask, the impersonal 'I' but the garb of authority that enables the speaker or singer to express the 'collective conscious', the ethic and values of the community. Notice the pervading sense of collective experience in the works of these writers. The collective 'we' is a moral datum, the 'I' emerging only when there is a detectable excommunicant. Not only in the question of poetic knowledge—that is, the manner images of reality are apprehended—but also in the nature of the poetic devices, these poets show

how close they are to the tradition that nurtured them. What is most significant in Kunene's

Beautiful tree of Jomela,
You sheltered us from northern winds
And devoured little plants.
You stood alone on the hill top
Where the afternoon dances with its red feathers

is not the personification of the tree, or its apparent symbolic use, but the fact that the idea of a living tree is not only part of traditional African belief but is also part of *everyday* thought pattern. The fact of a tree walking is not an intellectual construct but a reality that does not depend on any rationalist evidence to authenticate it.

These three are in the tradition of the best poets from Africa.

TABAN LO LIYONG:
EATING CHIEFS

By M. MICERE MUGO

The most immediate impact of Taban lo Liyong's
Eating Chiefs is perhaps the power to arouse in the reader
a nostalgia for the now almost extinct 'evening around
the hearth' of African traditional setting. For those days
when myth, legend and folk-tale narration was a vital
part of traditional African society's routine entertainment. Liyong is so close to the tone, rhythm and style of
the traditional narrator that it is often difficult to
distinguish between his voice—the voice of the artist—and that of the narrator. This is good. It clearly
illustrates, among other things, that after all not all that
hard digging may have to be done to recover what is
lying buried under our 'Excavation Sites'.

Mind you, saying this is not to maintain that in *Eating
Chiefs* Taban lo Liyong has broken fresh ground. Other
African writers before him have already done
so . . . Achebe, Ngugi, Okot p'Bitek—but more so,
Wole Soyinka—to mention the most obvious. All these
have in their own way made use of anthropological
collections. From his plays, specifically: *Kongi's Harvest, The Strong Breed* and *A Dance of the Forests*—so
thoroughly steeped in Yoruba mythology, legend and
tradition—it is surely obvious that Soyinka is involved in
the artistic preservation and interpretation of anthropological material. More important, the plays are presented

235

in such a way that this specific traditional background gives meaning and relevance to wider and contemporary issues. Hence, one hopes that the author's statement: "It is my aim to induce creative writers to take off from where the anthropologists have stopped" is not a claim to pioneership. *If* Liyong has broken fresh ground, it is in the sense that he has *retold* rather than *drawn from* the oral literature of his people. However, the point is, he has done it in a very meaningful way—expertly blending their flavour by maintaining the aroma of the old and enriching it with the fragrance of the new.

Mythologies make up some of a nation's most permanent forms of artistic expression. Rightly preseved, they can provide a literature for all times. They can become the safe in which a society's social and inner life/meaning are hid. In *Eating Chiefs*, Taban lo Liyong has involved himself in this vital process of preservation. And not only that; many pieces in this book contain a great deal of challenging material: they address themselves to some of the most pertinent issues facing us to date.

The book is divided into three parts. Part One mainly consists of stories and poems narrating what could perhaps be called 'the gradual self-dispersion of the Lwo peoples'—their migration movement. Most of the pieces tell the old tale of brother quarrelling with brother, division resulting and each taking the opposite direction to search for his fortune. In this section, two notions that seem to stretch the reader's elasticity a bit too far are raised. The first is the 'Child of culture' idea from "The Spear, Bead and Bean Story." The idea is forced, one feels. The author seems to be striving to establish a theory, to prove a point about the quality—the validity of the culture he is writing about . . . something like that. And is this necessary? The other one is the story, "How

Nyikango went to Heaven.'' It is very unconvincing and out of keeping with the rest of the pieces, to say the least.

However, what is of greater consequence in this first part is the quality of a lot of the prose and poetry. Listen to this smart juxtaposition of riddle and double-meaning in ''The Spear, Bead and Bean Story'':—

''A man is not a man without his spear. With his spear he can defend his own and win his wars and kill his game. In our spear, our manhood resides. In our manhood, our spears are found . . .'' Beautiful. Liyong's style is in keeping with African speech rhythms, patterns and modes of expression. Here is another lovely example of interplay between/play upon-
. . . deliberate ambiguity, riddle and puzzle, accompanied by appropriate movement. (It comes from ''Nyilak, the Famous Girl of the Plains''):—

''Nyilak stood fixed; fixed down by that lustful stare/(-the beast moved forward and backward; Nyilak moved backward and forward)/Then they rested; the creature went backwards; Nyilak went homewards/True to her promises she had never met a man.'' Here we have a very complex devise that is rather intricately mastered.

One of the most appetizing qualities of traditional tale-telling was the use of parable. This devise, Liyong really successfully recaptures from time to time in this book. To give several examples . . . From ''Gods favour those Born to be Kings'' apparently, Kijok, in his desperate efforts to win the contest with his brothers (in these particular lines, the beer-drinking part of it) he: . . . ''pulled and pulled and thought there was a taste of beer/He halted a while and found only bitter saliva of anxiety and rage/He pulled again but almost pulled his cheeks in.'' In ''The Spear, Bead and Bean Story'': . . . ''the daughter vomited and had induced dysentry for three days and nights and for three days and

nights the bead did not come out. She almost passed her
intestines out. . .'' Perhaps while at this, we might as
well cite two more from the third section of the book, for
it is impossible to resist that piece of advice by the
cunning elder of the fugitive 'clan' to the young hunters
in ''To you Crazzolara'':— . . . ''Whenever a young
man kills a large animal like the elephant, giraffe, hippo,
buffalo, rhino, lion or leopard for which a *tyer* is due the
chief, the young man shall not blow his whistle to indicate that he has killed the beast. . . . But whenever a
young man kills a rat, he shall whistle up to heav-
en. . . .'' Delicious! Very typical African humour! As
is the description of Apwoyo dancing: . . . ''And he
blew the horn. And he danced and danced. And he
sweated a whole lake. . . .''

Part Two is the section that probably best fulfils the
proposed function of the kind of literature transmuted by
Liyong in this book. He says that in order to live,
. . . ''our traditions have to be topical; to be topical they must be used as part and parcel of our contemporary contentions and controversies.'' Whatever this statement specifically refers to, to a socio-political-oriented
mind, the second section of the book deals with some of
the most fundamental concepts regarding government,
leadership, acquisition of power and the whole business
of the exploiter versus the exploited. For, surely the
Obibis (greedy devourers) of this world sooner or later
force their victims to strike—to reverse the situation—so
that the Obibis too taste of . . . ''the bruises and cuts
only his victims had known'' . . . before. And are
there not millions and millions of citizens in this world
who would cry with the men and women of ''Kid-
napped'': ''Here we are . . . dying of hunger/And Ba-
ratogo cannot provide for us/Here we are, all getting sick
and old: signs of pain/And our Chief cannot give us an
ear.'' ??? How about the brand of politics in ''The Path

of Reason is a Twisted Thing"? Or "Taming the Savages"? Don't we recognise the dirty gymnastics of power politics—the unjust triumph of material ambitions, mundane values? Don't we witness a confirmation of "the survival of the fittest" theory in operation? The story of "Obura the Just" does not happen often enough in the world we know! These collections tell of very familiar and living situations. They function as parables. Some of them are so grim with the horror of life's injustice that it is a treat to turn to a piece like "Recent Occuring"—a hilarious anecdote, the irony and dry humour of which combined, make the poem a superb off-colour joke. Such farce too! A similar but much more complex style makes "Types of Reasoning" one of the poems I have most enjoyed reading. The narrative is rather cleverly balanced: one aspect of it is bursting with energy and drama (the conceited chief's part); the other is considerably calm and sustained (this is the collective voice of Padere elders). The platform opens with the conceited chief, absolutely in love with 'self' and thoroughly drunk with greed for power. He comes struting and striding like a peacock, trumpeting from so high "up there" that he identifies himself with the deity. But his loud-mouthed blowings misfire because they are checked in time by the cool, reasoning; but firmly warning collective voice of the elders of Padere . . . Beautiful contrast and balancing, climax and anticlimax. Effective deflation, in which the over-acted part of the braggart becomes melodramatic–no, turns into farce, before the dignity of the elders. The emptiness and bankruptsy of the chief's values is thus embarrassingly exposed.

In this piece, the elders fully play their traditional role as the official critics of society and its rulers. This proper execution of the critic's role contrasts sharply with that of the old councillors in "Nyilak" who 'dared not mutter as the bread at court was sweeter." Incidentally, if someone gets into a situation where she/he is looking for a verse-speaking piece, try this poem.

Part Three contains more stories of Lwo migration, while 'looking' at some of the societies (formed by the movement) in function. The reader is given a glimpse into some of the mores, the values, along which they operate. It is introduced by a motto which, superficially read, seems to state the exact opposite of what it should: *Ok Ichiem Gi Wadwu*—"Thou shalt not Commune with Thine Brethren." However, the accompanying stories and poems eventually interpret the paradox. Recurring statements—though they appear variably worded in different pieces—continually reinforce this motto. The motto's overriding message seems to be that, blood and social ties should not be turned into bonds that tie the people down to a small circle of acquaintances; but that men should constantly be creating new brothers, forming new friendships. In other words, relationships between human beings should not be merely determined by such limiting factors as historical events, geographical placements, social groupings, and what have you. . . . It is an appeal for a sense of 'the greater family'. In "Lacek Obalo Kaka", Atiko, who is wounded by the humiliation he has suffered at the hand of his own brother, is taught by painful experience (after "a brother came forward in the form of a friend from Ometta") that "brothers are born as well as made." In similar spirit, "Angulu" is a call for the young generation to enact and record history anew—the history of its own epoch, that is—rather than stagnantly feed and dwell on the events of the past, for: "It is meet and right/That each age should create its friends and enemies/without the briefings of the old."

Fresh, meaningful relationships; goodwill and the generosity of a large heart . . . all these, are part of the above recurring theme. But, needless to say, the above observation is not to establish that all the writings in this section can be fenced within the framework of the outlined themes. Each poem or story carries its own specific message. For instance, three of perhaps the most appealing of all the writings contained in this section touch on other themes all together. "Omera, Cip Aye Otera Itim" is a beautiful song by a rebel girl who can obviously put together the two and two of the whole business of African preferencial male-child treatment. Oh, It's delightful! It echoes the 'melody' of Okot p'Bitek's *Song of Lawino.* "The division of Labour among the Pari" contains good news for women still fighting for liberation. I mean, it is good to hear of a society in which women are so liberated! Lastly, that superb story of "The Birth of the Heartbeat" dedicated to Lubuc, the famous Ugandan Ding Ding dancer. I dare say that those who have seen the dance, the Heartbeat of Africa, do not blame Apwoyo all that much for being so thoroughly captivated by the beat. Criticism is rather levelled at his shirking of responsibility—failing to fulfil the male duty of providing for the family; to put first things first.

THE PLAYS OF SARIF EASMON

By E. TAIWO PALMER

Sarif Easmon has been almost universally acclaimed as Sierra Leone's leading writer, and his plays have been performed successfully, not only in Sierra Leone, but throughout West Africa. But whether this reputation is entirely deserved is a debatable question. This article will try to demonstrate that Easmon's artistry is defective and that although the issues he deals with are relevant to the African situation, the conclusions he arrives at and the values he endorses are repugnant to most Africans.

Easmon's first play, *Dear Parent and Ogre* which, like all his works, is set in his native Sierra Leone, deals with class-consciousness, social snobbery, and the conflict between the generations. On the surface, Easmon seems to attack all forms of hereditary privilege, and the attitudes which these help to foster, and proclaims that in the future the dominant class in Africa will be, not the artistocracy, but the meritocracy—the group of young men and women who, regardless of origin, have pulled themselves up by their own exertions. In the play, Dauda Touray, an aristocrat of the old school, bitterly opposes his daughter's determination to marry Sekou Kuyateh, who comes from the poor, beggarly class of Yalies. Sekou is now a flourishing pop star with an international reputation and Siata, the daughter, is determined to marry him, even if this results in a clash with her father. For his part, Dauda wishes Siata to marry Mahmoud, his new political ally. After a series of incidents in which, *inter alia,* Dauda and Mahmoud narrowly escape death by drowning and are subsequently accused by Siata of planning an attack on Sekou at Lumley Beach, Dauda is brought to see reason. He consents to the marriage and everything ends happily.

This outline of the play seems to confirm Sarif Easmon's modern liberalism, but when the play is thoroughly considered, a few awkward questions suggest themselves. The first concerns the accuracy of the details to the facts of Sierra Leone Life. The aristocracy from which Dauda Touray is descended was in all probability a Susu or Madingo aristocracy whose sphere of influence was confined to a small area of the Northern Province of Sierra Leone; they could not therefore have shaped the destinies of the whole of Luawa for centuries, as Dauda claims in the play. As Easmon implies, this Susu aristocracy would have despised the Yalies, who were a group of professional singers belonging to the same tribe, but their modern descendants would almost certainly not behave in the way Dauda does. In the first place, they would have been removed from the real centres of power for generations; secondly, although many of them would probably be occupying positions of responsibility and importance, they would still be rooted in their tribal culture and traditions and would not strain after the pseudo-Western "Culture", "Sophistication" and "Refinement" that Dauda seems to yearn after. Thirdly, they would certainly not demonstrate Dauda's social snobbery.

Dauda's brand of aristocracy recalls the old Creole aristocracy rather than a Susu one. The Creoles are descended from liberated slaves who settled along the Sierra Leone Peninsula in the late Eighteenth and Nineteenth centuries. Some of these families came to occupy positions of power and influence and could be said to have formed an aristocracy. But their influence was confined to the Peninsula or Colony area, and their modern descendants, though retaining some of the aristocratic flair, have also been removed from the real centres of power, and very few would practice Dauda's conscious social snobbery. Moreover, Easmon falsifies the structure of political parties in Sierra Leone. It is unlikely that Mahmoud and Dauda would have belonged to opposite political parties based on class differences. They both seem to belong to the same tribe (although Mahmoud is half-Creole) and from the very beginning they would both have belonged to the same party—a party largely based on tribal loyalties. The shaping force behind political parties in Sierra Leone today is tribal loyalty, not class differences. Class distinction, in the sense it is known in some of the Western democracies, hardly exists in Sierra Leone. Our major problem is tribalism, and this Easmon almost completely ignores in the play. The fact is that Easmon exaggerates the class problem and ignores the tribal.

Turning to the details of the play itself we discover that these issues and themes are not only imperfectly conceived, but also inadequately pursued, and this becomes most obvious when Siata's role is considered. Siata is intended to be Sarif Easmon's standard bearer, for she is the girl who champions the cause of the meritocracy against the aristocracy, and Easmon seems to give her his complete endorsement. But if we examined her carefully we would discover that she demonstrates all the vices that Easmon associates with Dauda's brand of aristocracy—social snobbery, materialistic concern for fast cars and champagne, and a certain yearning after Western values. Siata is not in the least concerned with the fortunes of the meritocracy; she champions Sekou's cause, not for any idealistic reasons, but simply because she is in love with him. Furthermore Sekou is not an ordinary meritocrat; indeed, strictly speaking, he is not a meritocrat at all. He is a glamorous pop star who has got to the top of his profession and won the hearts of London, Paris and New York by virtue of his having a lovely voice. For all practical purposes he is a member of the aristocracy himself, in spite of his humble origins, for he speaks like them and is addicted to champagne and luxurious cars just like them. It is surely not very difficult for a girl like Siata to champion the cause of such a man; there is a sense in which she is as obsessed with his Rolls-Royce as with his face.

We get an even better insight into Siata's real character when we consider her treatment of Mahmoud Sawaneh, the only real meritocrat in the play. Mahmoud, a competent young man of tremendous determination, energy and industry, is a Trade Union leader who has pulled himself up from his humble origins to become leader of his own political party and subsequently deputy Prime Minister. And yet when the possibility of marriage to this genuine meritocrat is mentioned to Siata she exclaims: "Daddy are you trying to insult me? I—marry that—that—half-Creole, halfslave—and one-hundred-percent demagogue! DADDY!" It would have been perfectly acceptable if Siata had objected to Mahmoud on the grounds that she was not in love with him; but as it is, her outburst is the nastiest thing said by anyone about anyone else in the play, and it is motivated by consciousness of social superiority and tribal difference. Siata's response seems even more atrocious in the light of subsequent events, for as the play progresses, we see that Mahmoud is anything but a demagogue who bullies the trade union movement and whose eyes are solely set on power, as Siata claims. Indeed, he even saves Siata's father from drowning in a feat of selfless heroism.

Dauda was clearly intended to be the reactionary, snobbish, aristocratic ogre, and it is true that he is made to say some very snobbish things in the play. But he recognises Mahmoud's worth to the extent that he is prepared to form a political pact with him, and after the drowning incident Mahmoud becomes his best friend and associate—the only person he is prepared to accept as a son-in-law. This does not suggest much consciousness of class. The truth is that Dauda, the supposed aristocrat, appears to much greater advantage in this play than Siata, the supposed champion of meritocracy.

Sekou, Easmon's treasured meritocrat, is an ineffective and rather feminine young man who utters nothing but sentimentality whenever he speaks. If Mahmoud had not come to his aid to help carry the standard of meritocracy, we would all have been sent rushing into the arms of the aristocrats for confidence and assurance. Moreover, Sekou is himself a snob. In spite of what Easmon tells us, he is secretly ashamed of his own father. For instance, in one of the scenes of the play (Act two, Scene two) Sekou is seen having a discussion with the members of the Touray Family when his father walks in unexpectedly and Easmon tells us, in what is supposedly a stage direction, that "he was a little put out, but certainly not ashamed of his dad." Why, in that case, is Sekou "a little put out", and why does Easmon need to stress that he is not ashamed of his dad? Sekou then goes on to say to his father in the presence of the entire Touray family:

> Father, you don't need to go playing your balanyi for a living. I send you enough every month, surely. I saw the improvements you've made in the house. I had hoped you'd give up all this and live a little more comfortably.

If Sekou were the decent young man Easmon thinks he is, he would not have said this to his father in the presence of virtual strangers. The truth is that Sekou is ashamed of the fact that his father plays a balanyi for a living. Dauda's son, Saidu, who also professes sympathy for the meritocracy, is nothing but a humbug—a parasite who hangs on to Sekou, not because he respects his capacity for work, but because he can make money out of him.

It seems, then, that with the exception of Francoise, Dauda's French wife, all the characters who are supposed to champion the cause of the meritocracy, are unattractive and demonstrate little real concern for meritocrats. The main reason for this is that in spite of the lip service he pays to the idea of a meritocracy, Easmon himself and almost all his characters are attracted to the values of the artistocracy, associated as these are with Western value judgements. The tenor of the entire play, the behaviour of most of the characters, and the atmosphere of the Dauda home both before and after the crisis, undermine Easmon's professed intention at the start. One of the major problems in Africa today is the difficulty of instilling into young and old alike a proper sense of values, a serious concern for the things that matter, and a sense of priorities. Easmon's work offers them false values—luxurious cars, champagne, nostalgia for Paris and New York—all adding up to a quality of life which is not only foreign, but for the average African impossible of achievement because it is so expensive. And these are the values of his aristocratic class.

However, the main objection to Easmon's work concerns not so much the nature of the values he endorses, as the defectiveness of his art. *Dear Parent and Ogre* conspicuously lacks action and a coherent plot. From the beginning of the play right up to Act Two, Scene One, there is very little action deriving from the interrelation of characters and issuing from the dialogue, and in order to get the plot moving Easmon contrives an accident—the report of the drowning. Again and again we shall discover in Easmon's work that he can get action only by resorting to incidents of this kind. And even after the announcement of the accident action is generated in Easmon's stage directions rather than in the dialogue. From Act Two, Scene One to Act Three, Scene One, the play stagnates again until another "accident" occurs, this time the attack by hooligans on Sekou at Lumley Beach. From this point onwards the play sags in interest until the end.

Since at the start of the play Dauda objects to Siata's marriage with Sekou, the movement of the play should surely be towards a change of heart on Dauda's part. We expect certain incidents to occur which will shock him into a realisation of the worth of the meritocracy in general and Sekou in particular. But nothing of the sort happens. What brings about the change of heart is the discovery that his wife and daughter intend to leave him. We are informed that relations between the three have deteriorated since the attack on Sekou, for Siata and Francoise think that Mahmoud and Dauda are responsible; hence the decision to leave. But we have been permitted to see nothing of this process of deterioration in the Dauda household, and in any case we are informed towards the end of the play that Siata and Francoise knew all along that the man who planned the attack on Sekou was Foday Touray, not Dauda or Mahmoud. So why the cooling-off of relations? Why the threat to leave for Paris? Dauda's change of heart is not convincingly motivated and the overall impression is that the plot of this play is very crudely managed.

Sarif Easmon's language is stylised, pretentious and archaic, and its main effect is to make his characters sound ridiculous even when they are at their most serious. A single example will do to make the point. This is Dauda giving an account of the drowning scene:

When the ferry gathered speed and began really to

rush at the first boulders in the rapids, I was so
terrified—my emotions overshot mere funk. At the
first teeth-rattling impact with the rocks, the feel of the
pontoon just vanished under my feet. I must have
flown like a shell from a cannon. Up-Up-Up with,
very oddly, a feeling of detached exhilaration. Then
the river rushed up at me. Ugghhh! Why is water so
monstrously wet and cold when it comes on you unexpectedly? . . . And now I could not believe the vast,
serpent coils of whiteness that surrounded and en-
gulfed me, roared in my ears and sought to dismember
me—I could not think this cruel, vicious thing could
be water! But then—I could not think at all . . . I
confess I screamed like mad as I was swept over. . . . No doubt it was there that I got this wound
on my head. I must have been concussed. . . . (Act
Two, Scene Two.)

If Sarif Easmon's intention had been to satirise Dauda at
this point he could not have chosen a better device. But
satire is out of the question because as the scene
progresses we realise that he gives Dauda his unqualified
endorsement. The conclusion one arrives at is that the
comic effect is not deliberately intended, but has been
achieved by crudity of technique. Easmon does not seem
to be in touch with the feel of the language as it is spoken
by normal men, for his characters often speak in a way
which recalls neither a modern African nor a modern
Englishman. He has no conception of "register" or the
appropriateness of linguistic devices; his language is not
the language of dialogue but of debate and declamation.
Here for instance is a comment made by Siata to her
stepmother:

Well said, ma belle maman! But here, dear Francoise in this home where the base that singly and

jointly Europe and Africa can offer have been given a
new vitality—HERE I should have hoped such ser-
mons were unnecessary. (Act One, Scene One).

For humour Easmon often resorts to cheap Oscar
Wildean witticisms such as this statement by Dauda, ''I
carry my pride as I carry my drink—I never allow either
to intoxicate me''.

The weakness of Easmon's characterisation is partly
demonstrated by the fact that his characters are always
involved in actions which are psychologically implausi-
ble. Is it possible that Sekou, who seems such a
well-bred young man, would reveal to Siata and her
family the contents of a confidential letter, containing
disparaging remarks about Dauda and the others? Is it
possible that Siata would tell Francoise, in Dauda's presence, that Dauda had been involved in the murder of a
handsome Yalie, especially as she seemed at that time to
have no reason for divulging such information? Is it
possible that Foday, an educated man, would reveal his
snobbery in such a stupidly blatant way? The whole point
about class snobbery is that it manifests itself in all sorts
of subtle forms, not as obviously as Foday demonstrates
his.

But by far the most damaging indictment against Easmon as a dramatist is his infringement of the cardinal rule
of impersonality. Impersonality is the essence of the
dramatist's art; he must disappear completely from the
scene and allow his characters to demonstrate his themes
by their actions and dialogue. He must create by becoming characters quite other than himself. However, Sarif
Easmon's imagination is such that he cannot stay outside
the work he has created. Consequently his characters
become mere puppets who are continually manipulated
by him in order to demonstrate his thesis. The presence
of the author in this play is even more strongly indicated

by the numerous stage directions which account for
almost a third of the play. An overabundance of stage
directions is necessarily a bad thing for it is both an insult
to the intelligence of the actor and a limitation of his
freedom to interpret the part as he sees it. It can have a
cramping effect and does not make for a good production. But the matter is much more complicated than this.
Let us look at one or two "stage directions":

(1) *Françoise* (whose consciousness is painfully
stabbed by Siata's sobs), . . .

(2) *Saidu* (He is very worried, both at the prospect of his father's death, and the
almost equally terrible responsibility
of heading the Touray clan). . . .

(3) *Dauda* (The effect of this statement on Mahmoud is devastating. It strikes straight
at all the complexes that hold his character in one piece. A shudder runs
through him. His features twitch, and
his voice shakes as he tries to
reply). . .

How does one act in order to show that what has just
been said strikes at all the complexes that hold one's
being together? How precisely does one show that one's
consciousness is painfully stabbed? How does one show
that one is worried at the thought of the responsibility of
leading the Touray clan? It needs only a little thought to
make the reader aware that these are not stage directions
at all, but Sarif Easmon commenting on the play and
interpreting its every act for the benefit of the reader. Yet
this should be unnecessary in a properly constructed
play. Mahmoud ought to act and say things which tell the
audience that Dauda's recent comment has a devastating
effect on him. We should be able to gather from Saidu's

words and general behaviour that he is worried about becoming the head of the Touray clan. But Sarif Easmon needs to comment because he has failed to create sufficiently interesting situations and dialogue capable of carrying his meaning without his intervention. His stage directions, therefore, are partly an attempt to eke out the deficiency of his art. Some of the stage directions give information which is already obvious as when, for instance, we are told in a "stage direction" that Foday has inherited the worst of the Touray pride. We do not need this "direction" to tell us that Foday is the most stupidly snobbish of all the Tourays. Some give directions which the most stupid actor should have been aware of in any case, as in this one:

> *Sekou:* (continues in deep passionate tones) Even my music would cease to have meaning if life had not the promise of you. (Act Three, Sc. One).

An actor who does not realise that he must say these words in "deep passionate tones" should not be in the business. Some of the stage directions are used to give information that should have been given in other forms. For instance, we are told in one that in the days before Mahmoud, Dauda had been anxious for Foday to marry Siata. How is an audience watching the play on the stage and not reading it in a study expected to know this? The truth is that three-quarters of the stage directions are unnecessary; they are only made necessary by the defectiveness of Easmon's art.

This fondness of commentary correlates with an addiction for "showing-off". In this play, Easmon "shows-off" his knowledge of music, especially Wagner's, of Byron, of French, and of Continental pleasure resorts, in a quite unnecessary way. Indeed, it is clear that the most powerful character in Sarif Easmon's plays is Sarif Easmon himself. One must also mention that a number of the scenes are irrelevant and point to the author's lack of control over the details of the play.

A well-made play is a composite of plot, action, characterisation, dialogue and themes properly conceived and adequately worked out. We cannot say a play is good because its author seems to be saying good things. A play is much more than a collection of moralistic statements on certain themes put into the mouths of certain characters. We expect to see these themes demonstrated through the characters' actions and dialogue and through a skilful working-out of the plot. Judged by these standards, *Dear Parent and Ogre* seems a failure.

In his second play, *The New Patriots,* Sarif Easmon quite justifiably sets out to attack the corruption, tribalism, political incompetence and mismanagement which were so rife in post-Independence Africa. There was a tremendous need in Sierra Leone for someone to mobilise all the disgust that ordinary citizens felt, not only towards the regime of the day, but also towards the practice of politics in general. Sarif Easmon supplied that need, and wrote what could best be described as a tract for the times. The Nigerian novelist, Chinua Achebe, had written a similar work, *A Man Of The People,* in which he mercilessly exposed the corruption and immorality which characterised Nigerian politics, and he was later hailed as a prophet in that the calamities he forecast at the end of the novel came true with the 1966 coup. Easmon's work could also be described as prophetic since some of the charges he made against Ministers were fully borne out in the lurid details revealed by the various commissions of inquiry, set up after the second Sierra Leone coup in 1967. These facts help to explain the play's popularity; playgoers and readers felt that Easmon was articulating the sentiments that they themselves felt as they surveyed the mess that politicians had made in many parts of Africa. It is true that Ministers were corrupt and used their positions to amass wealth; it is true that judges of the Supreme Court were put under extreme pressure to give verdicts favouring the government of the day; it is true that civil servants were victimised; it is also true that certain Ministers were openly tribalistic in their outlook. These are the facts of history, and audiences from Freetown to Lagos applauded the play's realism. But they would still have applauded had Easmon merely read these facts out in a public lecture or written them up in an article for the local press. What was being applauded was the truth of the play's allegations, not the playwright's literary achievement. The literary critic who looks on the play as a play on the stage, or reads it in the study, is likely to come up with an entirely different verdict.

If Easmon chooses to communicate his views in a play, and not in a speech or an article, then he is expected to conform to certain dramatic criteria and he must expect to be judged by those criteria. We need therefore to consider how satisfactory The New Patriots is as a play, and not as a piece of propaganda or polemic article. The play can only be regarded as satisfactory if one considers morality plays satisfactory, for it has all the trappings of a morality play—the dramatic equivalent of a "moral fable" in which "the moral is peculiarly insistent". Its conclusion is the morality type conclusion, in which rewards and punishments are distributed as if the characters could be strictly categorised into "black" and "white"; it is a conclusion which seems to ignore the complexity and double-sidedness of most of the characters as we have experienced them. Furthermore, in this play, there is an excess of preaching, of thesis-stating and sermonising and each of the characters is liable at any point in the drama to come forward and deliver a "speech" on the evils of tribalism, corruption in government circles, the need for an independent judiciary or the incompetence of the cabinet. The following remark of George's could be taken as an example:

> Politics is not a prize in a vacuum, man. It's people who make politics possible. In a few years Kelfah will be a voter. Don't you think you owe it to the thousands like him who voted for you, to worry your head even a little to find out what they think and feel? Do you think you have become God because you've become a Minister? Anyway, whatever you say, nobody is going to lock Kelfah up. (Act One, Sc. One.)

One's overall impression is that the moral in this play is much too insistent.

In a sense *The New Patriots* is an advance on *Dear Parent And Ogre,* for its plot is much more closely knit and much more expertly constructed. The leading characters, George, Barbara, Byeloh and Hayford junior, are all introduced in the first scene, so are the main themes of corruption, ministerial incompetence and tribal consciousness. It is also suggested that in spite of his smooth exterior, John Hayford is quite capable of double-dealing in matters of love. In Act One, Scene Two, the themes of corruption and tribal feeling are further developed, and we already begin to see the consequences of John Hayford's philandering. In Act Two, Scene Two, we see the full extent of the clash between Mahmeh and her father, caused not only by John Hayford's licentiousness, but also supposedly by Byeloh's tribal consciousness. In the next scene the full extent of the corruption and fraud in Byeloh's Ministry is revealed, and the clash between him and his permanent Secretary, John, comes to a head. The third act brings the nemesis, with Byeloh paying the penalty for his misdeeds. He loses his daughter who marries his greatest enemy John Hayford; he loses his best friend, Barbara, who marries George Hayford, and he also loses his job. At the same time, George Hayford is hailed as the hero of the hour. From this survey it is evident that Easmon has developed greater assurance in his handling of plot than was evident in the earlier play.

Furthermore, there is more action in this play resulting from the interplay of characters and dialogue. Scenes such as those involving John Hayford and Mahmeh, or John Hayford, George Hayford and Byeloh, or Mahmeh and her father, are powerful, and have their fair share of interest and suspense; but they do not owe these to any trumped-up action or violent accident, as is often the case in *Dear Parent and Ogre*. There are also fewer psychological implausibilities, and although psychological penetration is still not Easmon's forte, he has improved on his characterisation. The study of Mahmeh, Byeloh's daughter, who is torn between love of John and her father, is subtle and convincing, and Barbara is much more acceptable as a good woman than Francoise in *Dear Parent and Ogre*, or Makallay in the novel, *The Burnt-out Marriage*.

The New Patriots then, has some virtues, but it also has glaring weaknesses and it is doubtful whether it survives them. The most important of these is the lack of adequate demonstration of some of the qualities attributed to the leading characters Byeloh, John Hayford and George Hayford. The result is that to the reader, the moral judgement offered at the end seems inadequate and wrong-headed. For instance much is made of Byeloh's hatred of the Creoles; he is supposed to harbour a pathological hatred for his Creole permanent Secretary, John Hayford, because he envies him his pedigree, and his cleverness and superiority, even over the white man. While it is true that Byeloh says some very nastily tribalistic things in the play, he does not entirely act like a man who is tribally conscious. He behaves with marked respect and affection for Barbara with whom he was brought up in a Creole household; he is fond of Barbara's daughter Vi, and his relations with John up to the point of the inquiry are cordial, as far as we can see. Towards the end of the play, George Hayford accuses Byeloh of having conjured up every plot in the book against John; but we have been shown very little of this process of plotting; we have seen very little demonstration of this hatred of John in particular, and the Creoles in general.

We are also informed that Byeloh has been involved in fraudulent practices and that in order to conceal these, he has had to "steal" a certain file and extract several leaves from others. At the end of the play, the file is discovered, and it is proved to have been locked up in Byeloh's home. But we would have liked to see much more solid demonstration of Byeloh's corruption than the information of the missing file and its late discovery in his home. Momoh Seisay's corruption, for instance, is convincing, because he tells us of it himself; he boasts about it and gives us a list of some of his activities; this is why he emerges as the real villain of the play—the man without a conscience and without scruples.

Byeloh, on the other hand, has a conscience and he does have scruples. After the Prime Minister lectures the Cabinet on the need for honesty in the Administration, he seems to have been the only one who was struck by the P.M.'s statement:

But to be frank, Momoh, the P.M. worries me. It is something more than conscience that's wrong with him now. He was almost in tears when he addressed us today. He was so distressed to point out that if we arrange fiddles, we're taking the money right out of the country's general development fund. Put like that it makes one feel like a thief. I was mightily uncomfortable when he said that the man who offers a public servant a one-pound bribe is sure he can compensate himself by robbing the country of up to a hundred pounds. (Act One, Sc. Two.)

Very few African Ministers would have the honesty to admit this. Byeloh also sees the unfairness of increasing the up-country allowances of Ministers' threefold, while rejecting the workers' claim for a wage increase of ninepence a day, and he suggests that the increase be granted: "I think we should be more sympathetic to the workers' case. After all it is the people who put us in power." This is the most human statement made by anyone in the play, including the self-righteous Mr. Justice Hayford. When Seisay suggests that the country needs a dictatorship which would bring the press to heel and shoot all troublemakers, Byeloh replies: "I know that government too: you'll have the whole population and its dictator all living together in one big jail. I hope we don't ever have that kind of thing here". Byeloh is a man of compassion, and he is not nearly so stupid as Easmon suggests he is. One of the blackest marks against him is his brutality to his daughter Mahmeh, after the discovery that she has lost her virginity to the libertine, John Hayford. There is no doubt about the extent of Mahmeh's suffering during this painful scene, and no one would condone Byeloh's meanness in planting the tape-recorder which reveals the damaging information or his harshness in calling Mahmeh a harlot. But we would be reacting wrongly to the scene if we did not realise that it called for a more complex response than this. For Byeloh does have a point. In his tribe and his society, the loss of virginity before marriage is a heinous offence, all the more heinous because the girl in question is the daughter of a paramount chief—the supposed guardian of all that is sacred in the tribe. This is what Byeloh means when he exclaims: "Ha, a thing of sacred note to your tribe, that was of so little account to you, you could lose it in the bush like a wild animal". Yet, he is contrite and repentant afterwards; he begs Mahmeh not to leave the house and when she does, he follows her to Barbara's and begs her forgiveness. One is not suggesting that Byeloh does not have faults; obviously, he does; but he is by no means as wicked a man as Easmon would have us believe, and he certainly does not deserve the harsh punishment he gets at the end. Nor is one suggesting that the pre-coup regime in Sierra Leone was innocent. It has been shown to have been corrupt, incompetent and tribally biassed. But an author writing a play about this should demonstrate the corruption, incompetence and tribalism within the context of the play. It is not enough merely to talk about it.

It is typical of the art of Sarif Easmon that the villains he is determined to condemn always turn out to be more attractive than the heroes he single-mindedly endorses. This is because the venom he directs against the villains always seems to be in excess of the bad qualities demonstrated; moreover the author seems to blind himself to their virtues and consequently appears personally involved in the wrangling and bitterness. Similarly the degree of idealisation accorded to the heroes is always in excess of the virtues demonstrated. This is certainly true of Easmon's portrayal of Mr. Justice Hayford. The Chief Justice is conceived as a man of high and unshakable principles. He is one of "the two men in the whole country who are above corruption" (the other is the Prime Minister). He is determined to keep the Judiciary independent and is prepared to tell the Prime Minister so to his face. He behaves impartially in conducting the inquiry involving his son and the Minister, Byeloh. He is the champion of the workers' cause and during the riots he is commissioned by the Prime Minister to soothe tempers and restore order, and he is subsequently hailed by all—workers and aristocrats alike, as the hero of the hour.

There is no doubt about Mr. Justice Hayford's moral uprightness, but this is perhaps the only attractive quality he possesses. In the course of the play his snobbery, his pompous self-righteousness, his vindictiveness and his lack of tact and good manners are obvious, even though Easmon does not seem to be aware of them. In all of Easmon's works, there is usually a rather "aristocratic" individual, who is intolerably snobbish and given to champagne and Western or pseudo-Western manner-isms. Mr. Justice Hayford must be the most nastily snobbish of all. He is full of his ancestry: "We Hayfords would be the cream in any society it may please God to set us. And I, George of that ilk, I'm the cream floating on that cream. No Violetta. George Hayford is not poor in any sense, least of all in having had the friendship of your parents—a couple he's always considered his equals in birth, in culture and all the good things of life that the uncultured these days affect to despise". George talks about the Hayfords in a way that the Earl of Salisbury would never dream of talking about the Cecils.

If George were the "cultivated" man Easmon claims he is, he surely would have realised that it is bad form to continue to punch an opponent when he is down; for George could be cruelly vindictive. At the end, when the unfortunate Byeloh has been reduced to nothing and is virtually in tears at the feet of Barbara, Violet, John, Mahmeh and the Judge himself, Mr. Justice Hayford cannot resist the temptation to rub the medicine home:

Bye: Why am I alive when my all is dead, and my one-time so-precious blood rises in treason against me? My own child! Oh,

	dear Bee, the one good that parents can do for the world is to bring the cruel race of mankind to an end by one protracted and universal act of abortion!
George:	Then your parents should have started that dirty ball rolling! Unfortunately for your country they did not. But even for filth God finds some use. Without you there would have been no Mahmeh. Her goodness compensates the community for the evil you have done.

Inevitably, in any discussion of Sarif Easmon's work, the question of the definition of "culture" arises. For Easmon, the word clearly means adherence to certain Western values—champagne, Western music, Western literature and Western clothes. When, for instance, George enters the stage for the first time, we are told in "stage direction" that he enters with natural dignity, that he is very elegant in a West-end London tailored suit and that he laughs in a rich cultured and very pleasant tone. We are not, of course, given any clues as to what a cultured laugh might be, but it is obvious that for Easmon, George and his son John are the epitome of culture. Whether the cultured man must be able to demonstrate an acquaintance with Western values is a debatable point, but most people would agree that good-breeding in the sense of decent, pleasant, good manners extended to all, and an ability to be tactful and to put people, especially inferiors, at their ease, are essential ingredients of culture. Judged according to these criteria, Mr. Justice Hayford is a most uncultivated man. He behaves towards Byeloh with studied rudeness. When Byeloh meets him at Barbara's during the first scene and greets him, he merely nods stiffly, and on one occasion he says to Byeloh: "Take it easy Mr. Minister. Neither the law, nor the Police was designed as a toy for a politician's second childhood". This is Sarif Easmon's "cultured" man.

Mr. Justice Hayford, then, has some of the most unpleasant qualities one would ever expect to find anywhere, and yet Easmon continues to give him his complete endorsement and to make him the hero of the hour. His son, John, gets similar treatment from Easmon. He is portrayed as a latter-day Knight Errant, rushing to the defence of the damsel in distress, dealing redoubtable blows to left and right, effecting an astonishing rescue and receiving the thanks of all-and-sundry for his bravery and gallantry. He is also presented as a well-bred and "cultured" young man, a most brilliant administrator and one of the cleverest Africans of his generation. But the reader knows, from what he experiences in the play, that John is a hypocrite, a libertine and a humbug. He has a double standard in so far as behaviour to girls is concerned for to sophisticated Creoles, like Violet, he behaves with the utmost propriety because he respects her, but he has no scruples about seducing the Mende girl, Mahmeh. And it could not be claimed that he seduced her because he loved her and wanted to marry her, for on his own confession he was not sure he was in love with her until the last moment when he was about to rescue her. Yet he pretends to his father that he is an anchorite with the highest moral principles. Moreover, the reader fails to experience his brilliance as an administrator, his cleverness and his "culture"

In this play Sarif Easmon claims to be attacking tribalism, among other things, but as usual in his work he ends up by demonstrating a tribal consciousness as venomous and nauseating as the very evil he would deplore. All the Creoles emerge as sterling characters and all the provincials as villains (with the exception of Mahmeh who, like Mahta in *The Burnt-out Marriage*, is claimed for Creole-dom) as if some of the most incompetent and corrupt members of the pre-coup regime were not Creoles. Sarif Easmon seems to give all the Creoles a pat on the back and to tell them what "jolly good chaps" they all are, and what a "shocking shower" the other lot are. Sheer animus is the force which informs his attitude in the play; his personal feelings have not been given an "objective correlative".

In *The New Patriots*, Sarif Easmon started with a simple intention—to expose the corruption, incompetence and tribal bias of the Ministers of the day and to set over and against these Ministers of the day and to set over and against these the brilliance and moral fervour of some of the people these Ministers despised. In conformity with the morality-type conception of the play, the good characters are idealised and the bad ones subjected to scathing denunciation, and at the end, rewards and punishments are handed out in accordance with this strict division of the characters into two moral categories. The play would have been perfectly acceptable had Easmon fully demonstrated the corruption and the incompetence on the one hand, and the moral excellence on the other; it would still have been acceptable if, realising the complexity of the characters on both sides as they actually appear in the play, he had altered his proposed conclusion. But in the absence of both of these, it is reasonable to suggest that Easmon's art is defective and that the venom he directs towards some of the characters is unduly harsh and unjustified.

Easmon has clearly not been able to eliminate some of the faults observed in the earlier play. There is still the same pretentiousness of language such as this statement of Barbara's: "Really, we women spend all our lives heaping fuel on the fire of men's self-conceit". The fondness for words for their own sake even leads to, at least, one misunderstanding of English idiom: "One

Minister does not make a Government any more than one swallow makes a summer.'' There are the outdated pseudo-Oscar Wildean witticisms such as this one: "Although the ideal of a gentleman like the sterlingness of the £, has long been off the gold standard, I'm still old-fashioned enough to consider myself a gentleman. . . .'' There are the spurious comments and stage directions telling us what should have been demonstrated in the play, the accidents contrived to introduce excitement and the undramatic set speeches.

That Sarif Easmon's work has been over-rated in Sierra Leone is hardly surprising considering the fact that Sierra Leone audiences are starved of drama, especially indigenous drama. But one of the most pressing problems in Africa today is the difficulty of establishing and insisting on standards which are universally acceptable, a problem which confronts us, not least, in the sphere of literary criticism. We have an obligation to make readers and audiences aware of the difference between the good and the bad, the great and the mediocre, and we will only do this if we apply the same criteria to the study of African Literature that we would apply to others, and if we stop praising works for patriotic, political or sociological reasons. The most important test must be the quality of the author's literary achievement and by this test, Easmon seems to fail.

THE DEVELOPMENT OF THEATRE IN NIGERIA 1960–1967

By ERNEST EKOM

Until about 1960, talk of modern theatre experience in Nigeria refered to the concentration of dramatic experiments in Ibadan, centred on the University College Arts Theatre, and, to a lesser extent, in the other Nigerian regional capitals. The common feature was that they were all amateur directed.

Two groups of amateur dramatic societies used the University College theatre-house: the University College Dramatic Society, a student group, and the Arts Theatre Production Group, formed in 1957. Between them, they produced plays ranging from the Greeks, through Shakespeare, to Bretcht.

Outside the University, there were other amateur groups. In Ibadan, were based *The Players of the Dawn*, later absorbed in a newer group, *The 1960 Masks* of 'Wole Soyinka. In Lagos, as in Enugu, Kaduna and other principal centres, there were long established amateur dramatic societies, mainly among the non-African expatriate communities. Their theatricals served mainly to entertain a narrow circle of friends.

What might have passed for a professional theatre company was a group like the Hubert Ogunde Concert Party, consisting of "touring . . . entertainers specialising in extravagant melodrama, spiced with dancing and music and heavily laced with morals. . . ." ("New

Theatre Review'', 1959, art. M. Banham). And that they are still.

Spirit of 1960

In 1960, with Nigeria's independence, a new spirit was infused into every aspect of the national life, by the urge for progress connected with the attainment of nationhood. Artists sought to express the new national awareness in their work; and the theatre usually provides an excellent medium for such expression.

Propitiously, two Nigerians who were to influence the local theatre scene considerably, appeared on the scene, working in two widely separated areas of the country. 'Wole Soyinka, the dramatist, was based in Yorubaland—in Ibadan and Lagos—where he was doing post-graduate research. John Ekwere, actor-producer, and also a graduate in English, worked in Enugu in the eastern territory.

The 1960 Masks theatre group was born, Lagos based, but largely using facilities and material at Ibadan. The group's first production at the Arts Theatre, Ibadan, was Soyinka's own prize-winning Independence play—''A Dance of the Forests''. In Enugu, John Ekwere revived an old existing group, the *Ogui Players* into the *Eastern Nigeria Theatre Group.*

Thereafter, despite limitations of theatre facilities, financial support, indifferent audiences and dilenttantism, the amateur theatre in Nigeria gradually settled down to evolving into a modern theatre of indigenous experiences.

In tracing this growth of the modern theatre in Nigeria in the post-independence years, it is convenient to examine the development under three broad heads: the University theatres, MBARI activities, and the popular *concert groups.*

The University Theatres

Nigeria's oldest university, the University of Ibadan, has been the focus of most of the drama activities that may be linked with the universities. It ran the only School of Drama in the country, offering full-time courses in drama: theory, acting and production. But the school dates only from the 1962–63 session.

The Ibadan achievement is in giving amateurism a definite goal, and a respectability that it had long lacked among the generality of possible audiences and performers.

Play productions were usually considered as "concerts", where the word meant the "variety concert", and as entertainment, rated inferior. This concept is dying hard. The university groups, however, helped in the new realisation of the seriousness of what a production sought to do. That besides entertainment, each time a playgroup put up a production, they are attempting to re-enact on the stage the way society lives; expressing its ideas, actions and shortcomings with the clarity which the selectiveness of art makes possible.

"Theatre-on-Wheels"

The chief agency in effecting the continuing process of re-education of performers and audiences alike has been the University travelling theatres—the "Theatre-on-Wheels"—pioneered by the University of Ibadan Travelling Theatre.

The travelling theatre was initiated by the Student Dramatic Society, Ibadan, in 1961, following successful campus experiments in make-shift theatre, which involved taking plays round to the student audiences in their halls of residence. The dining halls became temporary playhouses for the productions, which used no scenery and minimum of equipment.

The play for the first road tour in March 1961, in which the Travelling Theatre covered 2,600 miles, was an adaptation of Moliere's famous 'Scapin'. Moliere himself largely borrowed the play from the Italian comedians—the travelling theatre of his time. So the "strolling players" of "comedia del arte" arrived in West Africa with "Suberu" (the title of the Ibadan Travelling Theatre's adaptation).

The Travelling Theatre was an experiment designed to spread the experience of good theatre to places outside the cultural centres like Ibadan, Lagos and Enugu: to reach as large audiences as possible, at prices they could afford. At the same time, it was a demonstration to schools and colleges and community drama groups of what they could do within limited facilities towards establishing a popular contemporary modern theatre in Nigeria.

Drama School

The establishment of a drama school further strengthened the amateur theatre, while providing the first signs of professionalism. It converted the Travelling Theatre into a highly successful medium of popularising modern theatre, in the form of experimental theatre.

For the theatre workshop is an invaluable part of the drama school's more organised training in modern techniques of production, acting and writing, involving not only undergraduates seeking practical experience for courses in theatre, but all classes of people within and outside the university.

The 1965 production of the Travelling Theatre Ibadan, for instance, was a song-and-dance adaptation of a popular Nigerian novel, "Danda" (author: Nkem Nwankwo). It involved established musicians, painters, intellectuals and domestics; provided training ground for actors, set designers, choreographers, playrights and producers. In performance, it enthralled both the Nigerian who had some experience of a Broadway production, and the local taxi driver who had wandered into the performance purely out of curiosity.

University of Nigeria

An interesting development of the Travelling Theatre productions was the rise of an orchestra of talented students, with some professional guidance, who provide musical backing to productions. The University of Nigeria, which has a Music Department, developed the idea into a full-blown production of the South-African musical "King King", late 1962. Thereafter, there appears to have been a change of emphasis in the University of Nigeria, Nsukka group of musicians to choral works —with resultant loss to the drama movement there.

By early 1965, however, the University of Nigeria drama circle had joined in the travelling theatre experiment, with its own production.

Students come and go, however; a student has a limited number of years to study at any university, and even the drama student has other academic demands made on him. By and large, the university is, nonetheless, the only place where a reasonable measure of continuity can be counted on in amateur groups in a developing economy with uncertain job opportunities (as the drama enthusiast lived on some other vocation). There were always better opportunities for replacement.

In the six years, since 1960, the student amateur dramatic societies in the universities in Ibadan, Lagos and

Nsukka—particularly in Ibadan—had shown a remarkable improvement in acting skills, writing and student productions.

In June 1965, the first students taking full courses in drama at Ibadan's School of Drama graduated. Within a few months of the graduation exercises, there was the first concrete instance of the school's success, in the emergence of a professional trio, "Theatre Express". And before the eclipse of the civil war, another graduate of the 'dramatic circus', Sonny Oti, was trying out theatre for a living in Port Harcourt and the eastern communities.

But the success of the attempts at professionalism were yet indeterminate.

Mbari

The great weakness of amateur drama in Nigeria was the lack of co-ordination: of a co-ordinating centre or organisation. It was this kind of orientation that succeeded in making professionals out of the traditional dancers, notably, the Atilogwu dancers.

Despite their interest and their positions as cultural centres, the universities could not fill this need. The universities have a primary function to society which, while it touches on the nation's cultural life, makes demands far beyond and to the exclusion of active "promotion" of this culture in the sphere of business and public enterprise.

Such involvement, therefore, had to come from outside the universities; from government or private organisations or individuals.

One such possibility was the government-sponsored agency, the National Arts Council, with its regional branches. The approach of these Councils has been, however, too empirical to promote any real development in the arts.

The annual Festivals of the Arts produced brief periods of intense activity succeeded by protracted inaction. They encouraged competition, no doubt, in the tradition of the Greeks; but without a comparable communal acceptance of the form as among the Greeks, such competition tended to split, rather that unite, the tiny proportion of the citizenry struggling to popularise modern theatre. It is not surprising that the method has contributed to establishing the indigenous dance—a widely accepted communal artistic form—but failed, within the same period, to improve the theatre.

Competitive elements alone, in the present stages of development of the theatre and related arts in Nigeria, segregate rather than share experiences, and co-ordination is impaired. The venue for creative exercise all the year round, for local theatre and the performing arts, which neither the universities not the Arts Councils had been able to provide was offered by MBARI.

MBARI is a club for African writers and artists, which was founded in Ibadan in 1961 as an independent forum for co-ordinating efforts in developing the arts. MBARI originates from the ancient religious cult in Owerri districts,[1] where it is the name given to unique shrines that house assorted mud sculpture by renowned local artists expressly executed in honour of the goddess "Ala".

Modern Mbari promotes arts exhibitions and arranges publications of short, select new writing (mostly poems and plays); and sponsors productions of talented work by new, unknown indigenous playwrights. Thus, in the Nigerian theatre scene, Mbari functioned like the Royal

[1]Now in the East Central State.

Court Theatre of London, catering for new playrights; and without *Mbari*, the play "Song of a Goat" (J. P. Clarke) might not have gained recognition when it did, and the Nigerian theatre might have missed the impetus that single play gave to it.

Before the 1967 civil war, there were four MBARI Centres in Nigeria: in Ibadan and Enugu; and in Lagos and Oshogbo (where they were called "Mbari Mbayo"—an obvious attempt to give the concept local colour). The Enugu MBARI helped to make the Theatre Group based there, led by John Ekwere: a group whose performance was such that it represented Nigerian theatre at the first Commonwealth Arts Festival in London (1965).

The Mbari Mbayo centre at Oshogbo, established by the German scholar Ulli Beier (one of the founding members of MBARI) has inspired and played a special role in the success of Duro Ladipo's Yoruba Folk Opera company based there. The centre at Ibadan is the headquarters of MBARI.

In all these centres, the organisation itself has still lacked one vital facility: good, modern, equipped theatre. The theatre and folk music groups operating under MBARI's umbrage usually have had to depend on "theatres" elsewhere for their productions. These "theatres" and *halls* built for exhibitions and lectures or ballroom dances, with a low platform and a few spotlights at one end. (An improvised open courtyard theatre, reminiscent of Elizabethan inn courtyard stages, had been used consistently by the Eastern Nigeria Theatre Group, as a solution to the problem posed by existing "theatres" in any serious, imaginative production.)

The "theatres" only suited those groups who were not concerned much with the aesthetics of stage production, hardly demand of the audience to suspend their disbelief, but depend on spectacle, the broad joke and dance for audience attention—the popular concert troupes.

The Popular "Concert" Groups

It is significant that the concert groups are confined to Yoruba country. An examination of the factors producing this class of "theatre" provides some, but only part, of the explanation to this development.

When in the forties, West Africans like Hubert Ogunde and Ogunmola started off their small troupes of variety artists, performing from village to village, they soon found out that they were on to a good thing. They were satisfying a widespread longing for light entertainment so lacking then, as now, in most communities—especially the more urbanised communities as in western Nigeria. The cinema was yet a rarity even in the principal cities.

In the later years, the incidence of western education and thought created even more leisure, even in the villages, with traditional means of recreation and entertainment fading at the same time, to become an affair only brought up occasionally for show.

Travelling acrobats and magicians have all striven to fill the gap in communal life, especially in the decades immediately following the Second World War. Most of these were ex-servicemen who had picked up the tricks in their sojourn overseas, and following demobilisation could not really fit back into the pattern of village life.

The more enterprising of these entertainers had developed other ideas for more varied entertainment, particularly as, after the first few occasions, the old tricks of sleight-of-hand had become predictable, and unpopular. One-man shows or small troupes of two or three grew into bigger groups; and the need for higher returns to cope with the new demands of organisation kept the rounds to the bigger urban centres. Pidgin English crept in to spice performances and to reach the diversified audience.

By the sixties, Hubert Ogunde's Concert Party was launched on countrywide tours. (Ogunde had by this time discovered a tactful way of preserving his group and beating competition: marry all the girls before training them, and use the brothers in the family—evolving a family circus!) The Ogundes have thrived on this "slapstick comedy", though artiste Ogunmola, and subsequently the immense talent of Duro Ladipo developed it into a more serious and coherent art form: incipient Yoruba folk opera.

The performances of the main tradition of the "concert" groups have stayed close to the variety concert, consisting of singing, dancing and clowning, held together by the thin thread of a melodramatic story. The themes of these farces strike an interesting parallel between the concert groups and the novelettes of Onitscha market literature.[1]

The parallel may be taken further to point the interesting absence in former Eastern Nigeria of folk theatre development or activity in the "comedia del arte" tradition of Yoruba's Ogundes and Ogunmolas; while, on the other hand, intense literary activity was absent in the western and northern parts of the country.

One reason, already indicated, must be the fact that the Yorubas had the most highly developed sense of urban life and so more readily adopted the western forms of entertainment, helped no doubt by the closeness to Lagos and the existence there of the adoptive culture which supports the variety concert. Added to this, is the effect

[1]TRANSITION 19: Onitsha Market Literature (Donatus Nwoga) pp. 26-33.

of church drama: of the Virgin Birth, the passion play, stations of the Cross, etc. which is most clearly noticed in the improvisations of the "concert" parties.

Duro Lapido's achievement was in secularising the medium, turning the song, mime and talking drum into exploring and expounding Yoruba folk history and myth.

The Efiks of Old Calabar, who have been exposed to similar cultural influences and pressures as the coastal Yoruba, retain a deep fondness for live concert and the kind of "sophisticated entertainment" represented by play-going. But they had been too diffused to develop their widely renowned fold traditions and dances into an established folk art medium, the way the Yoruba had.

In the eastern part of the country, generally, folk theatre has been relatively undeveloped, although numerous groups, besides the Efiks, still preserved interesting forms of folk drama, several of these unique. (J. P. Clark, the Nigerian poet-playwright, in a 1966 address to a symposium of the English Association of the University of Nigeria on "Some Aspects of Nigerian Drama" analyzes some of these forms of theatre.)

Meanwhile, the drama of the masquerades, the "Odum play" of the Okrikas; and other age-old rites connected with the seasonal cycle and the gods in the basically agricultural society, especially among the Ijaws and Cross River folk, all await fusion into a theatre that will reflect the people's roots and be acceptable in the mainstream of world theatre today.

Further Development

Theatre involves the two inseparable aspects of acting and writing. A play is just so many words in a book, until it is given full life on the stage. Without the plays, of course, there can be no live theatre houses either. In discussing the development of theatre in Nigeria, it is thus relevant to consider whether Nigeria does have the artists and writers to support a national theatre.

A theatre of indigenous experiences has to be built from plays with themes growing out of the maze of the life of the local people. It cannot rely on plays written primarily for Broadway or the West End theatres, or any other great theatres outside the African experience. Even the greatest of such plays—great because of their universal themes—have to be adapted for a meaningful local performance; because the play written for a different culture, dwell on situations alien to experience of the local audience, even if the issues are widespread human failings.

The local experience can only be best interpreted—or the international human riddle best expressed in local terms—by the writer who has been involved with the way of life most of his own life.

Between 1960 and 1967 Nigeria had two established and internationally reputed playwrights: 'Wole Soyinka and J. P. Clark. In his serious plays, Soyinka fuses Yoruba myth with a modern based conception of life, to createa highly symbolic statement of his vision of life. His most successful play, in terms of theatre, "Brother Jero", was however, that in which he had shorn off most of the symbolism for a hard, biting comedy in the vein of "Tartuff" (Moliere). "The Road" (1966) combines the symbolic statement and the hard-edged irony of the popular comedy.[1] Clark's first verse tragedy, "Song of a Goat" is still that by which he is widely known, although he has written two more plays since then (1961) that have been produced successfully in Nigeria and London's West End.

---

[1]Since then, there has been "Kongi's Harvest", written under the shadow of the Nigerian crisis.

Both writers are university men, who have been through courses in English, and their work demands sophisticated treatment. One or two other university men, with similar backgrounds (a grounding in Western literature) were also emerging as Nigerian playwrights, in 1967. The most significant of these had been Frank Aig-Imoukhede who, in the three years before the Nigerian civil war, had written two successful plays. (The first of them, "Ikeke" established the Lagos based theatre-group, *Theatre Workshop.)*

Writing at a less sophisticated level was James Ene Henshaw, a medical practitioner. His are the direct, heavily scored statements, thin and requiring much build up in production; but which, when successfully produced, do have a strong popular appeal. They contain something the masses can readily understand and respond to. The play titles in themselves are an indication: "This is Our Chance".

Considerable experimental writing, mainly of one-act and short plays, had been going on in Nsukka and Enugu, as in Ibadan and Lagos. But the country still needed playwrights and plays to establish and sustain a modern theatre of indigenous experiences.

During the period, the question of what direction contemporary drama in these parts would take had become an issue of literary criticism. Would it follow the method of building on the rich traditions of folklore, or would it adopt the themes and props associated with the clash of civilisations so characteristic of other kinds of emergent African writing particularly of the French-speaking community? . . . An artist will write what his intuitive wisdom prompts him to write, conditioned by his experience of humanity, which necessarily has to start with those he lives with most. For the artist brought up in Nigeria, these will be his African compatriots, be they Bini, Ewe, Ibo, Hausa, Yoruba or Ekoi.

One can hardly expect uniformity, however, in African theatres, even the West African theatre. Despite similarities in historical background and traditions, divergences in customs and beliefs, even if small, exist, besides marginal differences in the cultural and political response to the traumatic experience of colonization.

Without seeking to be coteries, the local theatres from one country to another will seek to be within the communal experience, and only in as much as these experiences are clearly similar will the resultant theatre be broadly African.

Actors

The prevalent attitude to acting as a career in pre-war Nigeria has been largely contributory to the dearth of actors and actresses which is current. Acting was not considered a respectable "thing", especially for women, and the usual attitude even among those engaged in the existing theatre was that of amateur dilettantism.

In the course of the first half of the sixties a few girls had, anyway, braved professional attachment to the theatre through special training overseas. Girls like Olga Adeniyi-Jones and Frencesca Perreira; the cousins Yinka and Turrie Akerele, Elizabeth Osisioma and Edna Izuora, who took professional qualifications in drama in addition to some other disciplines. The trained male actors also had similar backgrounds. Many more had attained semi-professional perfection through long years of association with the leading amateur groups and innate interest in the stage. But the existing theatre was only a "pastime" and could not offer a living.

Theatre Artists

It was only in respect of stage designers and theatre

artists that the theatre scene in Nigeria wa extremely promising already by 1967. There was already a well established core of imaginative painters and graduates of the schools of fine arts and architecture. Modernistic painters, Demas Nwoko and Uche Okeke, were doing designing of remarkable originality and excellence for the leading theatre groups: designs that have stood up well in two international, highly competitive arts festivals—the Commonwealth Arts Festival in 1965, and the first Negro Arts Festival (1966) in Dakar.

In Lagos, in 1967, organised professionalism was emerging in Nigerian theatre, with the theatre promoting business, viz. Eldred Fiberisima Productions. The logical sequel to the universities' successful experiments in amateur theatre—the blooming of the experiments beyond theatricals—has to take place outside the campus.

Problems of Development

Two things still bedevil the theatre movement in Nigeria. Money: the lack of it; and the absence of theatre houses. At a time when all government and private planning is concerned with what is considered the priorities of economic development, the arts is not considered a rewarding area of investment!

In 1967, Ibadan still had, as in 1960, the only modern theatre in Nigeria, in the Arts Theatre of the University of Ibadan. (It seats only 304 and its lighting and stage equipment already needed improving.) There were one or two good theatres elsewhere. But in each case their location and proprietorship inhibited their usefulness to the theatre development . . . the Jos Theatre, owned by and serving only the mining folk; or the Shell-BP Theatre in Port Harcourt.

The situation demanded the installation of public

theatres in the main centres of the nation's cultural life. But MBARI could not finance a theatre house, as the organisation was run on a shoe-string budget comprising small grants from arts patrons.

A third, but less obvious problem, was the dearth of experienced producers. This was, however, a problem that increased experimental activity and discrimination in the audience and in the participants would ultimately solve. It was complicated by the intense competition that marked the new movement.

With the growing numbers of trained theatre people becoming available what was needed, though, was barely two well-managed, well-directed theatre companies that could get to make a living from their productions eventually.

Development in the arts often poses a paradox. The arts has always needed patronage: from past kings to present-day wealthy businessmen. Still the arts, and particularly theatre, flourishes best in freedom, which modern commercialism is not always able to grant it. Thus, for the theatre movement in a developing country like Nigeria, the necessary and crucial financial help coming from business is desirable; but it is fraught with the dangers of commercial interests which could impair developing standards. This, however, is a chance that has to be taken.

Direct government local grants are a most probable source of capital for funding the intial development of a national theatre. Establishment financing is not free from clogs, too; in this case, the stifling flair of bureaucratic controls.

What Kind of Theatre?

The ideal of the new theatre in Nigeria is to reach the vast masses of the folk in the streets, the village schools and communities, along with the handful of the sophisticated elite.

The ideal kind is a theatre that provides a home for the highly sophisticated as well as for the new-comer, not because their circles consider it the thing to do, nor because of financial rewards from being "with-it"; a viable kind distinguishable from the standard "big-production-run" type of established Western theatre; a kind that, like the theatre workshop is as much a training ground for promoting small and regular productions. It is the community theatre, somewhat as represented in the famous Karamu Centre in Cleveland, Ohio.

The community theatre in a developing society is, of course, a difficult proposition, not only because of the large financial resources required to sustain it, but also because very tiny proportions even of the educated adults in the towns, are theatre conscious. The immediate areas of rewarding effort in the circumstances are thus the school children and the handful of clerks and administrators, engineers, doctors, lawyers and business executives whose support, even if only indirect, is necessary for wider experiments and fulfilment.

In preparing its plays and tour programmes, the University Travelling Theatre has always given special attention to satisfying the school audiences. Schools in remote parts of Nigeria thus had the opportunity in recent years of watching at least one production of the university travelling theatres.

But the student performers can only be on the road once a year, and barely for a few weeks. The next pressing development is that such travelling performers consist of full-time performers, equipped with a self-contained caravan, who can be on the road throughout the dry months, at least.

Already the "Theatre-on-wheels' scheme developed by Mr. G. J. Axworthy, first Director of the School of

Drama, Ibadan, and his staff in the 1964 tour has become a tremendous success. Allowing for productions designed for performance in the open—with football stadiums becoming the ideal "theatres"—the innovation did overcome the problem of suitable playhouses. Audiences of thousands have thus been entertained at single performances.

The schools' bias did not end with reaching the schools and their communities through the travelling theatre. The Ibadan School of Drama provided one and two-year Certificate and Diploma courses for prospective teachers of drama in elementary and secondary schools and colleges (high school) and many school teachers in Nigeria had taken these courses in the four years up to 1967.

The objective has been to encourage and improve drama activities in the schools, in the belief that the established school drama group soon involves the whole community round the school; and even if this does not yield a regular theatre in the communities, it produces future adults with some feeling for theatre.

Aid to education

Drama in school is, of course, important in other ways: it is aid to education. Acting, in particular, helps the child to give expression to his natural creativeness, teaches him self-reliance and the habit of careful observation; and above all, clear speech.

A player, it is realised, must communicate promptly and effectively with his audience, otherwise the action is lost. A play, too, presents aspects of our everyday life, and so the good actor must also be the keen observer of humanity's foibles.

The kind of theatre suited to the Nigerian conditions (like any other developing community's conditions) of social economic and cultural development will evolve gradually. It will be influenced by the kind of plays which feed it, the nature of the theatre houses, prevailing social conditions and attitudes, and similar factors. Its ultimate realisation has to provide a fitting replacement to that missing portion in communal life created by the dropout of traditional means of leisure; it has to preserve valuable elements in the nation's past in the idiom of modern theatre—in an original theatre of African experiences for the whole community.

A TALK WITH
YAMBO OUOLOGUEM

Yambo Ouologuem is the descendant of a Dogon family who were rulers of Mali (central Africa) before the arrival of the French, and then, as now, owners of vast territories there. He came to France in 1964, studied at an elite school, the Ecole Normale Superieure, taking degrees in literature, philosophy, and English. A publisher as well as a writer, he produces school manuals for African students.

Bound to Violence, his first novel, which won the prestigious Prix Renaudot, is set in an African principality named Nakem. The name is imaginary, the country is real. Ouologuem presents his hero, Raymond Spartakus Kassoumi, as the summation of the millennial history of his birthplace. In a brief, violent fresco he paints Nakem's past. Nakem's chiefs are blacks, of course, but of Semitic origin. The structure of the country is feudal, with the chief and his notables at the top and their slaves at the bottom. When the French colonize the country, the notables arrange to have the sons of the slaves sent to mission schools and later, as puppets in the hands of the ruling class, push them on the political scene. The real and secret ruler of Nakem, the Saif, pulls the strings.

Much has been said and written about the oppressed Blacks. Ouologuem, from a new vantage point uniquely his own, speaks of Blacks oppressing Blacks.

A French magazine, *Plexus,* published an interview with Ouologuem, extracts from which follow:

284

Plexus: In Bound to Violence, you say of Raymond Spartakus Kassoumi that he is a "problematical individual." Do you identify with your hero? Do you consider yourself problematical?

Yambo Ouologuem: I wanted to present the "new wave" of so-called evolved Africans. They are in a position of contestation, both with regard to African things today and to African history, which they believe has been squashed by white colonialism.

P. But aren't there a great many things in your book which you might have identified with and expressed in the first person?

Y.O. I would never have enjoyed writing a book in the first person. I prefer to let the systems speak and reveal themselves rather than take myself as the unique point of reference.

P. All the same, if your book has been received with considerable passion, it's because it was taken as a personal testimony.

Y.O. I know nothing about a personal testimony. All I know is that up to the present, in my opinion, the Blacks have lived in the attitude of slaves. I felt it necessary to give back to their history its documentary character. I did not want to reduce African history arbitrarily to a dimension which is only a small part of it, namely white colonialism. White colonialism has been preceded by other colonialisms: first the colonialism of the black notables—and it should be remembered that it is through their notables that the black soul has become the Negro soul. Later, Arab colonialism reinforced the notables' colonialism by inserting it into the codified structure of the Islamic religion. Instead of the atmosphere of a thinking, analyzing culture, the norms of definition all centered on conformity. Thinking was conforming. The Koran, incidentally, endorses slavery and provides statutes for it. The Koran's ideology imposes absolute conformity to tradition, with strict adherence to the letter and no effort to apprehend the spirit. In Islamic schools, one learns the verses of the Koran by rote, by recitation. The two colonialisms preceding the white colonialism excluded dialogue from their structure. White colonialism, with its subsequent attempt at decolonization, introduced a new factor: Contestation. The Negro has come to arouse the bad conscience in the white man. "Negritude" makes its appearance as a combative ideology aiming to justify the black man in his struggle against a system of oppression originating with the white man. At the same time, absorption of white culture makes it possible for the black to rise above the black condition. White colonialism is repudiated, reviled and isolated, while at the same time its purse is used. This contradictory attitude goes along with extreme touchiness, to the point where one no longer knows what name to give to these men from Africa. Blacks? That's too pointed a reference to the color of their skin. Negroes? That is also resented. What we are left with is Africans. The Blacks of the U.S.A. even insist on being called Afro-Americans. There are all symptoms of the attitude of the slave since it consists in defining oneself by reference to another rather than to one's self.

P. Why did you write Bound to Violence?

Y.O. I think that one writes because of a moment when one reaches a certain density of being. . . . On the level of form, I wanted to make the epic speak, the tales of the griots, the Arab chroniclers, the oral African tradition. I had to reconstitute a form of speech filtered through a vision arising authentically from black roots.

P. Do you question the findings of ethnological works on Africa?

Y.O. Virtually all are questionable a priori. They do not allow reality to speak.

P. Bound to Violence doubtless gives a truer and better image of Africa?

Y.O. No doubt a truer one. I don't know about better.

P. If it is all right with you, let us take up the sexual problem to which you have given considerable space in Bound to Violence. In the West, we have our own ideas about black sexuality. We believe that it has retained a spontaneity that the whites have lost.

Y.O. In Europe and North Africa, virility has detached itself from the individual and become attached to property. In other words, you are a man, you are virile, not as a person by the name of X or Y, but as the owner of a car, an apartment, a house in the country, etc. It is evident that a woman also becomes an object for consumption to which one is entitled. She is regarded not so much as sexual as she is feminine. Erotic sexuality, on the other hand, becomes associated with the black or the exotic woman, and with the colored man, who is outside the notions of sexuality linked to money. Furthermore, it is certainly true that Africa is filled with sensual emanations and eroticism. Even politically, sex and blood played their role in the Africa of *Bound to Violence.* For the reason that, when the French, the English, and other Europeans arrived there, they came alone and their wives followed them only two years later. They turned to the village chiefs and the interpreters for bedfellows. But the notables always sent them women who were in fact agents, instructed to report to those who had sent them what the white man's intentions were. It was physical prostitution for the purpose of winning the confidence of the partner.

P. But they did not simulate their sexuality.

Y.O. They did not simulate. Sexuality with them is immanent. But they did have to force themselves to it. You have to know about certain African beliefs. White is the color of death, of mourning, of the state of non-being. The power of this thought is such that many people feel a profound revulsion when they find themselves in the presence of whites, of whom they say that they sold their souls to the devil. When the French arrived, there was a very real revulsion against the occupying forces, coupled with the fascination that goes with the images of fear.

P. You are defining here historical forces. On a more general plane, may one say that the Africans live their sexuality more freely and naturally, while the occidentals have lost their visceral spontaneity?

Y.O. Evidently. And they recover this visceral spontaneity when they are in the position of the man who pays.

P. Is African sexuality actually in that state of grace?

Y.O. All human beings are capable of that state of grace. It's more a question of the individual than a racial question. There are surely impotent men among Blacks. But, generally speaking, in Africa the body is not alienated from what is called eroticism over here, linked here to a commercializing of sexuality. When I say commercializing, I mean the art of dressing and preparing the body as if the body by itself could not impose its presence. One does not seem able to conceive of eroticism here without isolating certain parts of the body—the lips, the pubis, etc. But true eroticism is founded on an immediate apprehension of the other in his or her totality, physical and emotional: the miracle of the couple achieving union successfully.

P. You believe that this notion is getting lost in the West?

Y.O. I don't know. I'm not from here.

P. How, to change to another though parallel subject, can one explain the taboo which bans miscegenation in the West as well as in Africa?

Y.O. I don't know whether one can speak of a taboo, since it has been transgressed. But let us consider an occidental woman who feels alienated and treated as an object of consumption. As a rule, such a woman almost always belongs to the lower classes. When she contracts a mixed marriage, she revolts against a milieu she considers enslaving and barring her from full self-realization.

P. But what happens when an African marries a white woman, what are his motivations?

Y.O. There may be several. A retarded romantic attitude which tries to overcome alienation by wanting to pass for a white man with a black skin; or it may be the result of an intransigence of personality that seeks to affirm itself by determining its own destiny.

P. We have confronted Black with White in every conceivable way. Is there a problem that pertains neither to the fact of being white nor to that of being black?

Y.O. I do not orient myself in reference to whites nor in reference to blacks. I think that one is oneself, and that is it. Incidentally, there is no black problem. There is a problem of class conflict to which the black man lends the color of the contempt inherent in his condition; one should remember his history and see the tensions of today with objectivity.

P. As far as you are concerned, the fact that you are black does not condition your personality more strongly than any other fortuitous quality?

Y.O. That's correct.

P. Will you return to Africa?

Y.O. I shall return to Africa because I believe that one should abide by one's nationality without, however, falling into the cult of a demagogical nationalism. But I don't agonize at all about my own fate.

Reprinted with the permission of Harcourt Brace Jovanovich, publishers.

POETRY

ORDER OF THE BLACK CROSS

By OKOT P'BITEK

Out of the War of Freedom and Unity
We shall build a New Jerusalem!

The bones of the war-dead
Will be our bricks,
The skulls of the children
That starved to death
Will be our window panes,
With the strong concrete of human blood
We will build sky-scrapers . . .
We will paint the houses gray
With human brains!

We have so much building material,
We need no foreign aid:
No advisors, no experts, no mercernaries . . .
Thanks to the struggle
We now have our own experts . . .

The rebellion is over
The bloody conflict has ended,
We shall beat the tanks into tractors,
The war planes will spray the river-beds and swamps
And rid us of mosquitos,
The navy will become the national fishing fleet . . .
We will feed the people with high protein foods . . .

The machine guns and the rifles?
The Game Department will use these for cropping
    Our rich Wild Life . . .
Black woman,
Take courage and weep no more!

I saw your dry-stick baby die in your arms,
(Actually it had died long before!)
Your breasts, once a pair of ripe papayas
Are now dry like paper!
I saw your young husband blown to bits,
A piece of his right toe fell in my garden . . .
I know your old father has lost his wife,
They killed her after a brief rape under the granary . . .
But, Black Woman
Take courage . . .

Look, your Brother is our Hero,
He has been awarded the Order of the Black Cross
And has become A Free Man of our Capital City. . . .

No. The dead did not die for nothing
Your sufferings were not in vain,
We shall name the streets after the Heros.

O Jerusalem, New Jerusalem!

I see the peaceful River flowing through you,
There are no slums, no more decay,
No disease, no corruption. . . .

FOR CHIEF—A TRIBUTE TO ALBERT JOHN LUTULI

By DENNIS BRUTUS

So the old leonine heart is stilled
the grave composure of the carven face
matched at last by a stillness overall
the measure of bitterness, totally filled
brims to the tautness of exhausted space
and he who sustained a faith in grace
believing men crippled could still walk tall
in the thorn-thickets of corrupting power
and more dear the central humanity
than any abstractions of time or place
daring to challenge, refusing to cower
mangled even at the end, he lies quiet
his stillness no less an assertion of faith
and the indestructible stubbornness of will.

So the machine breaks you
and you fall
still fighting grimly.
    The years epitomize
    in this harsh act
    of many:
Should one despair
knowing how great the power
how unavailing opposition?

Yet your great soul
asserts a worth—
transcendant humanity.
There is a valour
greater than victory:
Greatness endures.

And the people mourn
the millions mourn,
the sorrowing land
is plunged in deeper sorrow:
When will the soft rains dissolve the entire
  landscape at dusk?
Sorrow and anger stir,
dull pain and truculent woe,
and bitterness slowly seethes
till fury cauldrons from pain—
Oh when will the blind storms rampage the
  landscape in the dark?

Return to us

  when sunset smoulders on the smooth horizon,
  when the trees are starkly black
  and beautiful
  against the red and mauve of the sky

Return to us

  when woodsmoke comes sweet and poignant
  from the fields at dusk
  after the winds of our fury have breathed
  on the smouldering coals of our anger
  and our fierce destruction has raged

O great patient enduring spirit
return to us.

O grave and statuesque man
stand along our paths,
overlook our ways.
   Goad us by your calm regard
   fire us with your desire,
   steel us with your will.
Spirit of freedom and courage
guard us from despair
brood over us with your faith.
   Fire the flagging and the faint,
   spur us to fierce resolve,
   drive us to fight and win.

Here by the pool my scarred ungainly body shrinks,
by blue glass depths, kittenish tinkling ripples
I cool my parched rigid spirit
with anticipations of champagne.

To lift, this once, the foaming goblet
in harsh joy, bright, brittle, unbending as glass
while in sere patches of the scraggly well-loved grass
in a loneliness desperate and vast
as shooting-star scatterings in glaucous space
for this one guest at least
they thrust down a mute vacant glass

Shatter underfoot
in a weaving of sorrow and joy
nuptial and lamentation,
the pitiful unprotesting glass
reciting the ambivalent prothalamium:

"If I forget thee, O Jerusalem
where by sad waters I sit down remembering"

let the glass-hard longing, anger, pain
shimmer and scintillate awhile,
the bright drops of joy-wine gush
while the sharp bright edge of action waits
and fury slakes her thirst a space.

Celebrate
the fierce joy of victory
and necessary wounding
that the day may sooner come
of our unexiling:
of our return.

VEGETATION DE CLARTE

By FRANÇOIS SENGAT-KUO

Te voici révillée d'entre les morts
que s'accomplisse enfin l'oracle des jours fastes
le bâton du pélerin se brise entre mes doigts las
quelle Parques dis a bâti malicieuse
cette muraille de Chine au creux de nos rêves?

    la lune pâlira aux abords de l'hiver
    et ton chemin sera spirale longuement
    et ton rêve dérivera vers le large
    incapable d'être le cauri et d'être la kora

ô nostalgie des terres vierges touffues de soleil
nostalgie de coquillages baisés d'algues et de vagues

    et tu reviendras épave mordue de sel marin
    au port connu où s'amarrent les voiliers
    et tu seras galet échoué sur le sable comique
    et tu seras boue adhérée au talon des passants
    et tu attendras la fièvre au front l'oracle
    l'oeil rivé sur la page bleue de l'horizon

nostalgie des oiseaux énivrés d'aurores
nostalgie de ruisseaux sursurrant sous la mousse
voice venir les jours fastes des éternels recommence-
ments

quelle Parque dis a bâti malicieuse
cette muraille de Chine au creux de nos rêves?

ton corps sera guitare sous les doigts du vent
et l'étoile filante allègrement tissera le pont
et ELLE reviendra parée, de tulle lunaire
comme à l'autel votif jadis les yeux fermés

ô biche alanguie le long d'un ruisseau
succulence des fruits muris aux abords de l'été
le baton du pélerin se brise entre mes doigts las
quelle Parques dis a bâti malicieuse
cette muraille de Chine au creux de nos rêves?

fétiche tutélaire au seuil du village
je te prends à témoin de mes rêves éclatés en pollen
le Yang-tsé-kiang déborde la muraille des Parques
je te prends à témoin de cette végétation de clarté
germée au plus intime de nos coquillages

AU MASQUE

By FRANÇOIS SENGAT-KUO

Masque ô masque tutélaire de mon village
je te salue comme le coq salue l'aurore
et je confesse ma trahison d'enfant prodigue

ils m'ont dit ô masque à l'âge de l'innocence
que ton regard séculaire brûle du feu de l'enfer
et que le rictus de tes lèvres est malediction
et que tu es mensonge et que tu es désordre

au bord de la route ô masque je t'ai déposé
comme un, voyageur fourbu une idole encombrante
et ma prière inquiète à la tombée de la nuit
Grands Maîtres du Livre et du Canon
que votre règne soit la récompense de mon voyage

voici mes pieds meurtris d'une longue errance
je viens à toi comme d'un désert calciné
assoiffé d'ombre et de sources vives
je reviens à toi la tête haute ô masque
mon éclat de rire tonnerre au milieu de leur fête
je te découvre nombril sacré de mon être
et ta beauté foudroie mon coeur de sa vérité d'homme
et tes yeux profonds s'allument en soleils primordiaux
et tes lèvres murmurent des secrets oubliés
Toi qui n'es pas fin mais recommencement
ô masque moi-même en face de moi
je te salue comme le coq un jour nouveau.

IN AETERNUM

By FRANÇOIS SENGAT-KUO

Sur le parvis Notre-Dame ensemble agenouillés
tu murmurais à l'unisson de la Seine
mon Dieu faites que je sois lierre à son cou
éternellement l'eau de source sur son front moite
faites que je sois l'ombre épaisse du baobab au coeur de
l'été
le champ de mil offert à sa faim O mon Dieu
faites que ses yeux soient mes yeux
son souffle mon souffle
sa soif ma soif
éternellement

Souviens toi
Souviens toi des carillons sur nos têtes d'anges
l'envolée triomphante des orgues aux jours fastes
je répondais
O Seigneur exauce ma simple prière dans sa nudité
que je ne sois pas à ses pieds le sable brulant du désert
mais la pluie tiède annonciatrice des moissons
que je ne sois pas le vautour de ses rêves d'enfant
mais le pourvoyeur viril d'étoiles sous la tente
que je sois O Seigneur le mage au coeur tendre
le chevalier servant aux heures de recueillement
le jardin éternellement fleuri de son âme
la main fraternelle dans sa main
bouche de sa bouche
coeur de son coeur
éternellement

Souviens toi
comme aux jours jadis des initiations sacrées
nous avons à l'aurore fait le serment du sang
bénis soient les coeurs accordés à l'ombre des cathé-
drales
l'anneau à nos doigts plus dur que granit
O Seigneur bénis ce que nul ne peut défaire
éternellement

Et tu fus mon amour lierre à mon cou tendu
ombre épaisse du baobab au midi de l'été
champ de mil offert à ma faim sans fin
et je fus tiède pluié annonciatrice des moissons
chevalier sérvant aux heures silencieuses
main fraternelle dans ta main
deux fois trois ans

Mais quels nuages soudain gros de quel orage
je confesse l'alchimie du coeur plus corrosive que l'acide
le rossignol étranglé au sortir de l'été
je confesse la source tarie au centre de l'oasis
le champ de mil ébloui de sauterelles
mais je confesse aussi mon amour
mon amour infini comme l'infinité de tes yeux
deux fois trois ans

Et ma prière au petit matin de Noel paix
paix sur terre et paix dans les coeurs accouplés
faites à nouveau O mon Dieu que l'oasis soit oasis
que l'hiver désolé lève des printemps triomphants
faites plus vivantes les fleurs cueillies au bord de la Seine
comme aux jours jadis des initations sacrées
faites à nos doigts l'anneau plus dur que granit
et bénis Seigneur bénis ce que nul ne peut défaire
in aeternum

L'INDÉPENDANCE

By FRANÇOIS SENGAT-KUO

Tu dis l'indépendance
ce jour là
nous nous sommes sentis baobabs
avec du soleil plein nos feuillages
tout verts
avec une sève nouvelle plein nos tiges
et nous avons dansé dansé
parce que de la nuit triômphait le jour
mais sur nos plus hautes branches
quelle nuée de sauterelles soudain
l'indépendance mon ami
n'est pas éclair fugitif
un éclat de rire dans le silence étale
un képi blanc sur ta tête noire
un fanion neuf sur un mât ancien
les vertus loquaces acclamées des troupeaux
la ruée des esclaves aux paradis des seigneurs
si ce jour là
nous nous sommes sentis baobabs
avec du soleil plein nos feuillages
tout verts
avec une sève nouvelle plein nos tiges
si nous avons dansé dansé
jusqu'au lever du jour
c'est que l'indépendance mon ami
c'est d'un peuple ressuscité digne

le serment du sang au petit matin
l'air des montagnes plein nos poumons
la liberté des fleuves d'aller à la mer
le droit égal des bourgeons de s'ouvrir à la lumière
la justice éclose sur le fumier du mépris
un champs offert à la force de nos muscles
la promesse féconde de moissons communes
chaque planète dans son orbite retrouvé
pour l'accord parfait de l'univers des hommes.

COMME LA MER . . .

By FRANÇOIS SENGAT-KUO

L'amour est comme la mer
sans cesse sur les plages de nos coeurs
déferlent ses vagues infinies

L'amour est comme la mer
il sépare et il unit
comme la mer les continents

L'amour a ses tempêtes
comme la mer a ses furies
tempêtes expiatoires de nos péchés

Mais la mer a ses jours étales
comme l'amour ses joies sereines
la paix des coeurs accordés au petit matin

L'amour est comme la mer
il lèche les plaies de nos coeurs
comme la mer les gravillons du large

ô mer enveloppe-la de tes mains innombrables
et qu'Elle se saoule de ton étreinte infinie
comme l'infinité de mon amour!

CHANT DE LA DANSEUSE NOIRE

By FRANÇOIS SENGAT-KUO

Tam tam bat
tam tam rit
qui donc t'a dit
ma danse obscène

coup de reins
à gauche
coup de reins
à droite
frappe du pieds
pirouette
frappe du pieds
pirouette

tam tam bat
tam tam rit
coup de reins
en arrière
coup de reins
en avant

qui donc t'a dit
ma danse obscène
frappe du pieds

pirouette
frappe du pieds
pirouette

tam tam bat
tam tam rit
vient la saison
des semences
qui donc dis-moi
qui donc la pluie
invoquera

coup de reins
en arrière
coup de reins
en avant
coupe de reins
à gauche
coup de reins
à droite

tam tam bat
tam tam rit
j'accorde la lune
et le soleil
qui donc dis-moi
de l'Univers
perpétuera
le mouvement

frappe du pieds
pirouette
frappe du pieds
pirouette
je suis la vie
qui donc dis-moi

fécondera
femmes et champs

tam tam bat
tam tam rit
je tisse le noeud
entre les morts
et les vivants
qui donc dis-moi
qui donc sera
le messager
des ancêtres

coup de reins
à gauche
coup de reins
à droite
coupe de reins
en arrière
coup de reins
en avant
frappe du pieds
pirouette
frappe du pieds
pirouette

tam tam bat
tam tam rit
qui donc t'a dit
ma danse obscene

LA VOIE ROYALE

By FRANÇOIS SENGAT-KUO

Mon coeur chemine
à petits pas de chenille
sur la voie royale des négriers
quelles balafres sur ton front opaque
scintille le message des initiés
oh que batte mon coeur tambour
au rythme des vagues tourmentées
qui l'emportent pirogue
vers des horizon sans visage

La plante a germé succulente
sur un terroir inconnu des aieux
voici que vertes sont les feuilles
et la tige à la sveltesse des cocotiers
salut ô germination première salut
je viens gouter a la douceur des fruits
on m'a dit que tes branches toujours
dispensent l'ombre étale des résurrections

J'ai pris ta main dans ma main
le chemin donne sur les lieux sacrés
paix totems protecteurs des chaumières
voici le pollen sur l'humus natal retombé
qu'éclatent koras et balafongs
que sur l'arbre totems des jours heureux
rayonnent sans fin vos soleils nourriciers

A vos pieds l'offrande propitiatoire
bénissez totems bénissez cette main dans la mienne
bénissez la retombée des pollens à l'aurore
la voie royale mêne à l'ombre de tes yeux
et chemine mon coeur à petits pas de chenille
et batte batte mon coeur tambour
au rythme des vagues paisibles
qui l'emportent pirogue
vers des horizons connus.

SI JE POUVAIS ÊTRE GRIOT A EL HADJ AHMADOU AHIDJO[1]

By FRANÇOIS SENGAT-KUO

de mes yeux au premier chant du coq
le leit de chèvre n'a pas déchiré la toile d'araignée
à l'âge où le cocon libère le papillon des champs
je n'ai pas cent fois ruminé la kola et le mbongolo
au tour de mon cou pas de collier de dents de caiman
et ma lèvre ne connaît pas au petit matin
le goût du vin de palme resérvé aux initiés
qui donc consacrera ma langue pour les chants sacres
si je pouvais être griot comme au temps jadis
je dirais au monde ta haute lignée de cocotier
je chanterais chanterais à la trompette d'Armstrong
la chevauchée de ton sang dans les veines de mon peuple
toi qui as conquis le tigre et dompté le perroquet
je dirais au monde ta majesté de baobab et ta grâce de
palmier
toi qui as la fierté du Mont-Cameroun au coeur de l'orage
et la douceur de l'Adamaoua dans la nuit étale
ô toi maître du verbe et forgeron des resurrections
si je pouvais être griot comme au temps jadis
je dirais ta chair fraîche conjagaison des limons
du Wouri indolent et de la capricieuse Bénoué

---

[1]The President of Cameroun. Note the interesting book: *The Political Philosophy of Ahmadou Ahidjo*. Monte-Carlo: Editions Paul Bory, 1968.

311

de la Sanaga sans fin et du Nyong mystérieux
toi qui te nourris de pluie féconde et de clairs soleils
qui connais la mâle saveur des coupes anciennes
et la succulence du miel butiné au crépuscule
je dirais au monde le secret de ton alchimie
qui au petit matin maria la savane et la foret
je dirais à tout vent ta haute lignée de cocotier
et chanterais chanterais à la trompette d'Armstrong
la chevauchée de ton sang dans les veines de mon peuple.

NE MEURT PAS LE RÊVE DES HOMMES À MARTIN LUTHER KING

By FRANÇOIS SENGAT-KUO

Ils disent qu'ils l'ont tué
tué Martin Luther King l'immortel
sur ma plus haute branche
du hibou écoutez le ricanement
ne meurt pas le rêve des hommes
comme plante privée d'eau et de soleil

Un jour il faudra se lever
marcher droit devant soi
marcher jusqu'à Johannesbourg
comme jadis Chaka au coeur de lion
il faudra dire aux éperviers
que dure est notre chair de colombe à leur bec
dure comme le silex du Kilimanjaro
dire que tu n'es pas mort
ne meurt pas la colère des hommes
par pendaison au petit matin

Il faudra se lever tôt à l'aube
marcher avec la raideur du sabre
marcher jusqu'à Salisbury
comme jadis Samory la tête haute
il faudra aux vampires apprendre

que notre sang doux est amer à leur bouche
amer comme écorce de baobab
dire que tu n'es pas mort
ne meurt pas la soif de liberté
à coup pistolet au petit matin

Un jour il faudra se lever
marcher droit devant soi
obéir à la chevauchée de notre sang
marcher droit jusqu'à Washington
il faudra dire au yankee triomphant
que le bois d'ébène a tari dans nos forêts
dire que tu n'es pas mort
ne meurt pas la faim de dignité
par morsure de chien au petit matin

Ils disent qu'ils l'ont tué
tué Martin Luther King l'immortel
sur ma plus haute branche
du hibou écoutez le ricanement
il dit Martin Luther King vivant
dans le poing fermé de nos humiliations
dans les sanglots de la trompette d'Armstrong
dans les plaintes de Myriam Makéba
et l'invincible sourire de nos espérances
car ne meurt pas le rêve des hommes
comme plante privée d'eau et de soleil.

THE REMINDER

By EYAN NZIE

Now that the feet point to the back
and eyes look skywards
and mouths dare not stop the entry of filth
its vomit
with ears rolled up like unopened flowers
we each shall be a world

hurrah for the sons of giants
owners of the earth
praise be the losers with hands of fire
my hand with yours
join hands you masters and you too, losers
dance to the madness and shed tears of laughter

But wait
how come we by these giant trees
and the dance among these sacrificial fires
built by them of the past
present
and to come

There he stood
a white cock in his left hand
a knife in his right
and the cock dances to the music of death
wings flapping

legs kicking
and the worshipstone sighs warm with its bath of blood
and they shall bring a cool breeze
and rain
and peace

Yet here we stand
our ears sealed safe
heads shaking 'no'
we fear we yet might see

THE ORPHAN

By EYAN NZIE

Grandmother
your face forever aglow with the light of your pipe
let me come nearer and peer into that face so full of
    knowing
and read the crowded scribble on your brow

in your silent thoughtfulness I hear the echo of
    happenings
past and to come
and yet your oath of silence in a world wrapped in its
    noise
    forbids you waste your breath
compels you watch in silent agony
your children fight over sacrifical meat
their backs to the shrine
soaking the earth in blood

Nne o
your pains will never end even after you join our
    ancestors
for they too see
and wonder why
and shake their hoary heads in sorrowful amazement
wishing they could say 'stop' without intruding

and I
so far away from home among faces you'll never see
hear the cry of my brothers weary with folly and
    yet unable to stop
I feel your pain
their pain
all piled on top my secret agony.

SALUTE OF THE WINGED SEED

By EYAN NZIE

Mouth open to the sky
and inside headquake rocks my broomstick feet
fingers locked and palmcushions behind my head
I lie on my back and vainly curse and scream
flaying the air with childish kicking feet
how well I know how little I could do from here
or even back among my forgetting brothers

we are few
those seeds from grass under the elephant's belly
blown off too soon for the hoofs of warring kings
thankful for the hills and trees and mighty rivers
between our thinking heads
and piles of abandoned bodies
wrapped around the stems of uncaring speargrass shoots
the restingplace of flies

and we sons of mighty Ayah
Nki, Nkim, Nkro and one time tameless Ekajuk
now for once shall we ask why
as strange sounds and the smell of death stifle laughter
    beyond the walls of bellies
and babies now must learn to run before they crawl
and children fearful of gun toting strangers
with large antelope-eyes implore our protection
their lips like mutes moving soundless

319

and here we crouch
in holes for ever acting conspirators each to himself
heads bowed to fear
sons of the many villages and springs
I shout my tearful salute to you from the heart of cold and
    death
I wait to hear your answer
in rain
or wind
echoing from across the sea.

CHILD OF THE TREETOPS

By EYAN NZIE

And you child of the treetops
hearer of secrets down below
eye that next to the sky stands as fleeting scenes of human
    episodes rush past to their end
which is the beginning
you who swam the sap of the silkcotton tree from the
    earth
worshipping its fertile sacrifice of egg and fowl and wine
    and yam
and crawled through the huge entrails of its trunk for
    immeasurable time
do you hear your mother groan as you sit leisurely among
    the topest branches
drinking the forest smell from bark and leaf dead and
    alive
she who at a glance saw the end in your planted umbilical
    chord

the time has come to hear the endless voice of
    Akpatankun
no longer swelled by sounds of village laughter
and if you find his language strange
turn to the dancing oilpalm tree
do not stop its dance with questions
look at the yellow funnel mushrooms spouting from its
hairy roots
and read the answer of a question yet unasked

your winged dream that leapt from mountain peak to
   peak
soaring miles ahead the enemy
and those springy heels that shot you off the earth
how come they grown so soggy and impotent
now that you need them o so badly

But I that am the undiscovered reincarnation of He
Ogah of the many roots and herbs
whose life suckled on the mercy of the roaring wind and
   the anger of unknowing men
to men who scoff at miracles and still demand one
I shall reveal
that
the bug you stepped on near the head of that spring
died with the rain in its bowels
and the stench of its tongue has driven the sun beyond the
   hills
only to be seen but never touched
and your dreams
hidden beneath that towering moss-covered rock
have merged with their warm protector and left you with
   their whitened skeletons

and if you still doubt
listen to the bark of the cowrie beads
your ears in your hand
your eyes turned in.

NNE, ENUNO ATUORA

By EYAN NZIE

Nne
you who sent me only with a ladle
in its belly the water from many roots and herbs
pointing to the glimmer beyond the eye
before the night's wet drops faded off the leaves
head of the firespring
and I
sleep-clouds before my eyes

I have walked
Nne
I have walked over baking sand
and knifedge rocks
through steaming deserts of mud
my blistered soles hoping
my bones gone mad with pain and tiredness no longer
    keep the princely pace you taught me
my eye stuck to the glimmer beyond the eye has found
    my feet caught in this hole
of cold
and death
and stench beyond the senses

Atuora
you who the knowing ones call
Ano

the beautiful
the good
warmth that from the inside comes to shine the earth
Atuora
It is you I call from beyond the mighty river
like I always have from my beginning days
and the power of your self buried in the memory of your
    rich brown eyes
shall at once come to me wrapped in the belly of the early
    morning breeze
let my worries over there hold still
and leave you to your never ending headache
eyan nzie
child who rides the giddy heights of treetops
forever conscious of the brutish strength of man turned
    god
and yet unable to stand the crap humanity gobbles

Remember Atuora
the ladle with water in its belly
protection for the body's all you said
know now
the sun and wind have dried up the belly
and the ladle gone with the last storm
now lives with the claws of the eagle
my plea for justice merely called the eaglemenofshame
who flap their red wrinkled necks before my front
mouths belching putrefaction
wings tough with the smell of shit

Nne
they try to soil the vision of my eyes
let the head of the firespring stay untapped
but my dream
Nne
give me your warmth enough to wrap my dream.

FROM THE INSIDE OF THE ELEPHANT

By EYAN NZIE

a live pile of shit
crawling chinwards
neckhigh
and solid odour no knife can cut zealously crowding my
    nostrils
my self
floats
back to you
land of darkness
night
and mysterious voices
earth dark with life
with shoulders that with ease carry the oldest stoutest
    rock and tree
where interlacing leaves and branches permit pin rays of
    sundust
on land where everyday sees progress from peace and
    liberty
to
dogfights
for power
and wealth
and outside beauty

shall you know your son
on return from this nightmare of fiendish ghosts
bereft of shame and sight
where justice hides shivering among the books
and I
without those robes of princehood
nor the touch which evil kills
with a shadow turned lumpy from the kiss of a snout

and when the cleansing spirit of palmwine vomits the
    reward of my travel
shall your ears hold it long enough for the head to eat
will you rather infect your eyes with more beautiful tales
oozing from the pit of half-digested facts sown by kindly
    malefactors
whose tongue is a nest of lies
housed in a metal snout wrapped in plastic
spitting bullets and fire in the name of law
and order
and peace

ha
have I seen things
have I heard voices
have I felt cold enough to freeze your balls
you wise ones who sit just beyond the eyes
heads bowed
brows wrinkled with knowledge of the stubborn wall
    between sight and action
my fathers
should I like a seed in the bowels of a crocodile patiently
    wait
answer me you who hold all answers
before my boiling head cracks.

THE RETURN

By EYAN NZIE

Once more on my back in the belly of the night
and insect voices from up and all around like a flood
lull me on to sleep

through the hole in my roof
I see the sky
and feel the moon
and hear again the long past songs of my youth

like birds
they've flown away
left the playground bare
my eardrums dead
and the village lost in silence

Maybe the songs are there
maybe they could not fly
It is my inside that is dead and nevermore can smile

ETAN

By EYAN NZIE

Listen to this voice
etan
does it sound like a voice heard in a dream
between wake and sleep

etan
this is who sat the night to watch your whooping cough
hurting to see those baby limbs tautly hungry for some air
and now you think the speargrass hides you
pissing on the tall waterpot behind the kitchen
ai ai ai
the harmattan surrendered all to the fire with the wind
   at his heels
like they think they see me here
with eyes exchanged for the glitter of gold
they say
the head that's bowed receives no blows
the bended knee loses no blood
and the trembling voice is human poetry

but I from many years back have felt the sting of blows
head bowed
knee scraping the sandy classrooms of maryknoll
how can they fail to see
my neck's tired
my face rebels against the wormdom of never looking up

and my knee will only bend now for a kick
and this voice that shall tease many years of your ears
shall never melt its spine

hold my hand
etan
and let our answer mingle with the air
those bombs
and guns
and joints you say you took from me
go check your store
a-e
check my skin
my shithole
my mouth
my armpits
my toes and my nestlike hair
those things you fear to see lie deeper
my friends
they come when I command

some day when the sun like a snail
rises with water on its back
and voices born and unborn join my threatening fists
look out
my friends
look out.

KOL DE KACH

By EYAN NZIE

Papa
kol de kach
dat hol fo wol
na deh de kol de kom

Pikin
kol de kach
de wol get hol
bot lefam
ilef smol taim
wen yu dong big smol pas so
yu sef go si seh wol bi soso hol
seh hol bi wol an wol bi hol

Papa, papa
wetin dat min

lefam pikin, trai slip.

GOUFFRE

By SOTÈRE TORREGIAN

Je sais rien sauf que j' suis venu
des terres de Notre Père des Moutons

*GULF

I don't know anything but that I come from
the land of Our Father of Sheep

HOLLOWEEN
(To Calypso beat)

By SOTÈRE TORREGIAN

I love you Halloween

The night when witches mope around the moon
   spying upon their faint once-a-year followers—
     is Halloween.
You will be a Halloween lady
I can see Halloween I cannot feel her.
When witches watch the wicked moon on Halloween
Last Halloween I killed a man . . . (E.P.)
All the kids will be Halloween.
I am as insignificant as you Halloween

SCHUBERT'S
GREAT GREAT NIECE

By SOTÈRE TORREGIAN

The shrinking sun of my telephone book
Increases the skull
Of earthly love

Ah Franz Schubert's great great niece has driven off
    in her white XKE
Along with her the 3rd Law of my Thermodynamics
    of love

Away the illusory
Waterfalls of world's-end

And the shrinking sun is in
My hand
Holding her name address
    and telephone number
I am the Wandering Jew of love

POEM FOR CAMILO TORRES*

By SOTÈRE TORREGIAN

1
You warred against those modern Manichaean sects
You were the machine gun of the Apocalypse
The cults
Of Onan and Isis in whose night I go open-shirted
In whose night I am a slave
You freed me
In winter of the marquees
The high priest's ear cut off
To the ends of the earth
Every poem written is victory
From here on today
Every poem written is in your blood.
Father by your machine gun we're made clean.

2
There is a black cloud
In the carts they've bought from the Cushman Bakery
I have seen the emigrants of 1970
With hardly a smile so well behaved in knowing the
   "new math"
You would not know they were children

*Camilo Torres, Marxist-Leninist Guerilla Catholic priest who led the
liberation forces in Colombia against US imperialism, killed in 1967.

334

Every one sees the half moon that is his sister
In the ermine of deceit
Pass by like the milk window of a train

Ah young scholars
Hiding your heads like forests I row among you
Like Danton
I am guillotined by my own name

Ah planners, burst your bowels!
Over your categories
Over Abe Lincoln
Over your decemvirage
Over your gym-shorts

ROSE ALCHEMICA
Hommage a Anne Sheridan*

By SOTÈRE TORREGIAN

You are skiing
You are holding the dummy's hand
You are Napoleon's sweetheart
You are skiing again
Attired in furs you enter the great hall standing in the
　　doorway

You are in a two-piece bathing suit showing off your
　　buttocks in a back pose
Again on the skiing trail
A young novice bows before you her eyes electric
You appear on the divan a siren
You are at home in front of a 1940's fake fire-place in
　　shorts
You emerge like Clytemnestra
With serpents spinning a sun on your breast

*Anne Sheridan, American Movie Star.

336

THE HOMECOMING

By FEMI FATOBA

In his sleep he hears them calling
Through his dreams, beating Home!
Home! Home! on drums, logs and gongs.
He does not see their faces but
He knows their call is for him.
His name echoes with the drums and logs
Carrying their message beyond his sleep
In his wake, even before the sun wakes
He sees their form in mirages
Oozing from their drums, logs and gongs;
Their palms beckoning to him
Beat, boom, bang—The son
Of the soil must come home!
Must come home!
Come home!
Home!
The heart of his village soil calls,
The blood of his people shout.
The son of the soil
Goes home to meet home.
There is nobody to welcome him.
The familiar footpaths are gone,
The houses, new, glister with raw cement
Grey like the static clouds which lower the village.
The roofs shine their corrugated iron-sheets
To the blazing eye of the sky—

Their old grass thatchings blown away
With the years of his absence.
The streets are empty and clean,
There are no people except a few men
Plastering the pillars of a tall grey building
And a little black boy turning a wheel
In the farthest corner of a narrow long lane;
Slowly silently turning a wheel
In a corner in the dark. He doesn't know him.
The men, when he asks them, don't know
Where his father is, "He went away"
One said with hard forehead and stony eyes.
They don't speak to one another
And their tools don't clatter.
The houses have double numbers,
His father's "Five" is missing. In its place
Is a grey cement house. The village earth
Calls him but the village cement—
Houses deny him;
They refuse to take in his heavy box
Laden with nothing and
The mudwalls which knew his birth
Are gone—washed away by dews of his long journey.
There are no green frons except beyond
The far far hills and mountains
There are no trees except electric—
Lamp-poles and beacons all new, grey
And cold on cemented grey pavements
He carries his heavy, empty box to leave
But the soil beneath the cement
Under his feet call out loudly—
Son you are home!
Welcome home!
Come home
Home !
Home to rest.

OLAWUNMI

By FEMI FATOBA

That pitcher bearcr
   at the stream,
who went home
   wet-limbed and pitcherfull
with a parched throat.

OLAWUNMI in my mother's name.

RIVERS AND ROADS

By FEMI FATOBA

When I walk at the intersection
of the river and the road
Let not my feet debate
The ages of the elements.

At the dawn of streams
I came, traveller in a shoal
On a common current
Till half knew death
Living on the green terraces of birth.
The other half stringed together
Like beads of frog eggs
Swam to other shores
Where death might be
More cruel or more merciful;
And I was left to wash
In the dew of Time
On a cold morning.
It was the day of words
And all I did was cry
The pain of birth.
The banks strengthened me
   bathed me
   fed me
And set my feet on the road.

The dawn leaves towelled me
The sun rose me
And time tocked
To the beat of my feet.
At the kneeling of Time, I
Gave birth to the Earth
The elements met at my feet
In the dawn of Being.
At the dawn of the breath, I
Laid my flesh on a black mound
Of earth, through my veins
The pulse of Nature beat.
At the dawn of the voice, I
Shouted a greeting to the world
The earth, wind, birds and beasts
Answered me through the lungs of the Day.
I looked about me, there
Was no horizon limiting my reach:
All was me and one
At the dawn of knowledge.

The dawn leaves towelled me
The sun rose me; shone me.
Like a morning mirage
The sun carried its colour
Beyond the head of dusk
But its youth not
Above the navel of dawn:
And the sky renews its age
With the flow of clouds.
The old road grows new
While the foot grows old
Pounding the dusty birth
Of the spine of the road.
The roads I walked
The rivers I waded through

All in the eye of childhood.
There is no despair, no hope
In the eye of childhood
There is no flood
In the knowledge of rivers
In heat, no drought
In time, no division
In landscape, no walls;
There is no sight, no blindness
Only a perception
Pointing towards the Gods:
Gods who robe in palm-fronds
   and drink no palm-wine
Gods who bathe in water
   and drink blood
Gods of tears and laughter living
   among their own creations
   All in the eye of childhood
   The sky was a prism focussing
   All light on my path.
I knew the moon among the stars
Radiant companions from the shore
The gentle and bold face of a mother
Seeing her children through the night.
The sun was a ball playing
In a bowl of water, into which
Figers poked like the eyes of a father
Looking at his child
With the eye of childhood.
But in the sun's cellophane eclipse
I was walked in roadstreams
Round the edges of greenfields
With signs saying:
DO NOT STEP ON THE GRASS.
It was my feet, in my fatherland
I spoke tongues lent to me

I bore names stamped on me
I saw my home
With eyes of alien lenses
And my home-eyes I used
For lands of alien names
I waded in muddy banks
Where shadows were short
And tracks faint.
  In the days of short shadows
  Heads are small.
The doors of the heads shut
And words came out in hammerfalls,
I asked the men in the skull
"What are you doing behind closed doors?"
"The deeds of you
  the deeds of you."

They answered in distant tones.
In the place of short shadows
Where legs stand like straws
In a passing stream, the sea wins.
Water wins
Under the bridges
Below the boats
In the column of throats
Water wins
When like a pebble
Man sinks below
And waves billow
In concentric circles—
The face-rings of death
  eye-rings of life.
  In the time of short shadows
  Sight is long.
At the noon of Time, I
Gaze to see those gone before me.

At the borders of a grey mirage
I see the earth open its mouth
And gobble her children.
My way lies in that road
And beyond the landmark mirage
Are the thrones of my Gods who
Cannot stretch their hands
To bridge me across. Their wrists
Are soaked heavy in hues of gold.
All glory to Gold
For whom I abandoned
Praise to my Gods, who were
Castrated before they made me
Praise to my heroes
Who I never knew alive
And to my race
Lost at the alter of Gold.
All Glory to Gold and
All gold to Deceit.
All praise to the trust in a teacher
Which kills the potency of the skull
All reverence to the noon-dew
Which drowns birds of early wings.
I, inside me
My thoughts have been immured
And when I wake my tongue
From the furnace of my inside
Words come out blazing
Wronged, reshaped and fighting—
Words not made of air.

Such rivers I waded through
Like tears in the face of the sky.
Such roads I walked
In the ecdysis of the earth.
I searched for my bearing

On the multi-laned roads among
The criss-cross of milling feet:
I looked for my limbs
In the billowing froth of words;
I know the rainstorm
Not to be a kith of dawn-dew
And the sun
Not to be the seed-bag of day.

Now let me kneel at fresh waters
And drink of a new essence
To lay again the spring egg of the Earth
To marry Time at a new Dawn
Let me shed my civilization
On a new road,
Let me love death
In whose view all fruits are ripe
For I have looked
Through the rear-view mirror of time
And the past is my epilogue.
There shall be blood dripping
From the toes of my walk
And saline sweat
From the sinews of my swim:
When I speak me
From the smithy of my inside
My words shall recreate me
On the roads I walk
In the rivers I wade through.
The roads lead me hunting
The rivers beckon me to fish
But I am a vegetarian
So let not my feet debate
The ages of the elements
When the bushes roast the meat
And waters boil the fishes.

NEWSPAPER REVIEW

By FEMI FATOBA

Newspapers of Britain
Unite!
You have nothing to lose
But unprinted pages.
 The editors swear
 they are not out to bother me;
 the message is short.
 Read the Times
 Admire the People
 Don't under-study our Observer
 Never never Punch our dogs
 we love animals very dearly.
 Take no notice when
 you see us lie in the Sun,
 you might get hurt.
 Since things seem strange to you
 we are always ready to help;
 for you we make the Guardian
 as well as the prints of the Economist.
 It is our avowed mission
 to bring you civilization by Express
 so sit down in the closet and
 enjoy our New Society and social security
 and we shall send you the Daily Mail
 through the powellian voices of the People.
But I, being their naughty African manchild

I peep and I see . . .
From their backyard sheets
Come the News of the World.
    For my peeping, they say,
    Since you want to venture out
    You must wear bowler hats
    and three-peace suits, moreover
    roll your brolly thin and smile
    smile at all, at all times.
I smile down the road
And read myself Private Eyes.
Is it not a hard job
I then ask,
This business of smiling?
I look at the picture-prints
I touch the letters and
The papers tear in my face
Like growling lions.
All the same I smile back
Permanently hard and when
I look at me, daily, in the face of their Mirror
I see a Sketch of a grinning monster.
I look at the prints of a black woman
They say I have a chip on my sholders.
Looking then at a copy of 'the' Woman
Comes a Telegraph of unsmiling faces
From the Vendors saying,
    Don't open the pages of our Woman
    even when She so requests.
At that my prejudice loses its colour.
The bowler hat shades
My face, even black men don't recognise me
And when I tell them I am black
They laugh: they too don't smile.
I walk the streets, boiling
Limbs buttoned tight in suit,

Grey suit lined with the New Statesman
Every page reeking of culture:
Hunger tears my stomach muscles
But I still smile, though contorted
I keep it up, knowing
That I won't know how to smile
Under bowler hats
With hot air on my brain.
I keep fanning though
With my Private Eyes.

LOOK

By FEMI FATOBA

Look at those men
Sitting, looking like heavenly souls
With smooth shaven chins;
Weighing the deeds of men
They being more than man,
Look at them in their thou-shall-not looks.

Look at them in clean clothes, in
Washed bodies that spill deodorants
To kill lice off men's rags;
And twitching their manicured nails
At men's throats or wearing
Gloves to hide the fingers that
Write men's fate with indelible prints.

Look at those men
Nodding their wigged heads,
Speaking with coloured voices
And winking their painted faces
That hide their identities from man.
Look, look at them!

Look at those men
Smiling with glassy eyes
That see not beyond woman's flesh,
See their shining shoes that mirror

The face of the sky in dimensions
Beyond a common comprehension,
Just you look at them.

Look at them in their glass booths
With heaps of stones behind their windows.
Listen to their hearts trumpeting at
The news of failure. See them blow specks
Off friends' eyes with mouthfuls of pepper;
Look at them, the hands that work our clock.

Look at their women
Sitting high like fresh angels
With high giggles like empty bottles
Forced down a pool of water,
With high trebles and altos
Discussing a neighbour's loss of her dog;
Look at them the backseat drivers.

Look at them at their fat tables
Feeding worms and cats and dogs,
Spilling gold down their synthetic gullets
And packing little children into suitcases.
Are these the species that gave me life?
Look at them chewing at my breath.

Look at them all sitting there
Looking at the world with distant thoughts,
Thoughts of angels and heaven and hell
Of how and what where and why,
Of then and there; never here and now.
Are they like us humans with excuses?
Look, look at them, just look at them.

OLÓDÌ

By FEMI FATOBA

The rich walk in company of the rich,
The poor play in company of the poor,
The evil-wisher associate with the man-hater;
He refuses to do with us,
We refuse to do with him;
The owner of ill head
Does his own apart,
He refuses to do with Us.

We refuse to do with him.
There are three people in his home:
The first eats with hoe, like slave;
The second sleeps on naked floor, like sheep;
The third rubs his hindhead on sand, like monkey;
He refuses to do with us,
We refuse to do with him.

Goats have no enemies in the street,
Sheep have no enemies in the market.
He falls into latrine pit
When talking about us behind our back;
We are no enemies of his but
He refuses to do with Us.
The carrier of leprosy
Lives in the bush,
We refuse to do with Him.

OLÓDÌ: The nearest equivalent English word is "enemy". In Yoruba it signifies a relationship deeper than enmity.

EARTH TO EARTH

By FEMI FATOBA

I can hear their footsteps; falling leaves
On soft grass and their step, like
The first drops of late rain on sifted sand;
I once was somewhere but not like them,
Then I was not bone not flesh but a thought
Whistling hopes into the ears of newly-weds;
Then I was better as I was expected
And was respected on my arrival.
Respect is now theirs that are no more
Late kings and ex-subjects
Each now a royal six-foot of deafening silence
All side by side feeding from a common dish of earth,
Riding our nights and memory with thudding
   weightlessness.
Awe is now theirs who percieve the mystery of darkness
With brains of maggots and eyes of cobwebs
And will not part with it for the bait
Of plastic flowers and decorated tombstones,
I once shall be somewhere like them, revered
Marrowless bones clad in silk and mahogany,
Gained and lost, a myth, a night bird
Cawing lullabies to young travellers of dusk;
Then a king ruling all and none, another king,
An adorned heap
Subject of the forces of denudation.

EXILE

By SYL CHEYNEY-COKER

It had become a different kind of city
a place where the women no longer laughed
a place where the summaries of a decayed empire
had replaced the freshness of the African life
they tried to save this last outpost
when black Pushkin would not save Russia
it was there that the first fruits of learning evolved
but they forgot the wisdom of Songhai
oh, what a people, a people that have not looked
at the bronze eyes of their Gods, my Gods
a people without blood, blood of their ancestors
they have their lodges and freemasons
but where are the museums and temples
where children may learn about the glories of Ghana
the caravans of Timbuctoo, the proud Dogons
     of the kingdom of Mali
Oh, Sundiata, your name on my lips
is as fresh as the morning breeze in April
this rage that burns inside my heart
this shame that drove me into exile
oh, when shall I breathe the air of the Guinea Coast
Freetown, oh "fair city," I miss you
on this night of remembrance.

SHADOW

By SYL CHEYNEY-COKER

The day
pregnant with the sun
the night
pregnant with the moon
have the shadows behind

my mother was
pregnant with my race
nine months
she carried the black seed
raped by the white fertilizer
which blossomed
without the shadow
the shadow of the race

MAKEBA

By SYL CHEYNEY-COKER

Miriam, we have listened to you on the heights of
   Kilmanjaroo
we have danced to you in Dakar, New York and Guinea
and now we have seen you
Xhosa woman, dark enchantress from Zululand
I have known the rhythm of your dance, dance of fertility
rhythm of the Xhosas born in the kraals of South Africa
your voice is the sweet juice of the dark pimpernel
it is the endless dirge of the Bantus in the gold mines
of Johannesburg
the dim light in the prison at Roben Island
it is the magic of death defying the butchers at Sharpville
last night, I hear Vervoerd
it was the voice of a pitiable race
give him blood, give him Bantu water
and let your melancholic songs lift him
up from the depths of apartheid's ghoulish sleep
Miriam the Makeha
tell our Gods you delight us with Liwa Wechi and the
   Click song
and silence not your voice in Toureland.

DECEMBER 25—A NEW THINK

By HAROLD HEAD

Their first Noel
Our genesis of hell

But slaves communally masturbate
to the rhythms of historical hate

Celebrating the offspring of a Jewish mother
whom Christianity has denied a human father

Thus he came immaculate
to help them to a testicled fate

while darkies ejaculate in silent fear
for massa collects dues once a year

No more time to rush to the world's largest store
for X-mass suicide more and more

Free Angela a thought for Xmas
de lawd wont mind
discelebration

20 KARAT DEATH

By HAROLD HEAD

The shrill of whistles
the crack of dawn
A human train/funnels us like endless
lava/into devouring
earth

Then the drills rev up
And hot blooded veins taut up
into inclement constriction
And flex again/as the man-made claws
harpoon holes into golden earth
of clay and stone/biting into unknown
depths to seek out more wealth
for surface death

Flex muscles shudder
and Black faces glisten
Solemn, and intense
with contempt.

AZANIA
(South Africa)

By HAROLD HEAD

The funk of your lands
now determines the value of swiss made
watches/& international relations
And the pebbles of your rivers
add lustre to tyrant necks
whose husbands pee down
the groaning weight/of our oppressive
condition/in air-conditioned boredrooms
tokenly yapping/"down with apartheid"
while the misery lives on
and on and on and on

Muntu soul/come back to me
and let it be
Azania
again/& again

BOESMAN AND LENA
For Ruby Dee

By HAROLD HEAD

"We walk . . . ; . . ."
"walk"
".........and walk"

Movement began
when his semen reached/your ovary
and formed a coalition
deliberating for nine months
And we were born
It doesn't matter when
Boesman and Lena
All the Lenas and Boesmans
all of us
Boesman
And Lena

Some in Georgia
others in India
And in the Congo too
Boesman and Lena
We walk
And now . . . be
where the Indian sea
meets the Atlantic sea

Yes/we walk
In flight
Afrain/of them
Away/from them
To where we began
Which is/ . . . a where?

To what?
Boesman and Lena
Walking/walking/walking/walking
to what?
to where?
But we walk . . ./
Boesman and Lena

Boesman makes a hovel
to where we walked
and they/build new jungles
of concrete death
We do not return
it is theirs

No backwalking
"jonga phambili"—(look forward)
as Outa says

Outa walked
and walked
Till he could walk no more
"How does one bury a *kaffir*"
we wondered

And again/we walked
and walked

Away from our birthright
into purgatory
it never ends

the South African liberation move/
ment/now walking
into exile.

FOLKLORE, MUSIC
AND
COMMUNICATIONS

FOLKLORE AND THE NEW IMAGE OF MAN: SOME REMARKS ON THE CONTRIBUTION OF AFRICAN LITERATURES TO WORLD CULTURE

By ARNOLD RAINER

The rich literary tradition of the African peoples played an important role in the National Liberation Movement as an artistic and political factor. It was and is still background, a source of inspiration, the example of popularity for many works of modern authors. It was that sphere of intellectual and artistic life which was relatively free from colonial deformations, and whose renaissance since the end of the 19th century has worked in the spirit of enlightenment and strengthened the ideological background of the liberation movements. In other words, its renaissance formed the intellectual basis for the preparation of African masses and became therefore an aspect of that very revolution.

This social relevance and spiritual influence of the folklore has been promoted by the specific manners of its creation and aesthetic efficaciousness. Joseph Awouma remarked in his interesting essay on popular fairy-tales:

"Un conte est d'abord la production du groupe social dont il est né . . . Le conte traduit donc certains types de comportements, certaines classifications sociales, certains faits réels qui n 'ont pu être inventés 'ex nihilo'. Il est aussi une sorte de tréteau ou l'on se permet l'ironie, la

363

critique sociale, sorte d'emitoiro ou l'individu peut parler contre les tabous, ou cortaines sanctions. Il a aussi pour rôle d'eduquer le citoyen, de former sa conscience morale et de le guider dans sa conduite quotidienne.''

Thus, the literary heritage of the African peoples became a forming element of the new social consciousness, because of its subjects, its content of reality and humanism, and last not least—through the representation of the African cultural tradition—because of its mission of enlightenment. Of course, this heritage has been integrated in the modern arts and literature and was one of its starting-points. This process marks in its literary aspects the beginning of a comprehensive cultural revolution. Before the political independence it means mainly the fight for the cultural emancipation from colonial deformation. By now, the main task seems to be the further development of national cultures, deeply engaged for the best of the African peoples. This Pan-African Cultural Festival gives the proof of it.

Consequently, the African literatures are showing their contribution to the national liberation. Within the framework of its artistic, aesthetic and psychological possibilities, literature is a part of the complex social process.

We are witnessing how the cultural heritage of Africa is transformed into modern, social and political oriented literatures and arts. There is no doubt, this is one of the most important tasks of this mentioned cultural revolution and, however, a very remarkable event in the modern and progressive world culture. It includes a message of humanism to all mankind.

In East Africa, for example, we are able to see how the literary tradition is loosing its partial obscurity—without loosing the sense for a rich and impressing history which is an evident factor of national consciousness. Regarding this problem, the famous Chinua Achebe wrote: ''The novelist's duty is not to beat this morning's headline in topicality, it is to explore in depth the human condition. In Africa he cannot perform this task unless he has a proper sense of history.''

Let me mention an example. Shaaban Robert (1909–1962), one of the outstanding poets of this century, became the father of the national language and modern literature in Tanzania, because he started with the transformation of the very old and noble Swahili literature into modern life. He wrote all his works in Swahili, an indigenous African language. Shaaban Robert must be understood as a ''classical national author'' (as Goethe termed it) whose poetry, essays and stories gave an important impetus to establish national feelings amongst the people. He was effecting strong emotions for the people's language, its indigenous culture, and its country, his search for equality of all human beings and for justice in social and cultural development in Tanzania today.

The problem with which many contemporary African authors are faced is the problem of romanticism. In fact, the overcoming of romanticism is the very success of modern African literature: I think that realistic writing in these days marks the beginning of a new period of African literary history. Realism is the new and most impressing achievement of post-colonial literature.

Ezekiel Mphahlele wrote about the necessarity of the writer's emancipation in order to overcome the myths of a given social group. That means to find out ways of a cultural development in which the tradition is an important element. On the other hand, it is impossible to look only back to the past. I should like to quote Mbelle Sonne Dipoko who analyzed the situation of African poetry of French expression. ''It is this . . . search for original Africa unadorned by foreign contributions which leads African writing in French to look so much to the past. It is a search for authenticity in which they get their people's dream of happiness all wrong. For the masses happiness was, as it still is, a dream: of better living conditions . . . , a longing for better days to come.''

We are happy enough to see the efforts of artists, writers, all men of culture, of the African culture in general. We come to the festival in order to improve. We want to see the humanistic message of the African culture to the entire world.

THE COLLECTION, NOTATION AND ARRANGEMENT OF LIBERIAN FOLK SONGS

By AGNES NEBO VON BALLMOOS

A folk song may be defined as the musical repertory and tradition of communities. It is the product of an individual, but in the course of decades is modified by others. A folk song develops anonymously, usually among the lower classes together with texts dealing with the various phases of daily life: Working songs, love songs, cradle songs, drinking songs, patriotic songs, dancing songs, mourning songs. It has certain characteristic features which represent the general national traits of the people. Tradition is the great element in the survival of folk songs. There might be social, educational, and political changes within a country, but old songs, old tales, and old customs persist despite the distractions of modern existence and the imposition of the reforms.

The interest of Africans is in exposing what has been rediscovered, recreated, and created of our great African heritage and culture. My contribution to this method of identification within and outside of the African continent is the collection, notation, and arrangement of Liberian Folk Songs. To accomplish this, these five main sources are used:

My repertoire, attending a festival or service, listening to a soloist by appointment, assembling a group to perform, and listening to tapes and records.

Of these sources, I prefer to rely on the first two for the following reasons: some of the songs in my repertoire I have learned and performed among the ethnic group of which I am a member. Thus, I have been a part of the life with which these songs often deal. The remaining songs in my repertoire were studied and performed among an ethnic group of which I am not a member, but I have lived among the people of this group for more than three years. I have therefore, a fairly good idea of the characteristics of the music, melodically and rhythmically as well as the manner of performance. Another reason in favour of the repertory source is the ease with which I can notate without the troubles of winding, rewinding and playing of tapes which can be time consuming.

The second source in the collection procedure which I consider reliable is attending a service or festival without the performers being aware of my presence for taping and observing them. Here the performer or performers are more free especially in a case where he is creating a new song extemporaneously. When an individual or a group is asked to perform for recording purposes, they tend to be stiff, artificial and sometimes frightened. As a result, the best that is desired is not reached. Sometimes one has to warm them up with alcoholic beverages.

After the collection of the songs, our next problem is to locate the tonal centre of the song in order to establish the mode or scale (Western) in which the song is to be written on a musical staff. First the entire melody which is usually very short and most times is without an additional texture—strictly monophonic, is written down on the staff in musical syllables. After a careful observation of all the tones of the melody, especially that of the first and last, tones and the relationship of the rest of the tones to the first and last, a key is established. Of course, there are songs whose sounds cannot be written in the Western syllables and as such on the staff. These songs seem to demand the construction of a new scale which will be used strictly for the indigenous folk songs of Africa. Such songs are not notated nor discarded, but kept on tapes for more experience in this type of work and for future observation.

Determination of the measure of units is our next step in the notation process of the folk songs; here we are trying to locate a sort of time signature by drawing a line before the tones receiving the strongest pause. At times we come across the presence of two or three time signatures within a single song. The polyrhythmic characteristic of these songs is one of the labels of modern music. In establishing the note receiving the strongest beat, we also determine the dynamic, tempo, expression marks, ties, slurs, and the shading of the melody.

Since our research is strictly concerned with vocal folk music, the consideration of the text is one of our prime concerns. Correct accentuation, clarity of pronunciation, emphases of important words which are the basic requirements of good vocal style are not overlooked, but are stressed to convey in musical language the general character of the text as well as its fluctuating shades or contrasts. Generally, the text is more important than the actual melody in most African vocal music, particularly in the case where a story is told through song. Because of the importance of the text, and the shortness of the melody, we have employed textual repetition in our arrangement process which will be discussed later.

Instruments used to accompany these songs are almost exclusively percussive. To name a few; the drum, saasaa, bottle, ordinary carpenter saw, reed; those producing pitch are wooden xylophone and a gourd, a string instrument with piasava fiber as its strings or tiny wires as strings. Some of the tones produced on some of these instruments are not obtainable on Western keyboard instruments. We occasionally find the use of the

Western guitar among the Kra and the use of the Western accordion and the mouth organ among the Grebo, the reason being that these two groups live on the coastal area and their music has been affected by Western influence.

(1. Comments on xylophone made by Liberian and tuned with aid of western visitor). (2. demonstrate the playing of few of these percussive instruments mentioned).

After our notational process of establishing the measure of units to determine time signature, dynamics, tempo, expression marks, location of the tonal centre to determine the mode or scale, dictation of the melody to determine its pitch, duration, motion and rhythm, the texts of the songs and the awareness of the instruments used, we now sit to recreate through arrangement with the following methods: We are aware that because of our Western influence and training, the originality of these songs can be lost if precautions are not taken in the arrangements. We also know these songs will not completely eliminate the flavour of Western influence. With these two influences present, we sit to produce something of more African nature and characteristics of the particular ethnic group from which the song springs. In our arrangements, we write for four vocal parts, soprano, alto, tenor, and bass. We retain the original melody but develop it through rhythmic, and melodic imitation and through textual repetition. Being aware of the monophonic texture of the songs under discussion, we harmonize sparingly at end of phrases and cadences without much damage to the one line flavour. We also employ the use of unison in many of our passages, this unisonism being one of the characteristics which so earmark the music of Africa. A form is derived from the original song, the development, and the coda. Some of the forms are: AABACAA and coda, ABBA, ABA.

(a) Play Beah Moo Fidii   —rhythmic imitation
(b) Kah Beneh Kah   —presence of two keys
(c) Go to Sleep   —development of short theme

Our intention is to collect and notate music of all the ethnic groups in Liberia, but so far we have had the experience in collecting, notating, and arranging few songs from the Bassa, Gola, and Krao. We have discovered certain characteristics of the music of the three groups mentioned.

The Krao settled along the coastal areas extending from the western to the eastern sections of Liberia. Because of the geographical location of the Krao, early and frequent contacts with the western world were made. These contacts no doubt influenced some of the music of the Krao. The Krao are musically talented and are usually referred to as the best singers of Liberia. Their melodic lines often move diatonically in pleasing thirds usually sung by two female voices with the harmonic structure built both around the pentatonic and major scales showing the influence of the west with the Liberian tradition.

(a) Play excerpts from Deh Blah Nyo Wiseh to show both the pentatonic scale and the moving thirds.
(b) Play excerpts from Wah Gee Tee Bee to show harmonic structure based on western scale.

Rhythmically, the Kra retained their African complexed rhythm. They commonly use the following instruments:

Tuku   —A drum used in dance music.

Wre	—A slit log played on both sides with small sticks.
Kreh	—A steel bell with a small steel inside of it to be shaken. It is used after the war by the victor to announce his victory. It is also used in war dance.
Sakrai	—A dried gourd with beads or dried seeds arranged around it to be shaken by hand. It is used in social entertainment.
Jawra	—Dried seeds arranged on strings. Used around the ankle during the war dance.
Munei	—A wooden xylophone used to accompany folk tales on the farms.
Nunwan	—A wooden horn (traditionally the African horn is made of wood) used on battle front to give messages of warning. It is also used during the war dance.
Guitar	—The Western guitar is also occasionally used by some of the Krao.

The Bassa belong to a language group known linguistically as Krao. This group can be found along the coastal area and central interior of Liberia. They are the producers of some of the finest sacred vocal music of Liberia. They are very original in their creation of these songs. Their melodic lines often begin on an interval of a major second, on a minor third (LA DO). The end of short phrase on a major third and complete cadence on minor third or an added sixth. Since these melodies and on thirds, there is a feeling of harmonic progression of a major chord which is not the dominant chord going to the tonio at the end of the song. The end of these songs often have the tonality of chord six going to chord one in the minor mode.

Their language has an influence on the timbre of their music. Their style of singing can be compared with that of the Ancient Greeks during the period of Organum. The Gola's melodic lines often move in perfect fourths and fifths and the tonality derived is strictly modal. Some of these songs are so highly modal that we find it very difficult to establish a tonal centre on the Western musical staff.

Play excerpts from "Kah Beneh Kah" to show the progression of the fourths and fifths.

Typical instruments of the Gola:

(a)	Ged	—A small gourd with dried seed string around it. It is played by shaking the body of the gourd against the dried seeds. It is used by the Sandie Society for social entertainment.
(b)	Sangba	—A small drum made of animal hide and hollowed log. It is played by placing it between the thighs of the player and a string hung around the player's neck supporting the drum between the thighs. This instrument has a very sharp sound and it is used for social entertainment.
(c)	Kee	—A small slit drum of hollowed log opened in the centre and played with two small sticks. It is used for social entertainment.
(d)	Gihn	—A very large slit drum of hollowed log used for Poro Society perfor-

mances. Usually used when the Poro boys are coming from the "Bush".

(e) Kongoma —A boxlike instrument with a triangular opening, pieces of flat steel string across the opening (three in number) plucked with the tips of the fingers of one hand the other hand with large rings on finger tips striking the wooden body. It is an instrument used for social entertainment.

Collecting these indigenous instruments for preservation, exhibition, and instruction is part of our research at the University of Liberia.

Our research began in 1966 with the arrangement of seven songs performed by the University of Liberia choir—the very first time in our history of indigenous songs being performed by our highest institution. The idea thrilled the entire community and we received encouraging letters of congratulations.

Play "Beah Moo Fidii" for the thirds and the chord progression.

Bassa music is almost exclusively based on the petatonic scale and modes which we have not yet labelled. One can hardly detect the flavor of Western tonality in the music of the Bassa. Their style of singing is very dramatic and interesting. The soloist sings a complete line, but a second voice surprisingly joins the soloist on his last tone of the phrase and sings a major third above the main line or melody. These musical statements are given three times by the soloist and the added voice before the chorus starts responding. Well, a Westerner might interpret this style of singing as the three statements for Father, Son, and Holy Ghost, but that is the most typical manner the Bassa perform their songs, especially their sacred songs. The secular songs of the Bassa have the same harmonic structure as their sacred songs, but it is not as organized as the sacred music. Another aspect of the secular music, particularly that of the dance music, is that the texts are shocking, and in most cases vulgar. These types of songs are usually sung by men. Typical instruments of the Bassa:

(a) Goon —A round drum made of hollow log, about two and one-half feet in diameter covered on both ends with animal skin.

(b) Sankpa —A three-foot long hollowed log, top covered with animal hide.

(c) Dukpa —Talking drum, long hollowed log, top covered with animal hide.

(d) Gbadi —Belly harp, made of gourd, sticks and small vine (string instrument).

(e) Hwede —Slit drum, a log hollowed, both lips are struck with two small round sticks.

(f) Doma —A four to six inch long piece of reed with a hollow through the entire length. Played by slapping both ends alternatively with the hand and against the thigh for deeper sounds. It is usually played by young girls during initiation into the Zoe Bush School.

It is a task and a challenge to make known to the world the great potentialities of Africa through these valuable research projects and through these Pan-African cultural festivals. Speaking in my area, generally, the music of Africa represents a vast treasure of musical art the significance and artistic values of which are just becoming apparent to the Western mind. While the Western music is interested primarily in the development of counterpoint and harmony, the efforts of the African are most exclusively directed towards text, rhythm and melody. African vocal and instrumental music have influenced the Western music chiefly through two channels: The Negro Spirituals and the Negro Jazz.

The chief difficulty encountered in the study of African music, particularly the Liberian indigenous music, is the lack of written sources. It can be compared only to the Ancient tradition of the Gregorian Chant which was essentially dependent upon oral tradition and which began at the time when the first attempts towards a more accurate fixation were made.

LIBERIA'S CONTRIBUTION TO THE SCIENCE ON COMMUNICATION

By BAI T. MOORE

Liberia's indigenous population, numbering sixteen major tribes including the Grebo, Kru, Bassa, Dei, Vai, Gola, Kpelle, Krahn, Mano, Gio (Dan), Loma, Belle, Mende, Mandingo, Kisi and the Gbandi has a rich heritage of oral traditions, music dances and plastic arts.

Two of these tribes, the Vai and Bassa made a distinct contribution to the science of communication in the 19th century, when they each perfected a Script which made it possible to reduce in writing, the Vai and Bassa languages.

The Vai Script

In 1816 (six years before the landing of the Afro-American Founding Fathers at Cape Montserrado), Dualu Bukele, a serious minded young man of Bankakolo, a small village near Lake Piso in Grand Cape Mount County, made an invention which was to influence the cultural life of many tribes in Liberia including the Vai, Gola, Dei, Mandingo and Bassa. The invention, a Script unlike any other system of written communication was regarded by the Vai as a significant gift from God.

The legend as to how Bukele invented the Script is as fascinating as the Script itself. It is said that the inventor was at one time employed as a runner by a European

377

slave trader who operated a slave factory on the coast near Robertsport (administrative headquarters of Grand Cape Mount County). This gentleman was in constant touch with other colleagues along the Grain Coast.

Quite often Bukele was given letters by his employer to take to his friends without a verbal message. Bukele sometimes returned to his employer laden with goods. This intrigued the inventor; the fact that characters scribbled on a piece of paper (kpolo) could convey a message between persons living far apart. Bukele pondered over the mystery until it became an obsession with him. He sat up night after night fasting and praying, just to unravel the mystery.

How Dualu Bukele got the Script

One night while Bukele was wrapped up in a dream, a person draped in white appeared before him and said, "Dualu, I have brought you a Script with which you, too, can now write your language." Bukele woke up very excited. He could still see the Script vividly before him. He called some of his friends and related what he had seen in his dream. He then started writing the characters in the sand with a piece of stick. As he could not remember the character for every sound, his friends (Momolu Dualu Wogbe, Dualu Tamia, Jaa Zaawo, Zolu Tabaco, Jaa Belekole and Kahn Bala) assisted Bukele by suggesting characters for the sounds that were lacking.

It is interesting to note some of the early Bukele characters which have survived to the present with minor changes. Example:

(1)   The word for any alcoholic beverage in Vai is *kpe*. This phonetic sound is represented by the sign (⭘⭘), two gourds on a pole. When combined with other signs like (᪲) and

(*ᴔᴔ*) you get kpeima, the word for white in Vai.

(2) The word for horse in Vai is *so*. It is represented by the sign (ꓬ), three vertical lines based on two parellel horizontal ones, one long and the other short. When combined with the sign (ꓑ) you get the word *sona*, meaning rain in Vai.

When some scholars first heard of the Vai Script, they came to the hasty conclusion that it was merely a pictographic system of writing like the Egyptian hieroglyphics. They were unaware of its highly articulate character and careful study has proved their first theory to be unfounded.

The people of Bandakilo were curious to know whether Bukele's invention was practicable for easy communication. When they were convinced that it was, they sent a delegation to Maja (King) Gotolo, who, at the time was ruler of the Gawula Section, Manja Gotolo gave the delegation a royal reception and permitted the Script to be used for communication throughout Gawula and the tribes beyond her borders.

Six months later a school was established at Bandakolo which was attended by almost every ambitious young man of the area.

How the World got to know about the Script

A British naval officer, Lt. F. E. Forbes who was travelling by land from the Gold Coast (Ghana) to Sierra Leone in 1849, observed the strange system of writing on the walls of huts in the Tombe section of Grand Cape Mount County. Upon his arrival in Freetown, Lt. Forbes immediately reported his unique find to the eminent German anthropologist and linguist, Dr. S. W. Koelle, then principal of Fourah Bay College.

Dr. Koelle made two trips to Bandakolo, the inventor's home. He met Bukele on the first trip and managed not only to learn the Vai Script, but to collect sufficient materials to publish a Vai Grammar. When Dr. Koelle returned the second time, the school at Bandakolo had been destroyed by war and the inventor of the Script dead.

Bukele's death did not dampen the zeal for the popularization of the Vai Script. The task of refinding it was continued by the inventor's colleagues and the students of the Bandakolo school. One of the latter, Ndole Wono, who was among the first graduates of the school is credited with producing the first written travelogue in Vai. Ndole Wono's father was Bassa and his mother Vai. As a young man, Wono divided his time between Jondu, his maternal home, and Bassa where his father lived.

Wono's travelogue is a vivid description of a trip he made from Jondu to Bassa. The account provides an insight into the tribal customs of the Bassa and Vai in the early 19th century. Parts of Ndole Wono's book contain moral teachings, among other things.

That other students of the Bandakole school made contributions to Vai literature is evidenced by the existence of diaries, biographies, collections of proverbs and legends dating from the later part of the 19th century.

In his book, "Reisebilder Aus Liberia" (travelogues of Liberia) published in 1872, Johnann Buerlikofer, a Swiss explorer employed by the Royal University of Lyden devoted several pages to the Vai Script.

In 1885, principally as a result of the work of two explorers, Clark (a Britisher) and the anthropologist, Maurice Delafosse, (at one time Consul General of the Republic of France to Liberia) the announcement of the existence of the Via Script was made at the Berlin Conference.

Towards the end of the 19th century, Momolu Massaquoi and a group of scholars simplified the study of the Script by means of a chart which was included in the curriculum of St. John's Episcopal Mission in Robertsport, Grand Cape Mount County.

In 1924, while serving as Liberian Consul General in Germany, Momolu Massaquoi met Dr. Agust Klingenheben of Hamburg University and got him interested in the Vai Script and language. This interest grew to the point of including the Vai language and Script in the University of Hamburg African Language Seminar. Professor Klingenheben later visited Liberia and spent a few weeks in Jondu confering with elder Zuke Kandakai, Chief Vaani Mabu and others.

Mr. S. Jangaba Johnson again reintroduced the Script in the Curriculum of St. John Mission during the period 1929–1931.

Among his pupils were two German scholars, Dr. Fritz Ronnefeldt, M.D. and Richard W. Heydern. Both of them had started the study of the Vai language and Script in Hamburg University before coming to Liberia.

Up to the time of his death a few years ago, Dr. Klingenheban published many articles on the Script in numerous scientific journals in Germany and England.

As part of its African studies program, the University of Liberia in 1962 conducted a seminar to standardize the Script. The need grew out of the fact that the older charts of the Vai Script were being debated by many scholars including Dr. Klingenheben, Zuke Kandakai, Jangaba Johnson and others and the only solution to these controversaries lied in the standardization of the Script.

The delegates to the three day Seminar which was held from August 15th to the 17th came from all sections of

Liberia where the Vai Script and language are extensively used. The following areas were represented: Tombe, Gawula, Gola Kone, Vai Kone, Bassa, Dei, Lofa Gola and Mecca Chiefdoms. Dr. Klingenheben and his wife, who flew over expecially for the seminar, represented Hamburg University.

Many scholars, historians and linguists have held the view that the Via Script is cumbersome and is therefore unable to survive in the face of the European alphabet. In his history of Sierra Leone, published in 1962, the historian, Christopher Fyfe points out that in the 1960's an English trader who spent some time among the Vai in Cape Mount found schools where children were still learning the Script. But to some observers it seemed to be forgotten by the early twentieth century.

All over Liberia, however, the Script is flourishing and is in constant use. "As early as 1913, F. W. Migeod observed that the Script was so popular with the Vai that if they came under European rule it is doubtful if they would abandon it".

Mrs. Gail Stewart, a Missionary teacher who spent eight years in Robertsport and an ardent scholar who has devoted much time to the study of the Script admits its popularity in the whole of the Vai country. She points out that, "Literacy in his (the Vai's) own Script generates a pride that no phonetic alphabet can give, a point which seems to be borne out by the habit of Vai writers of preserving all of their correspondence, from weighty epistle to the smallest note".

Uses of the Script

Besides ordinary correspondence, the Script is used extensively as follows:

(a) Keeping family records including births, deaths, marriages, divorces, wills, contracts, etc.

(b)   Recording oral traditions, clan histories, legends, biographies, proverbs, poetry, folktales, simple scientific phenomenon, travelogues, moral saying, etc.

(c)   Business and craftmen make use of the Script in commercial transactions. There are extensive mercantile establishments operated by Vai businessmen who maintain ledgers and other commercial documents in the Script. Several established tailors record the measurements of clients in the Script without any difficulty whatsoever.

A few years ago, a renowned carver in Robertsport produced a sophisticated catalogue containing pictures of carvings described in the Script.

The Robertsport branch of the Young Men's Christian Association for a number of years published a memeographed newspaper which contained a newsletter written in the Script.

This raises the question of the number of persons who can read and write the Script. The 1962 census of Liberia reveals that the Vai in Liberia number about 28,898. However, other groups in Liberia including the Dei, Kpelle, Gola, Bassa, Mandingo and Mende speak Vai. It is safe to assume that between 20 to 25 per cent of the people who speak Vai can read the Script.

The Bassa Script or Vah

While the Bukele Script was gaining importance in and beyond Grand Cape Mount County, further down the coast in Grand Bassa County, another form of communication known as the Bassa Vah was being nurtured to take its place in the field of written communication.

According to an authority on the Bassa Vah, Joseph

Gbadyu, "for over three centuries the desire to produce a system of written and more durable means of communication burned within the Bassa until, by the mercies of God, they developed the system called Vah". Mr. Gbadyu points out that the system consisted of signs, codes and symbols used to convey ideas, thoughts, emotions as well as, to give instructions. All forms of bodily movement winking, clearing of the throat, nodding and so on, were considered by the Bassa to mean "throwing Vah".

The next important step in the development of the Bassa Script was the use of leaves on which symbols had been made by biting with the teeth. The symbols on bitten leaves were left at road junctions to convey ideas. Mr. Gbadyu says that this system of communication is practiced to the present in some sections of Grand Bassa County.

All the developments cited above made a significant impact "on the minds of great thinkers and invention diehards like Jenni Dira, Beeboo, Jedu Zodeh Bodogbee and Tomaa". It was these early thinkers who began to scribble Vah symbols on the bark of trees, on animal skins, and anything they could get their hands on.

In 1910, a Bassa scholar, Dr. Thomas Flo D. G. Lewis who had given the Vah serious thought and study returned from the United States with degrees in chemistry and medicine. Despite the demands of his profession, Dr. Lewis worked ceaselessly to give the Vah a more durable form.

Mainly through the instrumentality of Dr. Lewis, a printing press was designed to produce literature in the Bassa language. Dr. Lewis is said to have produced a Bassa primer, a hymnal, a reader and a book of wisdom, some of which are still in existence. The printing press is now in Lower Buchanan, Grand Bassa County.

The invention of writing is considered an important step in the evolution of man. It is the dividing line between prehistory and the beginning of recorded history. The Vai Script and the first effort by the Bassa to arrive at a coherent form of written communication indicate that Africans had reached a high level of mental development and civilization to be able to perfect a system of writing to preserve their rich cultural heritage.

VAI SCRIPT

VAI SCRIPT

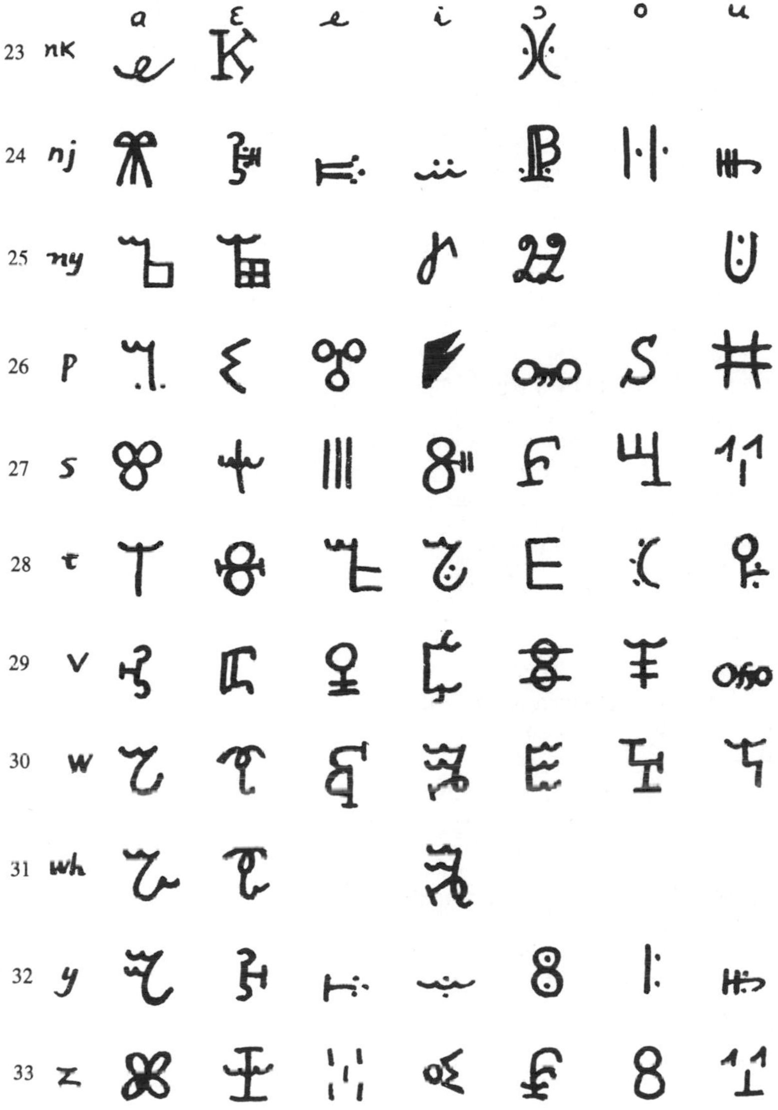
a ε e i ɔ o u
23 nK
24 nj
25 ny
26 p
27 s
28 t
29 v
30 w
31 wh
32 y
33 z

BASSA SCRIPT

BASSA CHARACTERS AND THEIR ENGLISH EQUIVALENT

1. ⋔ equals short "a", as in "far".
2. ℺ equals short "o", as in "God".
3. ⊙ equals long "o", as in "woe".
4. ⋓ equals "u", as in "coo".
5. ⋎ equals long "a", as in "nay".
6. ≺ equals short "e", as in "met".
7. ⅜ equals long "e", as in "me".
8. Ɜ equals "n", as in "darn".
9. ⋀ equals "k", as in "kite".
10. ⋝ equals "s", as in "say".
11. ⟶ equals "f", as in "far".
12. ട equals "m", as in "ment".
13. ſ equals consonantal "y", as in "yes" and "yea".
14. ⟆ equals hard "g", as in "gar".
15. ⋧ equals "d", as in "deed".
16. ⋓ does not correspond to any single English character but can be written as "kpa".
17. ⟶ equals "j", as in "Jordan".
18. ⅎ does not correspond to any single English character but can be written as "xwa".
19. ⋐ equals "w", as in "wire".
20. ⅁ equals "z", as in "Zorba" and "Zoril".
21. ⅃ does not correspond to any single English character but can be written as "gbu".
22. ч equals "l", as in "law".
23. ⅎ does not correspond to any single English character but can be written as "ch".
24. ⋎ does not correspond to any single English character but can be written as "whu".
25. ⊖ equals "t", as in "tor".
26. ⊼ equals "b", as in "bar".

27.   ⊏   equals "v", as in "Voodoo".
28.   Ⅱ   equals "h", as in "hinder" and "hen".
29.   ⅂   equals "p", as in "path".
30.   Ⴑ   equals "r", as in "rata".

Note: The first seven characters are vowels, the next twenty-three consonants.

BASSA TONAL MARKS ON VOWEL SOUNDS AND NAMES

1.   ˈ   high
2.   Ɔ   grave (low)
3.   :   mid
4.   ‾   mid-level (horizontal)
5.   ᶽ   high-low (high falling)

A printing machine made in Germany was introduced in 1910 and study materials were printed. Schools for children and adults were established throughout Bassa County. Today, Bassa script is widely used in correspondence.

COMPLETE LIST OF FRINGE PAPERS AT THE AFRICAN CULTURAL FESTIVAL IN ALGERIA IN 1969

Brutus, Dennis, *"Some notes: African culture and liberation"*.

Kennedy, J. Scott, *"African theatre"*.

La Guma, Alex, *"African culture and national liberation"*.

Markov, Walter, *"A propos d'Ibn Khaldoun, historien de la culture"*.

Mirimanov, V. B., *"Problemes actuels et perspectives du developpment de l'art Africain"*.

Morisseau-Leroy, Felix, *"Le role du theatre Africain dans le developpment"*.

Niang, Lamine, *"Negro-African culture and poetry—elements of the survival of our civilization"*.

Okpaku, Joseph, *"The artist and politics: the dynamics of contemporary African society"*.

Omideyi, Olaolu, *"The place of traditional music in African society with special reference to Nigeria"*.

Rainer, Arnold, *"Folklore and the new image of man: some remarks on the contribution of African literatures to world culture"*.

Tchernova, Mme., *"Sur le destin de l'artisanat"*.

Traore, Bakari, *"Theatre Africain: realities et perspectives"*.

NOTES ON CONTRIBUTORS

1. Stanislas Adotevi—is a Dohomeyean and a professeur of philosophy in Dahomey.

2. Rand Bishop—Mr. Bishop taught English for two years in Togo, and is currently teaching African Literature at the State University of New York at Oswego.

3. Houari Boumedienne—President of Algeria.

4. Dennis Brutus—He is a South African and currently teaches African Literature at Northwestern University, Evanston, Illinois.

5. J. M. Coetzee—Formerly an Assistant Professor of English at the State University of New York at Buffalo. He now teaches at the University of Cape Town, South Africa.

6. Syl Cheyney-Coker—Mr. Coker is a Sierra Leonean student at the University of Oregon, U.S.A.

7. Dr. Seth Cudjoe—Dr. Cudjoe who is a medical officer, is a member of "Akwampim Six" (a cultural gourp in Ghana) and a member of the Ghana Arts Council.

8. Ernest Ekom—After his graduation from Ibadan University where he did English and 20th century theatre, Mr. Ekom worked in the former Eastern Nigerian Braodcasting Company, and later as the first manager of the Ibadan University Travelling Theatre.

9. Ben Enwonwu—Mr. Enwonwu who was a cultural adviser to the Federal Military Government in 1969 is currently a Professor of Fine Art at the University of Ife.

10. Femi Fatoba—Mr. Fatoba is a lecturer in the Department of Theatre Arts at the University of Ibadan.

11. Harold Head—Mr. Head is South African and lives in New York.

12. B. Ezuma Igwe—Mr. Igwe who obtained his Bachelor's degree in English from the University of Makerere, East Africa, is currently doing his Masters at the University of British Columbia, Vancouver, Canada.

13. Ilunga Kabongo—Head of the Department of Political Science at The University of Louvanium, Zaire.

14. Mamadi Keita—Minister of Education and Culture (Guinea).

15. Mazisi Kunene—Mr. Kunene is a South African writer living in London.

16. Alex La Guma—Mr. La Guma who now lives in London is one of the foremost contemporary African novelists, and a leading spokesman against apartheid.

17. Henri Lopes—Minister of Education (Congo, Brazaville)

18. M. Micere Mugo—Mrs. Mugo who did her Bachelor's degree at Makerere, Uganda, is currently doing her Ph.D. in literature at the University of New Brunswick, Canada.

19. G.C.M. Mutiso—Professor of Political Science at Rutgers University, N.J.

20. Bai T. Moore—Liberian Deputy Minister for Cultural Affairs.

21. Agnes Nebo von Ballmoos—A lecturer in the Department of Music, University of Liberia.

22. Lamine Niang—A Counsellor at the Embassy of Senegal in Rabat, Morocco.

23. S. J. Ntiro—Commissioner for Culture (Tanzania)

24. Eyan Nzie—A Nigerian

25. Joseph Okpaku—Well-known Nigerian playwright and critic, is the president and publisher of The Third Press, New York.

26. Okot p' Bitek—A leading African poet and author of the highly successful epic poem SONG OF LAWINO. Mr. p'Bitek was director of the Uganda National Theatre and lecturer at Makerere University of East Africa.

27. Dr. E. Taiwo Palmer—Born in Freetown, Sierra Leone, Dr. Palmer was educated in Freetown, and received a doctorate from Edinburgh University, Scotland. He now teaches at Fourah Bay College (University of Sierra Leone), and has published articles on African Literature in African Literature Today.

28. Arnold Rainer—An East German, attended the Festival as an observer.

29. Eric Sellin—He is associate professor of French at Temple University. He has taught American literature at the University of Algiers during which time he also worked on a study of Francophone poetry of Africa.

30. François Sengat-Kuo—He is the Secretary General to the President of Cameroun as well as a teacher of Public Administration at the Ecole National d' Administration et de Magistrature at Yaounde.

31. Sotère Torregian—Torregian who works at Stanford University is a young American poet whose work has appeared in various magazines in campuses throughout the U.S.

32. Paulette Trout—Dr. Trout who, has taught at Yale, Columbia, Barnard College, and U.C.L.A., has published several articles on African literature in AFRICA REPORT. Dr. Trout who now lives in Cambridge, Massachusetts, is the Assistant Editor for African Literature in French for JONALA.